# FIT & HEALTHY PREGNANCY

## HOW TO STAY STRONG AND IN SHAPE
## FOR YOU AND YOUR BABY

KRISTINA PINTO

*with Rachel Kramer, MD*

VELO press

Boulder, Colorado

**velopress®**

3002 Sterling Circle, Suite 100
Boulder, Colorado 80301-2338 USA
(303) 440-0601 · Fax (303) 444-6788 · E-mail velopress@competitorgroup.com

Distributed in the United States and Canada by Ingram Publisher Services

Library of Congress Cataloging-in-Publication Data
Pinto, Kristina.
Fit and healthy pregnancy: how to stay strong and in shape for you and your baby / Kristina Pinto
with Rachel Kramer, MD.
        pages cm
Includes bibliographical references and index.
ISBN 978-1-934030-96-7 (pbk.)
1. Exercise for pregnant women. I. Kramer, Rachel (Rachel J.)
II. Title.
RG558.7.P56 2013
618.2'44—dc23
                                                                                2013018150

For information on purchasing VeloPress books, please call (800) 811-4210, ext. 2138,
or visit www.velopress.com.

This paper meets the requirements of ANSI/NISO Z39.48-1992 (Permanence of Paper).

Cover design by Maryl Swick
Interior design by Vicki Hopewell; composition by Vicki Hopewell and Jane Raese
Cover photographs by Brooke Duthie
Interior illustrations by Nicole Kaufman
Author photograph on page 315 by Kate Crabtree Photography

Text set in Archer

13   14   15 / 10   9   8   7   6   5   4   3   2   1

*For Henry*

# Contents

# PART II: THE FOURTH TRIMESTER

# Acknowledgments

Writing this book about fitness and pregnancy was a labor of love, and I'm grateful for the support and guidance I received from many people. I would like to thank my agent, Bob Kern, and my colleague in writing and sport Sage Rountree for shepherding my words to publication. I also extend tremendous gratitude to my editors Casey Blaine, Renee Jardine, and Connie Oehring for their valuable insights during the process of writing and refining.

I'm also grateful for the candor and generous time given by many athlete moms, trainers, coaches, and health professionals, particularly Dr. Rachel Kramer for her brilliant medical knowledge and compassionate care for women's health. I also deeply thank midwife Marisa Rowlson and coaches Deanna Pelletier, Jack Fultz, and Michelle Simmons. I appreciate the time given by Tracy Yoder at Running USA and by Bobbi Gibb, who talked openly with me about motherhood after her legendary Boston Marathon. For feedback on writing and running life, I am incredibly grateful to Emilie Manhart. I am honored to coach wonderfully inspiring athletes and to write for blog readers who follow *Mother Running Rampant* (http://kristinapinto.net), and I offer my thanks to them for their contributions to this book.

Thank you to Brian Sawyer for his partnership in raising a healthy and happy son and to my parents for teaching me to value mind-body fitness in family life through ballet, tennis, and croquet. Thank you also to Sarah Pinto, Mary Duquette, Mary Holt-Wilson, and Chrisanne Douglas for their loving kindness and honest presence. My deepest love and appreciation go to Dan L'Ecuyer for the incredible care and confidence he provides, both gentle and tough, in guiding me to strive and achieve in sport, motherhood, love, and writing. And, of course, my love and thanks go to the heart of my heart, Henry, who inspires and moves me every moment of my life.

KRISTINA PINTO

# Introduction

THE 2012 LONDON OLYMPICS seemed like a baby shower for fit pregnancy, a watershed for sport and motherhood. At the 2008 Beijing Games, swimmer Dara Torres had opened a door for women in sports to be highly visible moms, and the London Olympics picked up where she left off by placing mothers front and center. In no other Olympic broadcast had athlete moms been more celebrated, or perhaps more decorated. Beach volleyball star Kerri Walsh-Jennings took home her third consecutive gold medal, having become a mother of two in the years between the Athens (2004) and London Games. The 2012 medal favorites in the women's high jump included three moms of toddlers. Several of the most promising marathoners were also moms, including Kara Goucher of the United States and Romanian Constantina Dita, a 42-year-old mother of a teenager. No longer just waving flags tearfully from the stands, mothers were high-profile in the action and on the podium.

London was also a groundbreaking Olympics for expectant women. In no prior Games had a competitor participated at 36 weeks pregnant. Malaysian riflewoman Nur Suryani Mohammed competed in the 10-meter air-rifle event, saying later in a press interview that she talked to her baby daughter in utero every morning, asking permission to shoot without being kicked. "If the baby kicks, I have to breathe easy and let her calm down before shooting," said Nur.[1] Now, that's good advice for moms everywhere.

As a Muslim woman competing in Olympic air rifle while 8 months pregnant, Nur might have broken through several layers of ground in elite sports. At the same time, she represents the modern age in women's athletics. Today, many women are more likely to register for baby joggers and bike chariots than rocking chairs, and they're inclined to stay fit and active throughout pregnancy. As Nur put it, "I am the mother. I know what I can do. I am stubborn."

And yet many of us don't know how much we can do, and we encounter raised eyebrows and voices of concern that Nur and other expectant mothers also face as they strive for a fit pregnancy. This book offers answers to clear up that confusion, and it will help empower you for a healthy, active 40 weeks and beyond. It covers your mind-body wellness as well as the health and safety of the baby you're growing. And by presenting the most current knowledge on pregnancy and exercise and the advice and experiences of countless expectant women with active lifestyles, this book will equip you to navigate what can seem like the ultimate 9-month endurance sport.

At the same time that you'll learn about fitness that is safe and healthy for women with pregnancies that are progressing normally, reading this book will help you focus on *yourself*. The central tenet of a fit pregnancy is that you value your own experience and heed your individual body's cues in order to be strong, active, and healthy. This is your body and your pregnancy—no one else's. You're creating an ecosystem of flesh and blood, and your fit pregnancy won't look precisely like that of any other woman. This book reminds you to trust your body and focus on a balance between mental and physical health in order to be fit and healthy while you grow a baby.

Designed for veteran and recreational athletes as well as general fitness enthusiasts, the book digs deeply into each trimester, including the often neglected "fourth trimester" of postpartum adjustment. Each of these chapters covers the essential information you need to cultivate a healthy pregnancy and start toward motherhood. You'll be able to read about such key topics as:

* What's happening to my body?
* How do I fuel each trimester?
* How do I exercise safely throughout my pregnancy?
* How do I keep a fit mind during pregnancy?

You'll learn about fitness options for each phase of pregnancy, focusing on running, biking, swimming, stretching, and strength training. Chapters feature simple and efficient exercises to enhance your fitness routine as well as advice on building mental strength and finding calm during this period of change, both for yourself and for your relationships.

A distinctive feature of this book is the insight offered by the many moms who have been there before you as well as the expert contributions of coaches, trainers, midwives, and doctors. What's more, the book is rooted in the medical expertise of athlete OB-GYN Dr. Rachel Kramer, who offers current, balanced advice to guide you through a safe and rewarding pregnancy experience that honors your need for fitness and your care for your growing baby. You'll find her expert contributions highlighted throughout the book. Simply put, this book offers you the best of all sources: sound medical advice, a mind-body fitness guide, and motivation from other women who have walked—or worked out—in your shoes.

## What's in the Book

The first section of this book presents the most up-to-date knowledge on prenatal health and fitness. Chapter 1 introduces the current results of exercise science research with pregnant athletes, which will show you that exercise during pregnancy is not only safe but even ideal for mom-baby health and wellness. This chapter also discusses fertility and settles some erroneous ideas about fitness training and miscarriage. Information is your biggest ally when you face skepticism about pregnancy and continuing fitness activity, and this chapter arms you with what you need to know.

Chapter 2 walks you through the first trimester, helping you to surf the turbulent hormonal waves that can cause morning sickness, not to mention the physical and emotional changes of the first 12 weeks. It helps you navigate conversations with your partner and your doctor and explains the importance of setting an exercise base for the rest of your pregnancy as well as the usefulness of workouts for treating nausea. The chapter also offers workout ideas for strength training with resistance bands in the first trimester.

With Chapter 3, we enter the second trimester, or the "glow" phase of pregnancy, when you can take advantage of a new and fresh energy base with your exercise, especially if you focus on balanced nutrition and plenty of hydration. You'll learn about the fitness implications of specific pregnancy issues that are common in the second trimester, ranging from loosening joints to preeclampsia, as well as common mental challenges as your body changes. In addition to learning about safe and healthy exercise in the second trimester, you'll find a sequence of strength building exercises that use your own body weight as resistance to power your core as you head into the third trimester, when back strain is common.

Chapter 4 takes you into the home stretch as you experience the gravity-shifting gains and changes of the third trimester. You'll read about ways to treat back pain and guidelines for health and wellness during exercise in the final months, weeks, and days of your pregnancy. You'll also find information on fitness with gestational diabetes as well as other issues that can challenge your fitness plans, such as required bed rest. You'll find a list of suggested questions to help you choose your pediatrician and recommended questions for your tour of the hospital or birth center where you'll have your baby. Finally, you'll read up on sports specifics for weeks 28–40 and how you can use an exercise ball to stretch, strengthen, and prepare your pelvic floor for childbirth.

Part II of the book picks up from there with labor and delivery and a segue to a discussion of your fit motherhood during the "fourth trimester"—the first three months after your baby is born. Here you'll find advice and company for adjusting to your new family and your new identity as a mom while you aim to stay fit and healthy. This section informs and inspires, helping you to manage your physical health, exercise options, and mental wellness in this new phase of your life.

Chapter 5 guides you through the birth experience, explaining both vaginal and cesarean deliveries. The chapter also coaches you through the labor process with mental strategies recommended by athlete moms and discusses the choices you have in pain management. Finally, this chapter assists you with starting a list of items to bring to the hospital or birth center, to help you stay organized and calm.

Chapter 6 introduces you to the early weeks of the fourth trimester, that period of adaptation to a new lifestyle that finds you balancing family, fitness, and self. You'll read about breast-feeding, getting sleep, nutrition and hydration, weight-loss goals, and how to find yourself amid all that laundry and swaddling. You'll also learn what to expect and what to strive for when it comes to returning to exercise while managing fatigue and ways to stay calm and centered in the face of new motherhood.

Chapter 7 is designed to assist your return to more regular and effortful workouts and training goals, such as races or other athletic events. You'll read about what to expect from your body after the initial weeks of adjustment, including training and breast-feeding, sport-specific workouts that offer flexibility to busy moms, and racing in the postpartum months. In addition, advice on buying a treadmill, jogging stroller, and bike trainer will help you achieve more with your sport or exercise routine.

Finally, Chapter 8 takes on the mental aspects of life as an athlete mom with a baby or toddler. This chapter provides the motivation and inspiration of athlete moms who have created a lifestyle of fitness in their homes. It helps you navigate the challenges of nourishing a fit family with exercise and a balance of healthy foods and also explains some of the physical changes in a new mom's body. You'll also read advice and ideas for striking the workout-family balance through focusing on positive self-talk, scaling your goals, and modeling empowerment for your family. The chapter wraps up with new technology for success with the athlete-mom lifestyle and advice for boosting your fitness quotient with support networks (virtual and real-life) to help you achieve an indispensable endurance mom's "play group."

## The Author

As a developmental psychologist, mom, running coach, and marathoner for more than a decade, I have seen and heard countless stories of the power of sport in mothers' lives. Through my blogs, *Marathon Mama* and *Mother Running Rampant*, I discovered the legions of mother-runners on the roads and on the trails, many of whom were forging online connections with other moms, cultivating a social movement in sneakers. And with the uptick in the popularity of triathlon, you can now find more and more moms celebrating their love of fitness and sport on wheels and in the water. What I've learned from these women is that while being an athlete empowers each of us differently, we are unified by our need for sport and fitness, and we've become more committed to keeping that power in our lives as we have babies and grow our families.

The confluence of running, motherhood, and women's identity is an area about which I write with both respect and a good dose of irreverence. These are my passions and the source of much laughter as I coach other women in running. I teach the joy of getting out of your comfort zone to find the rewards of striving for goals many women never knew they could accomplish, whether it's completing a 5K or qualifying for Boston. Admittedly, my coaching has even included advice on how to spit while racing and how to paint toes with no nails.

When I had my baby, I didn't think I could manage training and motherhood and frankly couldn't imagine how any woman did. I'd exercised throughout my pregnancy by running, walking, swimming, and using the elliptical at the gym, and when I developed preeclampsia in my 40th week of pregnancy, I was quickly induced. As childbirth goes, I had an "easy" labor and vaginal delivery, due in no small part to a fit pregnancy, according to my doctor. My smooth birth experience gave way to a mentally tough postpartum transition, even with the joys of my new baby, who was born in Boston during the same October week that the Red Sox broke the curse to win the World Series. In a city full of exuberance, a crippling mix of fatigue and insomnia besieged my baby's first few weeks of life, and I developed clinical postpartum depression. My body and mind had been thrown for a loop, and I felt guilty that I couldn't find the bliss new moms were supposed to have. Before he was born, life had been only about my needs and goals, and I felt shell-shocked by life as a mother.

A typically frigid New England winter put us under house arrest in a small apartment, where I edited my dissertation and took care of a tiny baby who needed me in order to survive. I didn't want to go outside on the icy sidewalks with the stroller, and running felt crazy when I was so tired. I couldn't see straight to run and didn't know any women with new babies who did run. No one told me that mothers *can* run, and—more to the point—that sport actually helps motherhood. Far beyond that, it never occurred to me that running can feel as much a part of motherhood as the primal drive to protect our young. It was the end of 2004, and I had no clue that a mother, Catherine Ndereba, had won the world's most prestigious marathon that year. In my mind, motherhood entailed surviving the day with an infant who subjected me to intervals of crying with 90-second recovery periods of sleep.

It took six months to motivate myself to start running at all and a year to run a slow but liberating 10K. I hadn't realized that forcing myself out the door for short distances or locating a group of running mothers would relieve my depression and insomnia. I had no clue that even a daily mile alone might give me more strength to care for a baby who I swore was saying I was not his first choice. It was no fluke that my slow return to running coincided with greater adoration of my baby and a new love for being his mother.

On spring and summer and then fall mornings, we would run to the Charles River together, his voice undulating in the jogging stroller as we bounced across cracks in the sidewalk. Occasionally I would run alone while he played with his dad, and on those runs I felt like Winged Victory, but with my head firmly—finally—restored. I shed all of the trappings of motherhood with every step. My new-mom body was completely free, bouncing loosely like clothes in the dryer as I jogged slowly. Everything about my body was slack, as my bladder liked to remind me. But I was running, so I didn't much care.

This book has been a long time coming, both for me and for the topic of exercise, pregnancy, and new motherhood. In 2006, my boy planted the seeds for this book with the Cheerios he threw in my hair while we watched the Boston Marathon on TV. As I made lunch for him in his high chair, I watched athletes whose afternoon was looking pretty different from mine and welled up with tears as the exhausted people ran across the yellow line on Boylston Street. I wanted to be one of those people. I decided the marathon was within reach, since I knew how to run and my baby already had me exhausted anyway. And with a Cheerio to my temple, the seed was planted. My love of marathoning became a love of coaching, which was the perfect venue for merging my doctorate in women's psychology with my dedication to sport. This book is the result of that extensive work with other women and my experience as an athlete mom.

I've met many women who find strength and sustenance in sport and fitness, and this book is meant to underscore that they don't need to give up athletics when they decide to grow a family. The need for activity translates into a habit of the most awesome self-medication, whether it's running, biking, swimming, yoga, or some other cathartic activity involving your body—and pregnancy doesn't mean you must quit that healthy vice. Mother's Little Helper isn't a pill; it's a good sweat. This book is a guide to helping you find that zone of wellness as your body performs its ultimate feat of stamina and endurance: creating, growing, and delivering a baby.

## The Doctor

The sound, current medical knowledge that grounds this book comes from the expertise of Dr. Rachel Kramer, a triathlete, mother, and Yale-educated OB-GYN. Dr. Kramer has delivered thousands of healthy babies while helping moms achieve fit pregnancies with her commitment to fostering women's nutrition and exercise. She helps women with her unique skill as a physician who has successfully achieved a healthy weight loss of her own and built a dedication to endurance sport while raising two sons and practicing medicine.

Dr. Kramer's story of losing 116 pounds through better nutrition and exercise, becoming a triathlete and marathoner in the process, has been highlighted in the *Boston Globe* and on the *Today* show. A trusted doctor in Boston, she tells a familiar story to many women who strive for fitness and fulfillment in work and family. Having grown up as an overweight child who dreaded phys-ed class, Dr. Kramer gained more weight in medical school, eventually topping out at 286 pounds after her second son was born.

Her wake-up call came after lab tests revealed dangerously high cholesterol and a risk for liver disease, and she committed to achieving a more healthy body mass index (BMI). Dr. Kramer isn't shy about sharing her story with patients, inspiring them with her focus on the markers of good health and wellness, not the size of her jeans. And she didn't set out to become an endurance athlete, either. She started her journey into sport where many of us begin—in the gym. After establishing herself as a swimmer, she signed up for her first road race. Having now completed many races, including triathlons, half-marathons, and marathons, Dr. Kramer is a dedicated athlete who empowers women by paying forward the invigoration she gets from fitness and sport. As she puts it, "No one cheers for you at the gym. Where else do adults get people cheering for them?" Dr. Kramer herself walks the talk as a cheerleader for women's fit pregnancy, and she lends her wealth of knowledge, commitment to current research, and inspiration of countless patients to inform and empower you here.

## Summary

Despite many advances in what we know about exercise in pregnancy, misconceptions about its safety can be as stubborn as the lid on those pickles you're craving. Hippocrates taught centuries of physicians that much of women's activity (except maybe housework) could spell disaster for their reproductive health. Forget running a marathon; he believed a sneeze could eject a uterus.[2] He was, of course, wrong. Running won't shake out your uterus any more than a swim would drown your growing fetus. As it turns out, fitness is good for both pregnant mama and baby in utero.

Many people have lingering notions that pregnant women should be incubators, spending nine months at rest and living under one teeny, tiny gestational thumb. We hear that we have a "nesting instinct," and sometimes it seems we're expected to just sit very still and wait for the chicks to hatch. To most of us, though, the idea of prohibiting pregnant women from exercise seems absurd, given all that has been learned about the relationship between physical fitness and women's health. Not to mention, try telling a 21st-century active woman to sit for 40 weeks. Modern women are more attuned than ever to the mental and physical boost we get from activity and know a healthy and whole pregnancy thrives on a body in motion.

There are as many variations on the pregnant athlete's story as there are differences in pregnancies. Multiply that by the differences in doctors' perspectives on pregnancy fitness, and you've got a whole lot of cooks in the kitchen when a bun is in the oven. Some of us keep training for all 40 weeks, while others want to vomit at the sight of our running shoes and would like to tell the 40-week athletes where they can put theirs. This book is for every woman, and Chapter 1 is where the 40-week endurance event kicks off.

In addition to providing current information on training for experienced athletes, this book offers helpful guidance for women who are newly inspired to launch a fitness program, those who currently exercise lightly 0–2 days, or 0–2 hours, per week. More and more evidence suggests that maternal diet, weight, and exercise habits influence the genes of a developing fetus, setting a new baby on a course for future health obstacles and weight trouble. If you're turning over a new cabbage leaf and want to care for your prenatal and postpartum body, this is the book to help you create the healthiest sublet for your growing baby. Pregnancy isn't a 9-month free pass to avoid fitness and eat nothing but pie but rather is the perfect time to honor your health by committing or recommitting to a fitness plan that will lay the groundwork for your active and growing family.

This pregnancy guide doesn't rely on medical ideas from the 1950s—or even the 1990s. Rather, the most up-to-date research will provide you with the straight story behind exercise and pregnancy, allowing you to make informed decisions all along the way. Just as hydration is your best tool for fitness and performance, straightforward, reliable information about exercise and pregnancy will be your best training partner for a fit 40 weeks.

Pregnancy is not an illness, and you're part of a generation of women who won't take it lying down. You can be a new mom of a healthy, happy baby, and at the same time, you can have a body that stays strong and athletic. This book will get you there. Sport moms aren't on the sidelines. We're in the game, at every phase of life. If you follow some key guidelines, listen to your body, and trust the feedback it gives you, you'll be in great shape for 40 weeks of wellness that will place a healthy and beautiful baby in your arms—be still your resting heart rate. No Olympic medal will ever compare to that.

NINE MONTHS OF

# Health & Wellness

# 1
## Building the Base for Your Ultra-Event

CONGRATULATIONS! You are about to embark on the race of your life. And as with any tough endurance challenge, you want to go into it prepared. So many myths and misinformation surround exercise and pregnancy that you may feel as if you want to head for the hills—as long as hiking is okay. (Don't worry, it is.) This chapter gives you the real scoop on advances in research on sports science and pregnancy and will clear up misconceptions about conception and all that comes after. Not only will it give you peace of mind, but when someone asks why you're working out "in your condition," you'll be prepared to explain how exercise is actually a protective factor for expectant women and the babies they're growing. It's much more tactful than saying, "Hey, butt out."

Here's what you'll find in this chapter:

* Exercise and fertility
* Nutrition and fertility
* The interaction between fertility drugs and exercise
* The relationship between your body's health and exercising when you're pregnant
* How exercise affects your growing fetus
* Mental prep work for a fit and healthy pregnancy

By the end of this chapter, you'll feel better equipped to set off on your 40-week countdown to the biggest event of your life. Let's get you on the right track.

## How Does Exercise Affect My Fertility?

This book centers on pregnancy, but naturally, getting to that point is hugely relevant, and athletic women can have particular concerns about conception and fertility because the reproductive system responds to how much energy we expend by working out. We're not talking about how you get through a triathlon during your period or the nuances of core work with severe menstrual cramps. And we're not talking about the tricky business of using up so much energy at the gym that you have zero interest in sex.

Yes, conception is closely tied to energy, to the extent that your body needs enough nutrition, particularly fat, to compensate for your activity and stay in a healthy zone for conceiving and supporting the growth of a fetus. But while exercise intensity and volume are often held responsible for how easily an athletic woman conceives, there are several factors in menstrual regularity that can play out in fertility issues:

* Balance of energy use and fuel intake (calories)
* Body weight and composition
* Disordered eating habits
* Psychological stress
* Individual variation among women

When you have missing, infrequent, or irregular periods as a result of any of those factors, you might experience trouble conceiving, which is known as ovulatory infertility. It's like trying to make an omelet without eggs. Although working out is something of a scapegoat, exercise at high levels of training volume, particularly in endurance sports, can change the frequency and regularity of menstruation, making it hard to predict your ovulation. For example, one study of distance runners found that an increase in mileage from 30 to 42 miles per week was associated with the rate of amenorrhea (missing a period for at least 3 months in a row) going from 2 percent to 31 percent.[1]

The thing is, statistics like this can create the false belief that exercise causes ovulatory infertility, which isn't the case. Amenorrhea associated with exercise has to do with food intake and energy use and maintaining the balance between them. Exercise simply affects that balance, which wobbles when a woman isn't getting enough calories from fat to support her energy use. The result is a disruption in the hormones that direct her ability to conceive and may change her body mass index (BMI), which influences menstrual regularity.

## What's BMI?

You might be thinking, "Hold up; I thought pregnancy meant the freedom to gain weight. Why measure my body fat?" BMI, calculated from a formula based on your height and weight, can factor into fertility and healthy nutrition for supporting the growth of your fetus. If your BMI is either too high or too low, your periods can be disrupted, affecting conception. Specifically, a BMI that is below the 10th percentile, meaning your body fat is less than 22 percent of the total, means you could experience irregular periods or amenorrhea. Eating fewer calories than you use during the day can disrupt your body's ability to produce estrogen and progesterone, which regulate your menstrual cycle and by extension your ovulation and fertility. However, when your diet includes enough fuel to support your exercise routine and energy use, there will be no change in the hormones responsible for fertility.[2] The take-home message? If you're having house guests, you buy more groceries. If you're going to house a baby in your body, you need enough nutrition for both of you. Your kids won't just raid the fridge as teenagers—they'll do it in the womb, too.

On the whole, medical experts agree that there is no real evidence that exercise intensity threatens fertility—as long as you get balanced nutrition to maintain a healthy fat store. In fact, research shows that overweight women experience a higher rate of infertility than those who have lower BMIs, with 12 percent of cases attributable to being underweight and 25 percent to obesity.[3] What's more, vigorous exercise actually lowers your risk for ovulatory infertility, as long as you maintain a healthy BMI. Every hour that you exercise each week is associated with a 5 to 7 percent lower risk of infertility related to ovulation.[4]

Vigorous exercise actually **lowers your risk for ovulatory infertility,** as long as you maintain a healthy BMI.

If your doctor or midwife is concerned about your BMI being too low, you might be advised to decrease your workout intensity or training volume temporarily while you boost your calorie intake to meet your body's demands (based on what you're burning). If that's the case, don't fret about lost workouts. Consider replacing one calorie-sucking cardio workout per week with a yoga or dance class. You might not tap into your aerobic endorphins, but you can still achieve the delicious feel of a sweaty workout. This is a great time to try a new fitness activity you haven't been able to fit into your regular routine or specific training regimen. It could be your chance to try belly dancing and archery—just don't do them together.

Fitness isn't a threat to pregnancy; it's an asset. As long as your training or exercise program increases gradually in intensity and volume, it will be less likely to jeopardize your menstruation because the reproductive system adapts to changes in exertion and metabolism.[5] Older studies that linked exercise and infertility sampled women who started very intense programs or who had other complicating factors, such as stress or nutritional deficits.[6] More recent research that compares exercisers of various levels of intensity with nonexercisers finds that the rate of conception is similar between groups and that approximately 5 percent of women in both groups experienced infertility.[7]

With many women having babies later in life, fertility struggles aren't uncommon, and many women who are frustrated and emotionally spent from

## WHAT'S MY BMI?

General guidelines for women looking to balance fitness with pregnancy focus on sufficient fueling to stay strong and healthy to maintain a regular menstrual cycle. You can calculate your BMI on your own with the Quetelet index, a standard method used by physicians and nutritionists. A desirable range for a woman wishing to maintain menstrual health is 20 to 25.

1. Divide your weight in pounds by 2.2 to find your weight in kilograms (kg).
2. Multiply your height in inches by 0.0254.
3. Multiply that number by itself to get the meters squared ($m^2$).
4. Divide the kg by the $m^2$ to find your BMI.

For example, a 130-pound woman who is 5 feet 6 inches tall would have a BMI of 19 with the following calculations.

1. $130/2.2 = 59.09$ kg
2. $66 \text{ inches} \times 0.0254 = 1.68$
3. $1.68 \times 1.68 = 2.81 \text{ } m^2$
4. $59.09/2.81 = 21.03$

trying to conceive say they cut back on exercise as a way to feel some control over a situation that even doctors have trouble explaining with certainty. This is a normal coping response to a stressful and difficult experience. Ultimately, though, fitness activity is your ally because it relieves stress and helps you maintain a healthy body that can support the growth of a baby. When you think about your workouts, strive to find the mental space between exercise as a stress-buster and workouts that cause anxiety about your fertility. Whether you're a recreational athlete or an elite competitor, exercise jeopardizes your fertility only when it is the reason that your body doesn't have enough fat to ovulate and, therefore, conceive.

Most women likely will not have fertility trouble that is exercise-induced. Fertility might become more difficult for those who train at the elite level because their bodies have so little fat, but you can safely maintain a moderate to vigorous fitness program of 4 to 7 days of cardio and strength building exercise per week without concern about conceiving as long as you get enough calories from fat to menstruate. Such a program includes 30- to 45-minute workouts and longer sessions of up to a few hours for endurance athletes. It's all about fueling to replenish what is burned. However, as mentioned previously, new exercisers should always begin a program gradually, particularly if they're trying to conceive.

As you think about planning your 9-month ultra-event, try to establish a realistic sense of your fitness habits and physical baseline, whether you're concerned about fertility or looking to determine your pregnancy fitness goals. Print out a calendar and write down your physical activity for the month before conception to get a real idea of your workout baseline.

Establishing your BMI is another good frame of reference for understanding your fitness and health baseline, but keep in mind that the formula and results rely on your height and weight without taking into account your aerobic capacity, genetics, bone mass, or ratio of fat to muscle. Nonetheless, your body-fat percentage is important information to consider. A healthy woman is 20 to 25 percent body fat, and a specialist can give you a reliable measurement and analysis of your particular case using skinfold calipers, which might look like a torture device but are actually more like tongs.

Your individual body and fertility will probably have different needs and patterns for metabolizing food depending on the type and intensity of your different activities. If you'd like a specific dietary plan for your fertility and fitness routine, get the input of a nutritionist, fertility expert, and/or exercise specialist who can address the specifics of your lifestyle and health. When it comes to your cycle and fertility, individual variation is as important as the energy intake–use relationship.

## Does Nutrition Affect Conception?

At a basic level, you strike a deal with your body: On average, well-fueled bodies will accommodate a fair amount of activity volume so that women can make babies. It's safe for conception to maintain your workout intensity as long as you also eat enough calories and fat to fuel it.

Tara, a devoted runner, had her first baby in 2006. After a tough postpartum transition, exercise helped her handle life stressors. "Running was my primary form of escape." However, she had trouble with eating and stress, and her menstrual cycle didn't reestablish itself. Her doctor prescribed estrogen for her underlying fertility and depression issues. The estrogen acted as birth control, and Tara still didn't have periods and could not get pregnant.

Over the next few years, she focused on her athletic goals because "running provided me with the mental escape I needed to deal with my busy life." During that time, Tara and her husband adopted two girls and, through in vitro fertilization (IVF), had their fourth baby in April 2012. Through her ordeals with conception, Tara figured out that exercise is key to her mental and physical health and that her fertility was influenced by many factors, including stress, estrogen, and nutrition. Through the process of coping with infertility, she began to place more value on keeping her mind and body healthy with the sport she loves and a balanced diet.

Ovulatory infertility often points to a diet that can't support a healthy weight, and a dietary deficit is closely related to energy use, for example, your expenditure during workouts. In studies, the women who experienced amenorrhea (missing a period for more than 3 months in a row) had a negative energy balance: decreased protein, glycogen, vitamin, and fat stores, which are essential for telling your body it can grow a healthy fetus.[8] Energy intake and expenditure depend on healthy nutrition, so fertility issues are often tied to inadequate calories and an imbalance of protein, carbohydrates, and essential fats. If your menstrual cycle is irregular or you've missed periods for several months, consult your doctor and discuss the full range of possible causes and treatments.

Treating amenorrhea as a result of a low BMI includes increasing your calories and intake of unsaturated fats as well as eating a wider variety of foods or several (four to six) smaller meals throughout the day. Athletic women require more protein than the recommended daily allowance (RDA) for adults, and women with fertility concerns based on menstrual function have consistently lower protein levels in their diet. It is completely possible to be a vegetarian and get enough protein, but it's an area of nutrition to watch, especially if you don't eat dairy products. You can eat protein-rich foods such as beans, soy, whole grains, and meat substitutes to meet your needs.

The story is similar for carbs and fat. Athletic women require more carbs and fatty acids than the RDA for adults in order to replenish their glycogen stores, and women with fertility concerns based on menstrual function have consistently lower carb levels in their diet. Eating foods high in whole-grain carbs before and after a workout will make a huge difference in your energy and performance, not to mention menstrual health. Women whose fat intake is below 15 percent of their total nutrition can boost essential fatty acids with nuts, flax-seeds, and fish such as salmon and tuna.

Low levels of calcium, B vitamins, iron, and zinc often result from a generally inadequate diet. B vitamins are especially important because they help generate energy and strengthen and repair muscle.[10] Folate, in particular, is usually low in athletes and vigorous exercisers. If you are missing periods, you have lower estrogen levels, and it's even more important to get enough calcium and vitamin D to maintain bone strength. Women in endurance sports often take in less calcium than women in other fitness activities or sedentary lifestyles because many of these athletes restrict dairy to decrease fat and expend more energy than they replace with calcium-rich calories. This can cause a calcium deficiency, bone loss, and menstrual irregularity.[11] Remember, ice cream is your friend, especially if you have a BMI under 20 and are hoping to conceive. If you're an endurance athlete and have menstrual irregularity, you need to pay attention to getting enough of these micronutrients to keep you healthy and performing optimally. If it takes a prescription for a pint of Ben & Jerry's, your doctor will probably write one.

Many women committed to fitness experience troubled eating patterns and psychological stress related to body image, ranging from an overly restricted diet to a clinical eating disorder. In order to keep your fertility with regular periods, you need enough nutrition and calories. As an added reason for taking in sufficient calories, athletes with inadequate diets who face menstrual problems also often report injuries, poor athletic performance, and feeling very tired.[12] You can start to set a good example for the baby you want to grow by choosing to reject the tyranny of thinness and by focusing on health, wellness, and strength.

Most athletic women need 2,300 to 2,500 calories per day to maintain a healthy, stable body weight, but endurance athletes can require up to 4,000 calories every day when training for a marathon or triathlon. If you think you need to adjust your energy balance to help with menstrual regularity, meet with a nutritionist and/or your obstetrician (OB). You want to increase calories in small increments, such as 200 to 300 calories per day. Even if you gain a bit of weight, your athletic performance will probably improve because you'll have more energy to work with. A snack one hour before you exercise will fuel both the brain and muscles to maximize the workout, and a glass of chocolate milk is a simple way to refuel afterward.

Along the same lines, if you're a new athlete and your BMI is over 27, your energy output will probably improve if you decrease calories to lose weight in order to improve fertility. This approach will help to reinforce a new exercise habit and make it less arduous as you begin to get more fit. This is not a diet; it is a lifestyle change that will benefit your own fitness and get you to a body that is healthy, fertile ground for growing a baby. Focusing on wellness instead of restrictions in your diet can make a huge difference. Think about how healthy you would like your baby and children to be and treat yourself with the same level of care.

## How Do Fertility Drugs and Exercise Interact?

Often when women go off the birth control pill after having taken it for years, it can take longer than they'd like to get pregnant, and the delay can lead to worry and stress about fertility. Even for women with no fertility issues, it can sometimes take up to 12 months—or longer—to get pregnant. The causes of such fertility struggles are enigmatic to many women and their doctors, so people sometimes point to exercise as an obstacle to pregnancy. Although exercise in and of itself truly has no role in fertility, it can take longer to get pregnant after you go off the pill if you're burning a lot of fat through workouts.

If you find you need to turn to fertility meds, your provider will probably suggest that you approach exercise with caution. Many specialists advise women to restrict running to fewer than 10 miles per week when they're trying to conceive, but again, no research exists to support the idea that exercise threatens fertility. That said, fertility drugs may not mix well with aggressive workouts because they enlarge the ovaries from the size of a walnut to the size of, well, a much larger fruit. As they grow, the ovaries get heavier and can twist from the weight, which can be quite painful. Exercise increases the risk of that torsion. At the same time, exercise also increases blood flow throughout your body, and the uterus and ovaries want a good blood flow to assist fertility. As with keeping a healthy balance of calories and exercise, it's key to balance your body's desire for activity with its need for moderation.

Many women choose to scale back on running and exercise when struggling with fertility because it gives some measure of control. Some IVF research suggests that highly active women on IVF treatments have more trouble conceiving. A 2006 study found that women with 1 to 9 years of exercise history who worked out at least 4 hours per week were 40 percent less likely to conceive after the first IVF treatment than women who exercised less. Cardio workouts, in particular, lowered the odds of conception after the first IVF treatment for that group. Interestingly, though, women with years of high activity since childhood were just as likely to get pregnant as those who didn't exercise.[13] Despite these findings, many specialists still insist that there is no relationship between running and the success of IVF. Clearly, there is some ambiguity, and much more research is needed.

When you make your exercise choices during conception, keep this in mind and focus on what feels right for you. If you're pursuing IVF, you might want to scale back the intensity and volume of your workouts as you try to get pregnant in the months following treatment while not cutting out activity altogether. If training causes you stress over whether or nor you'll conceive, give yourself permission to rest, and look for stress-relieving physical outlets, such as Pilates, hiking, and yoga, that you can substitute for intense training.

## Is Exercise Really Okay Once I'm Pregnant?

Once you're expecting, pregnancy is no reason to give up fitness, and the fact that you are reading this book means you probably don't want to. What would you do if someone said you had to stop doing the sport or workout program you love? Dozens of endurance athletes answered that question in interviews for this book. Most said they'd lose their cool. One mom replied without beating around the bush, "I'd get a second opinion . . . and then run anyway." Fortunately, you're reading that second opinion, which supports your miracle of life in action: 40 weeks of healthy, fit, and safe pregnancy.

Maternal fitness is good for your growing baby as long as you heed your body's cues for adjusting your activity to create the fittest home base for your baby. This is the guiding principle throughout this book. However, you might experience some raised eyebrows when you're sweating through a run or walking into a spin class. Fortunately, research consistently shows that fitness activities and training are not just 100 percent safe but are even key to an expectant woman's mind-body, mom-baby health. A fitness-focused pregnancy is also your ally in the delivery room because maintaining exercise throughout pregnancy is

*Men on the streets used to yell at me that I was doing awful things to my baby by running. The babies are 8, 10, and 12 now.*

RACHEL | IRONMAN® TRIATHLETE AND MOTHER OF THREE

associated with shorter labor and lower rates of cesarean section[14] as well as quicker recovery after delivery.[15]

Here's your first one-line response to the naysayers: "Sitting on your couch for 40 weeks is probably more detrimental to everyone's mental and physical condition than exercising through a normal pregnancy." Indeed, research suggests that a sedentary pregnancy may be associated with hypertension, maternal and childhood obesity, gestational diabetes, some neurological disadvantages in early childhood, and preeclampsia.[16] So lace up those trainers while you can still reach your feet, because exercise is good for pregnancy, especially if you have other stress in your life—and who doesn't? There will be days when you're feeling too low to exercise, and that's perfectly fine. Respect your body's cues for what it needs throughout pregnancy.

When it comes to your workouts, you can feel comfortable getting your sweat on. We now know that both mom and baby do just fine if you follow the standard physical activity guidelines set by the U.S. Department of Health and Human Services,[17] which you'll read in the chapters that follow this one.

## Are There Risks to Working Out During Pregnancy?

Some research shows that standing for a long time or lifting heavy objects is associated with pregnancy complications (such as preterm birth), but exercise is more of a protective factor for women during pregnancy.[18] If you're in good health with no pregnancy complications, the American Congress of Obstetrics and Gynecologists (ACOG) approves a "regular, moderate intensity" exercise program[19] for all fitness levels, even for previously inactive women. You can continue activity as long as your pregnancy stays healthy and you feel good doing it, but it's important to regularly discuss the type and intensity of your workouts with your health care provider. Be willing to make adjustments in response to changes in how you feel over time.

Despite the misperception that exercise during pregnancy is risky for women and their babies, studies consistently show that those who work out when they're expecting tend to have better health outcomes during pregnancy and delivery. Here are some of the health assets found among fit moms-to-be:[20]

* Better cardiovascular function
* Less weight gain
* Lower musculoskeletal discomfort, especially in the lower back
* Better posture
* Fewer muscle cramps
* Better mood and self-esteem
* Lower risk of gestational diabetes
* Fewer instances of hypertension
* Better circulation throughout the body and to the placenta
* Less constipation and bloating
* Improved muscle support for the pelvis
* Lower rates of incontinence
* Stronger muscles, bones, and ligaments for labor and delivery
* More energy and better sleep

So are there any cautions besides not pushing yourself too far? Anecdotal evidence suggests that women already at risk for preterm labor might trigger labor with exercise, but those moms didn't experience the healthy, typical pregnancy that we're primarily focused on here. Exercise does not increase your risk for preterm labor,[21] and additional research finds that women who are considered "heavy" exercisers actually show lower rates of preterm birth than do women who exercise less often or with lower intensity.[22] After 37 weeks, active women deliver 6 days earlier, on average, but these deliveries are not considered preterm.[23]

**DOCTOR'S NOTE**

**Exercise**, even vigorous exercise, is healthy for a growing fetus, provided your body is accustomed to that level of exertion. Monitor your level of effort because overexerting yourself in a workout can be problematic. If you experience bleeding, hyperventilation, blinding headache, nausea, vomiting, or dizziness, stop immediately and contact your health care provider.

More intense exercise is associated with an increase in blood glucose in pregnant women, but there isn't a known impact on insulin level. It's thought that the glucose is produced in response to the need for it as a result of intense exercise, so there isn't likely to be a surplus that would cause a risk to you.

Exercising during pregnancy does seem to make a difference, with the best outcomes reported for women who maintain a consistent workout practice from early pregnancy through the third trimester, even if they adjust the intensity and type of exercise as they near delivery (see Chapter 4). For example, overall discomfort in late pregnancy appears to be lower in women who exercise more during the first trimester, and researchers have found that women with a history of vigorous workouts who continue to be highly active in pregnancy have lower resting heart rates and a better maximal oxygen consumption ($VO_2$max) throughout pregnancy than do moderate and nonexercisers.[24] There's a slight increase in $VO_2$max postpartum even among recreational athletes if they maintain just a moderate level of exercise throughout pregnancy.[25] However, while you can maintain (or even improve) your $VO_2$max, your anaerobic working capacity may be reduced in late pregnancy even if you've stayed active.[26] Still, the takeaway message—one that you will read throughout this chapter and this book—is that maintaining a consistent, moderate fitness program throughout pregnancy is good for you, your athletic body, and your baby's healthy development. In the chapters that follow, I offer guidelines and sport-specific advice to keep you moving through all phases of your pregnancy and beyond.

## What Level of Exercise Is Right for Me While I'm Pregnant?

Your level of exercise will vary throughout your pregnancy. Some days (or months) you'll feel like Wonder Woman, and other times will find you feeling like you ran a marathon when you only walked to the bathroom. As you'll read later, the first trimester (Chapter 2) can sometimes find you quite tired, whereas the second trimester (Chapter 3) will probably find you much more energized. This book will help you know how to respond to changes in your fitness needs and your body's response to activity, and the standard OB visits will be adequate for recreational and noncompetitive athletes to monitor a fitness program. More aggressive or competitive athletes should have additional monitoring throughout pregnancy if they want to reach beyond moderate exercise toward high-intensity and/or high-volume training.[27]

You might be wondering what counts as "moderate" versus "intense," or low versus high volume, and the answer is: It depends. A workout that feels intense to you could be moderate to another woman, and the type of activity you're doing plays into the distinction between moderate and intense. How your body responds to both pregnancy and exercise over those 9 months will be your individual story, and the rest of this book will help you read your own body's cues.

If you're a healthy woman with a regular, moderate workout program of 30 to 60 minutes 3 to 6 days per week, you can continue your fitness routine as long as your pregnancy is progressing smoothly. You can even build your exercise time to 150 minutes (2.5 hours) of moderate exercise per week.

When it comes to strength training during pregnancy, the guidelines set by the Department of Health and Human Services recommend 2 days per week of moderate, light muscle strengthening.[28] If you're also getting regular cardio workouts, focus your strength training on upper-body exercise, paying attention to strengthening your lower back during the first trimester. In Chapter 2, you'll read about how light free weights and resistance bands are a great option for building strength during the early months of pregnancy, but keep in mind that your balance can feel off when you're nauseated or getting bigger. Use a wide, stable stance while lifting, and aim for a higher number of slow reps at lower weights, as opposed to jerky motions with heavy weights. As you'll see in Chapter 3, you can also use your own increasing body weight with a stability tool (such as TRX or a chair) as a safe form of resistance for strength training, particularly when exercising your lower body.

TRAINING TIP  What kinds of workouts constitute "moderate"? Some cardio options in this category are: brisk walking (at least 3 mph, but not race walking), light jogging, water aerobics, and easy bicycling (slower than 10 mph).

If you're used to vigorous workouts in your program, it's okay to continue at that level. Activities considered to be "vigorous" include

* Race walking
* Running
* Swimming
* Aerobics (step, Zumba, dance)
* Biking at least 10 mph
* Hiking

Experienced athletes shouldn't strive to build the intensity of vigorous workouts during pregnancy and should listen when their bodies ask them to reduce their exertion as a result of exhaustion (not just feeling tired) or the other warning signs that appear below. This differs from the case of a woman who is new to fitness. As mentioned earlier, you can increase the duration of workouts up to a total of 2.5 hours over the course of the week and gradually build the intensity from a gentle (e.g., yoga, slow walking) to a moderate (e.g., brisk walking, slow biking) level. However, you should not increase the intensity of workouts that are already vigorous (e.g., running, swimming).

## What If I've Never Worked Out?

If you're new to fitness activities, congratulations on making the move to build fitness into your daily routine as you head into this 40-week fun house, where the mirrors sometimes seem distorted and it can be hard to find your bearings with fitness. When it comes to advice for those new to fitness, the Department of Health and Human Services offers a great maxim: "Start Low and Go Slow." Anyone who is training—whether new to exercise or a competitive veteran—must balance activity with recovery periods. It's tempting to overdo a workout when you've made a new commitment to fitness, but more is not always better, and it's key to realize that your body actually strengthens from rest between workouts.

Here are some guidelines for getting started:

* Build your program from a conservative base, such as walking on a flat treadmill before increasing the incline or walking hills.
* Your program should be based on your BMI (see earlier in this chapter) and individual fitness history. Talk to your doctor and consider working with a trainer who will personalize your workouts and keep you motivated and accountable.
* Educate yourself on prenatal fitness so you can perceive your body's cues regarding when to stop and when to persist with a workout. You're off to a great start by reading this book!
* Diversify your workouts to include cardio sessions, flexibility, and strength training. The variety will keep you motivated and build whole-body fitness.
* Trade sodas and juices for water (flavored water and coconut water are good alternatives), and carry a water bottle with you throughout the day.
* Seek medical attention if you develop warning signs of dehydration (headache, dizziness, nausea, blurred vision, cramping).

As a general guideline for beginning a new fitness practice, you want to keep your exertion below your maximum heart rate (see the sidebar on the next page to calculate your maximum). Strive to top out your workout exertion at 60 to 70 percent of your nonpregnant max as well as consulting Borg's scale of Rate of Perceived Exertion, which is explained in Chapter 2 (page 72). Keep your exercise plan light to moderate at first, measured by time, not distance. Gradually build your base of cardio exercise, such as walking, spinning, swimming, and prenatal aerobics, as well as light core and weight training to build muscle strength.

A great starting point if you are totally new to regular exercise entails a few weeks of the following program before adding 5 minutes per session every three days or adding another workout day to the routine:

## CALCULATING MAXIMUM HEART RATE

The Centers for Disease Control (CDC) recommend a simple formula for calculating a rough estimate of your maximum heart rate, which can then be used to figure out a target percentage of that max. To calculate your max heart rate, subtract your age from 220. For instance, a 34-year-old woman would have a max heart rate of 186 beats per minute (bpm).

To keep your activity in a safe range of 60 to 70 percent of your max, use the following formulas:

$$186 \times 0.60 = 111 \text{ bpm}$$
$$186 \times 0.70 = 130 \text{ bpm}$$

Keep in mind that because these heart rates are very conservative, you can use Borg's Rate of Perceived Exertion scale to safely increase your effort above this level, which may feel like you aren't exerting yourself (see page 72).

* 20 minutes of cardio at a conversational level, 3 to 4 days per week
* Low-weight strength training 1 to 2 days per week
* Flexibility exercises 2 to 3 days per week

Power walking, an elliptical machine, and an upright stationary bike are wonderful ways to begin a fitness program, and the exercises at the ends of Chapters 2 and 3 are ideal for starting a strength and flexibility routine.

Not only should you ease into a program (see Chapter 2 for more specifics) but you also need to consider various factors that can play a role in how your body adjusts to exercise. You're striving for balance, not overexerting yourself in any one area of your life. Give as much attention to sleep time as to work time, and make sure you achieve balance in nutrition and hydration as well.

## How Far Can I Take My Training During Pregnancy?

Although there is little empirical research on the upper limit of exercise intensity, athletes who are accustomed to high-intensity training before pregnancy

The following **general guidelines** for exercise during pregnancy will help to guide your prenatal fitness program:

* Warming up for 5 to 10 minutes is important to ease into a workout and determine how your body is feeling that day. Start slowly and build to more effortful exercise during a session.

* Exercising regularly on most days of the week is better for your fitness than a burst of exercise that's followed by days or weeks of no activity. A moderate workout of 30 minutes on most days of the week will be beneficial for most women.

* Generally speaking, if you're able to hold a conversation while you exercise, your exertion is in a safe zone. Use Borg's Rate of Perceived Exertion scale (see Chapter 2) to monitor your effort level, and don't exceed a 16 on the scale.

* The extra weight you carry as you progress through pregnancy will make easy exercise feel harder. Stop if you feel dizzy or exhausted.

* Drink a glass of water before and after exercise and drink based on thirst while you work out.

* Avoid exercise with a risk of falling or blunt force to the abdomen, such as downhill skiing or soccer.

* Be careful with any exercise that might strain your back, such as overstretching to touch your toes or the floor in yoga.

* Avoid sit-ups or any exercise while lying on your back after the first trimester.

* Always inform the instructor, trainer, or coach that you're pregnant.

and have an uncomplicated pregnancy can safely assume no adverse effects of maintaining that intensity once they're expecting.[29] Women have been physically active and making babies since the beginning of time. As long as you don't get overzealous with a new program or try to prove any points about what you can pull off with your exertion when you're expecting, your body knows how to manage exercise and grow a baby quite well and will let you know if you need to pull back.

If you are already engaging in vigorous activity, you can keep your workouts at that level during pregnancy, but be aware that you may need to make changes in your workout intensity based on your body's cues and responses to exercise. A fit pregnancy really can't accommodate dogged, disciplined severity with exercise. As long as you adjust your mind-set and don't try to push through fatigue, which is a common trait in endurance athletes, it's fine to maintain the status quo in your training intensity because your body is used to it. The chapters in this book will help you cultivate peace of mind when it comes to changes in your body's tolerance for various types and levels of exercise. Just remember that you're exercising for two, and your passenger will have a say in what you do.

That said, if you signed up for a race before pregnancy, you're probably okay to complete it, depending on how far you got in mileage in training. A veteran marathoner might be able to complete a marathon in the first trimester if her prepregnancy fitness level and experience with the distance mean she won't be taking her body to new and unfamiliar territory. She'll probably have to lower her level of exertion in training and perhaps switch to a walk-run plan for both prep and the race, but pregnancy doesn't necessarily mean she must sit it out. The safety and sensibility of running a marathon or completing a similar long endurance event will vary from woman to woman. Every woman is different and needs to talk about her situation and background with her doctor before they decide together if she can safely do her race. While running a marathon in your third trimester might get you a lot of attention, it doesn't mean it's the right achievement for you, and of course pregnancy is not the time to make statements about your endurance. Athletes who push their workout intensity to 90 percent of max heart rate may endanger fetal well-being,[30] so it's critical to stay cognizant of your exertion.

TRAINING TIP A workout should relieve stress, not cause it—whether in terms of severe soreness or pressure to work harder at it. A little postexercise soreness can empower you, but having to take the stairs sideways due to pain from going too hard too soon is demotivating.

If you've been a vigorous athlete, use Borg's scale in Chapter 2 to direct your exertion to a safe zone rather than striving for a percentage of max heart rate. There is simply too much variability in the max heart rate across a pregnancy and too much individual variation between women to say that a specific percentage of target heart rate should direct your exertion. ACOG states that because of the variability in a woman's heart rate during exercise throughout pregnancy, target heart rates are an unreliable measure of intensity.[31] Borg's scale (explained in detail in Chapter 2) is a more useful assessment of your cardiovascular output, and how you feel is a better measure of your physiological response to exercise.

Keeping your prepregnancy level of exercise intensity is a great goal, but if your body tells you it's exhausted or your joints start to bother you as your weight increases, you need to make a change in activity (and perhaps in nutrition). Have your doctor monitor your risk for anemia (more on that in Chapter 3), since increases in your blood volume mean you need to generate a higher red-blood-cell count to prevent anemia. The risk of anemia is greater for competitive (versus recreational) athletes who want to continue with high-intensity training, so stay on top of your iron intake and ask your health care provider to closely monitor your risk for anemia. If you exercise throughout pregnancy, you will sustain an elevated blood volume, and your red-cell volume and total red blood cells will increase to match that volume.

## How Do I Talk to My Provider About Fitness?

Thanks to the anecdotal cases of high-profile athletes, such as marathoner Kara Goucher and tennis player Kim Clijsters, who trained successfully through pregnancy, we now have a medical field looking to establish some reliable, empirical knowledge about the safety of sports and exercise for expectant moms. Still, there's a lot more ground to cover in studying exercise physiology during pregnancy, and researchers are publishing their findings faster than they are trickling into the knowledge base of practicing doctors, coaches, and personal trainers.

Fitness trainers often approach pregnant clients with extreme caution because of lack of knowledge about the safety of exercise during pregnancy. Colleen, an avid runner, remembers, "I got booted from a spin class when I was 5 months pregnant because the instructor didn't think it was safe for me, even

Be aware that **you may need to make changes in your workout intensity** based on your body's cues and responses to exercise.

though I had been exercising the entire 5 months." Similarly, obstetricians still often make very conservative recommendations, whether because of limited exposure to current research, liability concerns, or persistent biases. Approximately half of doctors surveyed in a recent study said they discuss exercise with all of their patients, and half also said that they recommend that patients limit exercise in the third trimester—even patients who have been active in the first and second trimesters—even though exercise research indicates that scaling back is not necessary in healthy pregnancies.[32] Still, many doctors are learning more about exercise and pregnancy, and women now feel more empowered to talk to their providers about combining fitness training with pregnancy. This book will give you advice on how to broach the subject with your doctor or midwife by bringing logs and a list of your training goals to your first appointment.

Keep in mind that some providers are quite cautious, and many of those who do recommend exercise in the first trimester tend to focus on aerobic fitness; a minority suggest resistance training, even though resistance training promotes muscular strength for labor and a quicker recovery after delivery. Many obstetricians also still stick to a heart rate range of 140 to 150 bpm, even though updated ACOG guidelines aren't that conservative, and many don't encourage sedentary women to start exercising at all during pregnancy, even though studies suggest that a gradual, moderate increase in activity promotes healthy gestation. A woman's likelihood of committing to fitness during pregnancy increases when her doctor actively encourages it, so it's important to have an informed provider who's on board with the spectrum of activities you can do safely to maintain your fitness.

Prepping for a fit pregnancy is about building a team of advocates: your provider, partner, friends, and family. They're your support on the sidelines, the ones who will run you in to the finish, and informing yourself will help you include them in your network of fitness and health. You might be driven as an individual athlete, but no woman wins a race without others around her to help propel her there. Not quite your race director but more integral than the guys telling you to turn left or right, your doctor or midwife is a key player on the course.

Doctors have come a long way in their support for exercise during pregnancy, which is key to your health, sense of control, and maybe even general sanity. And it's encouraging that many doctors admit they need to know more about the effects of training on pregnancy, with younger obstetricians more readily encouraging patients to exercise, particularly as a way to prevent gestational diabetes and preeclampsia (see Chapters 3 and 4). While OB-GYNs and midwives incorporate the research on exercise into practice, you're also going to be empowered with a vast information base about your own body and the baby you're growing. It's not just about biceps curls and squats. Knowledge makes you stronger, too.

When you and your provider discuss your fitness practice over the course of the pregnancy cycle, these should be the biggest factors for determining your program:[33]

* Type of exercise
* Intensity of exercise

* Duration of exercise
* Frequency of exercise

Come prepared for your chat about exercise. Think about what you would like your workout routine to look like in each of those four categories, and if you're not sure how conservative your provider will be, know your rationales for believing your choices are safe.

Take the following factors into account when discussing an exercise plan with your provider:[34]

* Age
* Physical condition
* Fitness history
* Risk for heart disease
* Orthopedic history
* Medications
* History of pulmonary disease
* Progression of challenge over the pregnancy

* Disabilities
* Obstetric/gynecological history
* Environment
* Intensity of planned workouts
* Desire to exercise
* Nutritional status

## When Should I Take a Pregnant Pause?

Your fitness practice will be most healthy for mind and body when you can see it as your individual plan without holding it up against an ideal. Try not to compare your own activity with what your best friend did when she was pregnant. Your body will tell you how it feels; attend to those cues. Strive for balance when it comes to the reproductive process and your exercise routine, and be willing to adapt to factors in your lifestyle such as stress, work, and family dynamics. If you can avoid being rigid with your fitness program, your pregnancy and your workouts will do you much more good in body and mind.

There are a few conditions that point to drastically reducing or eliminating exercise, and these are nonnegotiable:[35]

* Relentless vomiting
* Abdominal or pelvic pain
* Severe illness (e.g., flu)
* Vaginal bleeding
* Injuries

Other circumstances that could influence your workout efforts should be discussed with your provider at your initial visit. These conditions include:

* Anemia
* Arrhythmia
* Bronchitis or asthma
* Diabetes that isn't well controlled
* Morbid obesity
* Severely low weight or BMI
* Intrauterine growth restriction in this pregnancy
* High blood pressure
* Orthopedic problems or sports injuries
* Epilepsy
* Hyperthyroidism
* Smoking
* Any other medical condition that makes you unsure whether exercise is okay

## How Does Exercise Affect My Growing Baby?

Research shows that exercise, and even vigorous training, are safe for you throughout pregnancy. So go ahead, exhale. Not only is a fitness practice safe, but also it will improve your health during and after pregnancy. Even better, research shows that your fitness routine or training is both safe and healthy for your growing baby. Here's your next one-liner comeback for the doubters: "Fit mama, fit baby." Let those words help guide your 40 weeks, not to mention the postpartum family life you're going to build.

The research on the effects of exercise on fetal development has kept pace with studies of the impact of exercise on women's bodies during pregnancy, and results show that your activity brings benefit to the baby in utero. Babies of women who were active during pregnancy tend to be leaner at birth and exhibit somewhat better neurobehavioral maturation.[37] These babies also have lower rates of long-term weight issues at age 5 as well as slightly higher brain function during childhood.[38]

From early pregnancy through the third trimester, a fetus can tolerate your exercise very well because a woman's body adapts to pregnancy in a way that

❝ *I was still running 5 miles a day until the week before I delivered and . . . going to the gym and using the weights. Doctor said that as long as it was something my body was already used to, it was fine.*

KATIE | RUNNER AND MOM OF OLIVIA AND AIDAN

...way that allows you to acclimate to changes ...g your growing baby safe and healthy.

...the growing baby. For instance, your body ...ur core body temperature by cooling itself ...from your skin. Similarly, fetal heart rate ...returns to normal after you finish working out.[39] This and other fetal responses to your activity are temporary and have no permanent effects on the baby's development. Regular and sustained workouts can increase the placenta's volume in early and midpregnancy but have no adverse effects on any pregnancy outcomes.

What about intensity? Well, maintaining a fantastically sweaty and vigorous level of exercise does not carry any negative health consequences for your growing baby, either, as long as that level of exercise is familiar to you and your body. There are no significant differences in the fetal heart rate (FHR), Doppler health, birth weight, and Apgar scores among babies of vigorous versus moderate exercisers.[40]

The upshot is that training is good for your pregnancy health, and it actually benefits your baby as well. The base you're building for a fit pregnancy is achieved by the concept of wellness: doing what feels good to the body for the sake of mom-baby health. It's safe and healthy to train and work out, but scale it back if you experience any of the adverse symptoms listed earlier or if you feel depleted and stressed by it to the point that it fails to enhance your general wellness. As athletes, we feel empowered by our agency over our bodies in the world, and pregnancy is no time to lose that self-possession.

## How Much Weight Should I Gain During My Pregnancy?

A healthy woman should strive to gain between 25 and 35 pounds over the course of a pregnancy. An overweight woman will need to gain less, and a doctor will likely advise an underweight woman to gain a bit more (see Table 1.1). How

**TABLE 1.1** Recommended Weight Gain During Pregnancy

| PREPREGNANCY WEIGHT CATEGORY | BODY MASS INDEX | WEIGHT GAIN DURING PREGNANCY |
|---|---|---|
| Underweight | <18.5 | 28–40 lbs. |
| Normal | 18.5–24.9 | 25–35 lbs. |
| Overweight | 25.0–29.9 | 15–25 lbs. |
| Obese | ≥30 | 11–20 lbs. |

Source: Centers for Disease Control, 2012, accessed April 3, 2013, at www.cdc.gov/pednss/what_is/pnss_health_indicators.htm.

much weight to gain varies because your own specific prepregnancy weight and the number of babies you're carrying will direct how much you need to gain to support a fetus. For example, a woman who is considered overweight by her doctor does not need to gain more than 15 to 25 pounds, whereas a woman in the 10th percentile for her BMI could need to gain 30 to 40 pounds to nourish herself and a baby. A woman carrying twins should look to gain 35 to 45 pounds.

According to the Institute of Medicine, you need to gain only between 2 and 4 pounds during the first trimester.[1] That might be hard to manage when

## WHERE DO THE POUNDS GO?

If you wonder where the weight gain is distributed during your pregnancy, here's how it breaks down (on average):

| | |
|---|---|
| 7 to 8 pounds | { Baby } |
| 4 pounds | { Blood supply } |
| 2 to 3 pounds | { Breast tissue } |
| 5 to 9 pounds | { Fat stores for breast-feeding and delivery } |
| 2 to 5 pounds | { Uterus growth } |
| 2 to 3 pounds | { Placenta } |
| 2 to 3 pounds | { Amniotic fluid } |
| 25 to 35 pounds | { TOTAL } |

pregnancy looks like a free pass to cannolis by the dozen, but as it happens, "eating for two" isn't necessary, although there's no shame in a cannoli. Weight gain is a topic to discuss with your doctor or midwife, who knows your individual body type and needs.

## How Do I Keep a Fit Mind During Pregnancy?

While I hope this chapter has given you the confidence to have a fit pregnancy, expecting a baby can still be overwhelming, and the rest of this book will address specific ways to keep a fit mind through each trimester and after delivery. Pregnancy is incredibly exciting, but as you cross the starting line for these 40 weeks, be prepared for mixed emotions. A fit mind is as important to nurture as a fit body. You may at times feel out of control. Exercise can help ease the feeling that you are inhabiting a foreign body (or that an alien has taken over yours). Maintaining a consistent fitness routine—even when you need to reduce the intensity—can empower you to feel more in control of the process and your body's radical departure from the norm. In addition, focus on three areas you can control when striving to maintain your Fit Self with a body in flux:

* Your body philosophy: how you think about training and fitness in this new phase
* Your personal climate: what's happening to you on a daily basis
* Your social outlets: the network of relationships that empower you

### YOUR BODY PHILOSOPHY

Pregnancy is not the time to lose weight, get faster, or work toward new fitness milestones. The key is to let your fitness serve you, not control you, so you can better manage the mental flux that comes with your body's changes. There's no pride in masochism when you're pregnant; your body has enough going on. Elation, deflation, optimism, panic, hope, loss . . . they're all reasonable and normal responses to this major journey. Any time you can give to yourself with a physical and mental release through sweat will help you feel like the fit and fantastic woman you know yourself to be. And the time you devote to rest will reinforce that strength by giving your body what it needs.

## THE LOWDOWN FROM ACTIVE MOMS: STAYING CONNECTED TO YOUR FIT SELF

- Start a subscription to a fitness magazine.

- Run or walk races if it feels good, and cheer for friends if you can't participate.

- Volunteer at a local race.

- Donate to or raise money for a charity that promotes prenatal or maternal health.

- When it's time to buy new clothes, get fitness clothes first. They're more comfortable, and they remind you of who you are.

- Buy new trainers, put new songs on your iPod, and have fun buying a bigger sports bra.

- Treat days you can't bear to work out as rest days or days off, not as failures to exercise.

- Use social networking (Tumblr, Facebook, Twitter) to connect with other active pregnant women who can be a great source of support, information, and motivation.

- Start a fit pregnancy blog; it can be private, or you can share your story with the world. Read the blogs of other pregnant athletes, and use them to build your community.

- Evaluate your workout goals week by week, based on how you feel, rather than holding fast to expectations or rigid plans for the entire pregnancy.

Craft your own philosophy for what feels safe and right as far as workouts go. You may have been an Ironman competitor prior to pregnancy, but biking may feel too risky in terms of the risk of falling, so you may choose to stick to swimming and running for the next 9 months. That's perfectly okay. These are your decisions to make based on how your mind and body feel. It's normal to feel conflicted about such decisions, but know that the only right answer is one that leads to a body rewarded by exercise, not stressed out by it.

*Each morning I'd get up, tell myself that going for a run was good for me, good for the baby, and good for my high-energy rescue dog, and manage to get out the door. Running in pregnancy is like regular running—you rarely regret it afterward.*                                    STEPH | RUNNER AND MOM OF NATE

## YOUR PERSONAL CLIMATE

Entering this year of excitement and upheaval, you want to pay attention to several important areas as you focus on balanced mind-body fitness. Balancing it all might seem like patting your head and rubbing your stomach, and no doubt people will try that on you during the next 9 months. But multitasking is a calling card for most 21st-century women, and keeping your attention on several areas simultaneously is great training for feeding a baby while sending e-mail and making another pot of coffee. As you head into pregnancy with a mind for fitness, guide your workout choices by giving a moment of thought each day to the interaction of the climates that surround you (and are sometimes in conflict): your physical condition, your mental state, and your environment.

Understanding how these climates interact will help you land on the right action plan for yourself.

## YOUR SOCIAL OUTLETS

Finding positive, reinforcing social outlets will make a difference in your fitness and how you cope with any toxic elements that drag you down, such as negative comments about how you look or what training you pursue. Talk to other women about their experiences with fitness during pregnancy. Blogs and Twitter are great options for expanding your social reach instantly, as are local running clubs and personal trainers and coaches. Look for a trainer with a record of working with expectant women. This network will help you navigate the small frustrations and large stressors of pregnancy and celebrate your milestones—like when your "innie" belly button becomes an "outie." And they'll be a source of reassurance and support after the baby is born.

\* \* \*

Whether you're a fierce competitor or you've previously avoided all things sweaty, this is a new phase for your Fit Self. If you feel depleted and sick, you don't have to bike for 5 hours, even if you're a long-course athlete, which can be hard to accept when your athleticism has been central to who you are. Along the same lines, if you haven't been an active person up to now but want to be, resist your prior habit of an inactive life. Respond to your own anxieties the way you would talk to a friend; we're usually more compassionate with others than with ourselves.

Be mindful of your body's cues, your energy, and the new and improved woman you're developing while your baby grows. Some days, it might feel daunting or impossible. It might feel like you're losing your Fit Self to a lifetime in baggy shirts, but you're not. You are getting ready to cross over into Fit Mom territory, and that mom kicks ass. Pregnancy is your 40-week warm-up to achieving the mother of all race medals. Use pregnancy as an opportunity to revise your identity for the better by setting expectations that are good for body and soul.

## Chapter Summary

Despite eons of misunderstanding about the relationship between pregnancy and exercise, new research tells us that training during pregnancy is very healthy. More research is needed on the subject of fertility, fertility treatment, and aerobic activity, particularly running, but studies show that training is not associated with ovulatory infertility as long as your body gets enough nutrition and calories for energy and menstruation. As long as your pregnancy progresses smoothly, there are no adverse effects of exercise on you or your growing baby, and regular fitness activity can actually prevent back pain, gestational diabetes, preeclampsia, and stress. Likewise, there is no apparent negative impact of exertion on fetal heart rate or development. Just pay attention to your body's feedback, and don't strive for competitive training or activity that is new or more intense. Chapter 2 will help you learn how to read your body's first-trimester feedback and draft a training program that is right for your goals and fitness level . . . when you can feel as if a carnival has overtaken your body and mind.

## TO REVIEW ... THE DOCTOR'S NOTES

✳ A woman's BMI needs to fall between 20 and 25 percent body fat in order for her to reliably ovulate.

✳ Vitamins and minerals are best absorbed by the body in the form of food, not supplements.

✳ Folic acid, iron, and calcium are very important for athletes during pregnancy. You can obtain folic acid from berries and enriched cereal. Iron is found in enriched cereals as well as in dried apricots. Calcium is found in dairy products, salmon, and dark greens.

✳ If you have irregular periods, ask your doctor to check for thyroid disease or polycystic ovarian syndrome.

✳ If you are older than 35 and haven't conceived after 6 months, seek a consultation with a fertility specialist. If you are younger than 35, try to conceive for a full year before seeking help unless you have known fertility issues.

✳ If your ovaries are hyperstimulated (enlarged) as a result of infertility treatments, you will need to cut back on your cardio exercise. Consult your doctor about suitable restrictions for your type of exercise and your current level of exercise intensity.

✳ Pregnant women do not need to cap exercise exertion at a max heart rate of 140 bpm as long as they are hydrated. Instead, use Borg's Rate of Perceived Exertion scale, found on page 72.

# Your First Trimester

*On Your Mark . . .*

SCIENTISTS NOW KNOW that pregnancy health and exercise aren't diametrically opposed—in fact, they make great training partners for this ultimate endurance event. So how do you know how to cultivate a fit first trimester? Whether you're a veteran competitive athlete, a recreational fitness devotee, or newly inspired to create a healthy body for yourself and your developing baby, this chapter provides you with the information you need to understand and maintain a fit first trimester. Athletes at the ready: It's pregnancy go time! In this chapter, you'll read about:

* What's happening to my body?
* Special issues and complications
* How do I fuel my first trimester?
* How do I keep a fit mind?
* How do I keep a fit body?
* Gear to get you going

## What's Happening to My Body?

If you don't know the first day of your last menstrual period, an ultrasound in the first trimester will establish the beginning date of your pregnancy. Missing your period is the major telltale sign that you're expecting, and most pregnancy tests will yield a positive result by the time you've skipped one period in your cycle because by then, several weeks will have passed in your pregnancy.

During the first 12 weeks, your body is like a Tilt-a-Whirl on overdrive. Pregnancy changes your blood volume, heart rate, and stroke volume to allow the baby to get the nutrients and oxygen it needs. To do this, your capillaries expand, but the expansion outpaces your blood volume, which leads to huge upsets in your body's stasis, causing fatigue, nausea, and weird symptoms such as congestion and excessive salivation. Odd as it is, your hormones could make you spit like a ballplayer. Your energy goes toward the pregnancy, and you're probably going to be tired from the work your hormones are doing to grow the embryo. No passive job is quite so exhausting.

At about the time your embryo is forming eyelids, you're probably having a hard time keeping yours open. In addition to being so tired that you want to fall asleep in your dinner, you might experience shortness of breath because your body is oxygenating the blood as your blood volume increases. In fact, fatigue and needing the bathroom are sometimes the cues that tell a woman she's pregnant. Other signs of early pregnancy include tender or swollen breasts, so invest in bras that are supportive, soft, and comfortable, especially when it comes to sports bras. Buy them in a few sizes because you'll grow into the larger ones, and they'll be in your drawer when you need them.

You'll probably find that you have to urinate more often, particularly at night. Your kidneys are becoming more efficient by eliminating waste for two. All that talk about leaking when you laugh or sneeze? It holds a lot of water (so to

---

### DOCTOR'S NOTE

**One of my patients** didn't know she was pregnant until she ran a race and posted a dramatically slower time than was typical for her because she was so tired from the first trimester.

**TABLE 2.1** First-Trimester Changes for Your Baby and Your Body

## YOUR BABY

| FIRST MONTH | SECOND MONTH | THIRD MONTH |
|---|---|---|
| Baby is about 6-7 mm (0.23-0.28 inch). | Baby is about 25 mm (1 inch). | Baby is about 75-100 mm (3-4 inches). |
| Embryo attaches to the uterus, with some cells beginning to form the baby and others building the placenta. | Eyelids and inner ear develop. | Buds for all teeth appear. |
| | Ankles, wrists, toes, and fingers develop. | Nails start to grow on fingers and toes. |
| Arms and legs start to grow. | Genitals determine the sex. | Bones and muscles grow. |
| Spinal cord and brain form. | Major organs and systems are in the process of developing. | Intestines and internal parts are forming. |
| | | Skin has transparent quality. |
| Lungs and heart grow, with a heartbeat starting at the end of the month. | | Hands develop, faster than feet, and arms are longer than legs. |
| | | Spine is soft. |

## YOUR BODY

| FIRST MONTH | SECOND MONTH | THIRD MONTH |
|---|---|---|
| Fertilized egg attaches to uterine wall. | Symptoms from the first month become more obvious, particularly nausea and fatigue. | Umbilical cord attaches the fetus to the placenta and brings nutrients and oxygen from your bloodstream to the fetus. |
| Missed period | | |
| Fatigue | Vomiting | Nausea can worsen. |
| Bloating | Heartburn | Acne can develop. |
| More frequent urination | Extra blood is produced to support the placenta. | Change in breast appearance; larger and darker nipples possible |
| Nausea | | |
| Unusual food cravings | Higher resting heart rate supports blood flow to the uterus. | Weight gain typically about 2 pounds by week 12 |
| Swollen, tender breasts | | |

> " *Nausea eased when I ran. Running was a relief—it was the only time I felt semidecent until the nausea abated at about 15 weeks.*
>
> MARY | FIVE-TIME IRONMAN FINISHER; TRIATHLON COACH; AND MOM OF NOAH, JORDAN, AND LARA

speak). Try to drink less in the evening, and limit caffeine, which is a diuretic, to one drink per day to cut back on your trips to the bathroom.

Another less desirable feature of the first trimester is constipation, which happens because your stomach takes longer than usual to process food so that it can get more nutrients into your bloodstream for your growing baby. Heartburn and constipation are sometimes byproducts of the brakes on your digestion; frequent, smaller meals that are high in fiber can help stave off these symptoms. Your workout habit will also help to keep you regular—in mind and body—while everything inside you is changing and growing.

Not every woman experiences every symptom of the first trimester. So your fitness routine probably won't look like anyone else's, and it's important to let go of comparisons or standards you set based on other women's pregnancy experiences. While some women spend 12 weeks in the bathroom, others feel fine. You're dealt the hand you get, and how you play depends on what the cards show. One thing is pretty much universal: Making a human being is one of the most exciting events you and your body can achieve, so go easy on your expectations for yourself as a take-no-prisoners athlete.

## MORNING SICKNESS

Morning sickness (which can occur any time of day but often happens in the morning) is characterized by nausea, dizziness, headache, and sometimes vomiting. You might be glowing, but it's also normal to feel pretty dark. As your blood vessels expand, you don't yet have the blood volume for both yourself and your fetus. Your blood pressure and blood sugar decrease to nourish the placenta, causing you to feel dizzy and nauseated. Because the oxygen in your blood volume is going to aid the developing embryo, you're sometimes left tired and feeling sick. Higher hormone levels in pregnancy are also thought to play a part in the dizziness you might feel. Morning sickness eases up by the second trimester for most women, but it can really wreak havoc on your life and level of activity during those first 12 weeks. However, rest assured, it won't harm you or your baby and poses a medical problem only if you can't keep food or fluids down at all or vomit at least three or four times per day.

One of the best ways to combat nausea is with activity, and many women will tell you that getting out in the morning air for a run or a trip to the gym

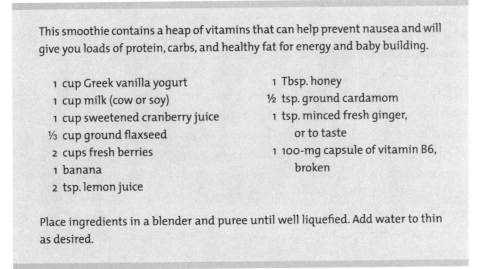

This smoothie contains a heap of vitamins that can help prevent nausea and will give you loads of protein, carbs, and healthy fat for energy and baby building.

1 cup Greek vanilla yogurt
1 cup milk (cow or soy)
1 cup sweetened cranberry juice
⅓ cup ground flaxseed
2 cups fresh berries
1 banana
2 tsp. lemon juice

1 Tbsp. honey
½ tsp. ground cardamom
1 tsp. minced fresh ginger, or to taste
1 100-mg capsule of vitamin B6, broken

Place ingredients in a blender and puree until well liquefied. Add water to thin as desired.

reduced their symptoms and helped them through the first trimester. It's not easy to work out when you feel nauseated, but you'll probably feel better afterward. A postrun smoothie could also help if it's packed with antinausea ingredients such as ginger. Your daily multivitamins can also make a difference, particularly vitamin B6.

To reduce your symptoms, ACOG recommends:

* Sleep as much as possible.
* Eat five or six smaller meals during the day.
* Avoid spicy foods and foods high in fat.
* Eat crackers before bedtime and when you get up in the morning.

## SPECIAL ISSUES AND COMPLICATIONS

### Extreme Morning Sickness

If you can't stop vomiting or suffer from debilitating nausea and dizziness, you may be diagnosed with hyperemesis gravidarum, which both sounds like and feels like a wizard's curse. When this leads to weight loss and dehydration, your doctor or provider will likely intervene with antinausea medication, such as a nighttime combination of B6 vitamins and doxylamine, which you can find over the counter as the primary ingredient in Unisom (Benedictin). Definitely consult your provider before turning to a powerful antihistamine to treat morning sickness, and be careful not to drive, chop vegetables, or e-mail your mother-in-law after taking Unisom.

In extreme cases, a doctor may prescribe Zofran, an antinausea drug given to chemotherapy patients. It usually isn't covered by health insurance and is pretty expensive, but if you're desperate and dehydrated, it could be well worth the money. In severe circumstances, your physician or midwife might even insist on an IV source for fluids to rehydrate you. You might also receive intravenous droperidol, which will give you a powerful combination of fluids, vitamins, and an antihistamine called diphenhydramine. Droperidol controls your nausea and vomiting right away so that you can eat and drink within a couple of days.

If you can't keep any fluids down, avoid exercise because it will dehydrate you further—although in this case, you probably don't feel like working out anyway. Call your doctor if you can't stop vomiting or you're debilitated by nausea.

## Bleeding

Spotting, such as light cervical bleeding during sex or exercise, is not uncommon in the first trimester. This kind of very slight bleeding should stop on its own, but always call your doctor about any bleeding you have, even spotting, because you won't know what the cause is without medical consultation. The two of you will determine the right response, which is often a pelvic exam, a blood test, or an ultrasound.

In the first trimester, bleeding can point to an ectopic pregnancy (a surgical emergency), miscarriage, cervicitis, or a subchrionic hematoma. In the second trimester, bleeding can lead to preterm labor; in the second or third trimester, it can signify a placental abruption or placenta previa. Don't ignore it. An abruption means the placenta has detached from the uterus, causing vaginal bleeding (and typically pain). The fetus may get less oxygen, and, obviously, medical care is urgently needed. Placenta previa occurs when the uterus sits so low that the placenta covers the cervix, causing vaginal bleeding, but usually without pain; this, too, requires medical attention.

## Depression

If you have a history of depression, now is the time to discuss it with your doctor or midwife, who will want to wean you off any SSRI medications in the first trimester to prevent prenatal complications and congenital heart defects that occasionally arise from antidepressants such as Prozac and Zoloft. Ideally, you will wean yourself off antidepressants prior to getting pregnant, as the biggest risk occurs in the first trimester. Beginning a stress-reduction relaxation session, whether it's active or sitting, will help with conflicting emotions in the first trimester. See page 63 for guidance on establishing a meditation practice to help you during the next 9 months. In addition to starting a meditation practice, consider finding a therapist and a support group of other pregnant women who struggle with depression.

## Diabetes

Because glucose levels shift easily during pregnancy, women with Type 1 or Type 2 diabetes will need to discuss their exercise options with their providers. Testing blood glucose with regularity and vigilance is key to a healthy pregnancy for this population, as is checking with their specialists about activity, glucose levels, and kidney health. The adrenaline from exercise can spike your blood glucose levels, so scaling back on the intensity of your workouts may be necessary, although your fatigue and other first-trimester symptoms might already restrict you from the exertion you have been used to. Your

**DOCTOR'S NOTE**

**Diabetics** should seek preconception counseling because diabetes needs to be under excellent control prior to pregnancy. You need to take at least 400 micrograms of folic acid every day for 2–3 months prior to conception to decrease the risk of neural tube defects. If you are a vigorous exerciser, you might need to use less insulin, so be sure to track your sugars. You also may need more insulin as the pregnancy goes on. Regular testing by your specialist is important so that you can change your insulin according to your test results. Always carry a ready sugar source in the event of a hypoglycemic reaction during exercise.

doctor might want you to test your glucose levels before, after, and every 15 minutes during a workout to gauge your body's response to the effort and to calculate your needed intake of carbs and insulin. Your preworkout glucose level might direct you to an easier effort that day, such as a walk or a gentle swim instead of a run. The best approach is communication with your provider and regular, frequent measurement of blood glucose throughout the day, particularly during workouts. Gestational diabetes is discussed in Chapter 4.

## Hypertension

Hypertension (also known as high blood pressure) during pregnancy, defined as a measurement higher than 140/90, can pose risks to your growing baby. It decreases the flow of oxygen and nutrients to the placenta, and it can lead to a placental abruption. There are different types of high blood pressure, however. Chronic hypertension occurs before conception or prior to the 20th week of pregnancy, and you will probably already be on blood pressure medication in this case. Consult your primary care doctor or OB-GYN about medications that are safe to take during pregnancy. Women with mild chronic hypertension should take the same exercise and lifestyle precautions as they did before conception. If you have chronic high blood pressure, ask your doctor if you should be on a Labetolol regimen to decrease the risk of developing preeclampsia later in your pregnancy (see Chapter 3 for more on preeclampsia).

While severely high blood pressure in late pregnancy indicates the need for bed rest, research shows that exercise beginning in the first trimester can improve the natural increase in blood pressure that comes with pregnancy, even among women who aren't active prior to pregnancy.[1] Walking for exercise for 30 minutes three to four times per week is enough to keep blood pressure stable. Resistance training is also known to keep blood pressure at a healthy level, but be careful to keep your weights lighter than you did before pregnancy, as over-lifting can increase blood pressure.

A moderate exercise program should be fine (see "How to Keep a Fit Body" later in this chapter), but discuss your individual case with your doctor. It doesn't take an extreme exercise regimen to show a positive influence on blood pressure, but your provider will assess your situation so that you can determine a safe level and type of activity.

## Immune System and General Health

Your maternal selflessness starts on day one, when your immunities to illness are lowered to keep the baby strong. You're asking your body to care for another body inside it, and all of your defenses are protecting the fetus like a fortress. Because you are directing all of your physical resources to the placenta and your growing baby, your immune system is more susceptible to viruses. For example, women with a history of genital warts might experience warty growths they didn't before, as a lowered immune system can cause flare-ups.

Given your weakened immune system, you should consider getting a flu shot. You don't want to get the flu, especially at a time when you may already be nauseated. The Centers for Disease Control and your doctor will advise you to get one; if for some reason the subject doesn't come up, ask for one.

By the way, it might seem as if you've caught a wretched cold from a weaker immune system, but the nasal congestion that's common during the first trimester comes from increased blood volume in your capillaries. The vessels in your nose expand with a higher blood volume and can make you feel stuffy with sinus pressure. Use a humidifier next to the bed at night to clear your sinuses.

## Miscarriage

Most miscarriages occur in the first trimester, predominantly due to chromosomal abnormalities. According to Dr. James Clapp, an expert in the field of exercise and pregnancy, regular cardio exercise throughout early pregnancy does not increase or decrease the odds of miscarriage,[2] which occurs in 10 to 25 percent of pregnancies, according to ACOG, regardless of exercise habits. That said, a woman with a history of miscarriage needs to discuss exercise with her provider, who might advise limiting exertion or the duration of workouts.

If scaling back helps to comfort and empower you, do so, but also know that you can safely work out without risking the loss of your baby. Chris, mom of two and a devoted yogi, chose to avoid most activities with any exertion during her first trimester after suffering four miscarriages. It helped her to control her circumstances, even though she knew that exercise doesn't cause miscarriage unless it involves a blow to the abdomen or a fall.

Miscarriage is an emotional, traumatic experience often accompanied by feelings of guilt and depression. Many women wonder what they did wrong and question their own behavior and bodies. *Did I eat too much chocolate, drink too much coffee? Did I exercise too much?* If you experience a miscarriage, don't swallow the pain of the experience. Find someone to talk to, and seek counseling through your doctor or recommendations from friends or family.

### Multiple Fetuses

Women expecting twins or more than two babies are considered to be at higher risk during pregnancy, but they can and should still pursue regular physical activity with the input of their doctors for as long as it feels good to them. Naturally, you're going to get bigger more quickly, so your symptoms of fatigue and shortness of breath will likely be exacerbated. However, medically speaking, you don't have to start modifying your exertion until 30 weeks, and you can get plenty of nutrition to support the development of multiple babies as well as your fitness routine. Research shows that unless complications arise during the pregnancy, women who carry twins can exercise to term with the same guidelines for safety as those with single fetuses.[3]

Just like a woman carrying a single baby, rescale expectations for your workouts and goals based on how you feel, and use this phase of life to focus on how much you appreciate the good sensations you get from movement and activity, not your capacity to meet predefined metrics for pace, distance, or calories burned.

## How Do I Fuel My First Trimester?

Contrary to stereotypes about expectant women, pregnancy—particularly the first trimester—isn't best served by a caloric free-for-all. Physiologically, your body has no need for extra calories during those first 12 weeks, although keep in mind that a woman active in endurance sports (or other activities) needs sufficient caloric replacement for what she's burning. Because your ideal intake depends on the forms and duration of your exercise, talk to your doctor about your specific training and eating additional daily calories when you're using energy through exercise. Table 2.2 shows the U.S. Department of Agriculture (USDA) recommendations for first-trimester nutrition.

When it comes to how and what you eat, aim to eat small meals every few hours during the day to avoid a drop in blood sugar, which is a risk in early preg-

## TABLE 2.2 Nutritional Guidelines for the First Trimester

*These USDA recommendations for a 28-year-old woman with a moderate exercise plan of 30 to 60 minutes per day are based on prepregnancy weight and are meant to be general guidelines. You can use the Choose My Plate feature on the USDA web site (www.choosemy plate.gov) to customize the plan to your weight and height. Please consult your provider for nutritional guidelines that are specific to your exercise volume, dietary needs, and desired weight gain throughout pregnancy.*

|  | 5'4", 115 LBS. | 5'4", 140 LBS. 5'9", 135 LBS. | 5'9", 170 LBS. |
|---|---|---|---|
| CALORIES/DAY | 2,000 | 2,200 | 2,400 |
| Vegetables | 2½ cups | 3 cups | 3 cups |
| Fruits | 2 cups | 2 cups | 2 cups |
| Grains | 6 oz. | 7 oz. | 8 oz. |
| Dairy | 3 cups | 3 cups | 3 cups |
| Protein | 5½ oz. | 6 oz. | 6½ oz. |
| Oils | 6 tsp. | 6 tsp. | 7 tsp. |

Source: USDA Daily Food Plan for the first trimester, 2012.

nancy because of the major metabolic changes happening. Eating small, frequent meals also helps prevent nausea and dizziness, particularly an hour or so before a workout and right after you finish, when your blood sugar is likely to be low. As you've probably heard, you might have particular food cravings or turn-offs because of the wild ride your hormones are on.

## CARBOHYDRATES

Carbohydrates are essential to fueling your performance as an active woman. Carbs will also help to fuel the workout going on inside your body as a pregnant woman. You need energy to fuel the activity in your uterus and any activity you pursue for yourself, especially if you're an endurance athlete. Your body is using more carbohydrates while you're pregnant, which can lead to low blood sugar when exercising, so replacing carbs immediately after a workout is essential.

Because your body's carbohydrate use corresponds to the level of exercise intensity, you'll want to focus on replenishing your calories in the form of complex carbs, such as whole-grain pastas, quinoa, nuts, beans, and brown rice, because complex carbs offer more fiber that slows digestion. Avoid eating simple

These foods will give you a 15-gram serving of carbohydrates:

1   banana
⅓   cup quinoa or brown rice
1   slice whole-wheat bread
¼   whole-wheat bagel from a bagel shop
½   cup oatmeal
¼   baked potato or ½ cup mashed potato
⅓   cup whole-grain pasta or brown rice
¾   cup unsweetened, dry whole-grain cereal
½   cup lentils, beans (kidney, pinto, black, garbanzo, white), or split peas

carbs (white bread, for example) as much as possible, and to aid digestion, try not to rush through eating meals in a short amount of time. While this can be hard if you're working and need to eat quickly during a busy day, relying on quick meals of simple carbs prompts unnecessary weight gain because your body metabolizes the sugars in simple starches such as pastries and muffins so quickly that you will find yourself hungry again before you leave the table. Whole grains take longer for your body to break down, keeping you full and giving you and the baby nutrients in the process. As an added perk, fiber can also reduce the nausea of the first trimester. If you can eat several smaller meals with complex carbs, your energy will benefit, you'll digest the food more easily, and you'll be more likely to get a quality workout because you'll burn the fuel more efficiently.

## PROTEIN

As an athletic woman, you should emphasize foods that serve as high-quality fuel for activities that burn a lot of calories. On top of complex carbs, you'll want sufficient protein from meat and/or legumes. If you're a vegetarian, you can get plenty of protein from beans and nuts. The difference between protein from plants and protein from animals is that animal proteins contain all of the essential amino acids, unlike plant proteins, which are incomplete. Because they consume more phytoestrogen, vegetarian women have an increased risk of hyposadias

If you get regular, vigorous exercise, you will need to replace 300 calories per day in the first trimester. Your caloric need will increase for the same level of exercise as you gain weight over the 40 weeks. You won't need any increase in the first trimester other than replacing what you've burned, but the same kind of exercise demands more energy (and calories) when you're heavier in the third trimester.

(a genital birth defect) in male babies.[4] However, this condition is fairly rare, and a vegetarian can find quality nutrition in fortified soy products. In addition, vegetarian women will want to pay extra attention to boosting vitamin B12, iron, and vitamin D.

Eating seafood is fine; however, you need to limit the types and quantities of certain fish to avoid intake of too much mercury. According to the Environmental Protection Agency, too much mercury can pose a risk to the development of a baby's nervous system. ACOG advises that you steer clear of shark, swordfish, king mackerel, or tilefish during pregnancy, as these fish are known to have abundant mercury levels; however, you can eat halibut, rainbow trout, wild shrimp (farm-raised have pesticides), salmon, canned light tuna, and catfish because the mercury content is much lower. For specifics on the safe quantities and types of seafood you can consume during pregnancy and when breast-feeding, see Chapter 4.

## HYDRATION

Hydration is one of the most important factors throughout a fit pregnancy, but it's especially critical in early pregnancy, when your vascular system pumps less blood relative to the expanded capacity of your circulation system. Over time, your body sorts out the deficit of blood circulating, and your blood volume and

TRAINING TIP  To avoid insufficient or excessive calories as your weight increases across pregnancy, keep a daily log of what you eat and your exercise to track healthy intake.

## PRENATAL VITAMINS

Ask any woman who's been pregnant, and she'll probably tell you that prenatal vitamins are like a gift from the gods. Usually prescribed by your OB, they help you feel as well as you can, and many women swear that prenatal vitamins are largely responsible for the great skin and hair that often comes with pregnancy. With that in mind, follow the dosage indications on the supplements you take. While the daily recommended intake (DRI) can be higher for some vitamins during pregnancy, high doses of certain vitamins, such as A and D, can do more harm than good to fetal development.

Your prenatal vitamins will give you the extra iron and folic acid you need because of increased blood volume and an increase in red blood cells. Folic acid (folate, a B vitamin) helps prevent neural birth defects, and prenatal multivitamins will usually provide the 400 mcg you need for the first 12 weeks, though fortified cereals are also high in folate.

You need extra iron during pregnancy because you're producing more blood to support your baby, and your red blood cells need more iron to send oxygen to your organs and to the fetus. ACOG recommends that you take 27 mg of iron every day. You'll likely find this in your multivitamins, but as an active woman, ask your doctor if you need iron in addition to the DRI found in your prenatal vitamin. Low iron can lead to anemia, which is a risk for women during pregnancy. Anemia jeopardizes the safety of your fitness routine because this condition is characterized by blood that isn't transporting oxygen well throughout your body, which is of course important to a safe and healthy workout. Symptoms of anemia include dizziness, shortness of breath, fatigue, and low blood pressure. Be advised that iron supplements can trigger an upset stomach and/or constipation, which are also common symptoms of the first trimester that you won't want to exacerbate. You can offset these side effects by gradually adding more fiber from fruits and whole grains as well as by drinking more water, which your active body needs anyway.

Here are some of the **top sources of iron** for pregnancy:

Pinto beans, ½ cup (5 mg iron)

Fortified cereals, 1 cup (3.5 mg iron)

Tofu, ½ cup (3.5 mg iron)

Pumpkin, squash, or sesame seeds,
    1 oz. (3.5 mg iron)

Beef, 3 oz. (2 mg iron)

Turkey, 3 oz. (2 mg iron)

Artichoke, medium (1 mg iron)

cardiac output will respond with an increase of about 40 percent, but during that process, your body risks dehydration. Dehydration can prompt uterine contractions, so it is important to stay hydrated when exercising. Drinking 8 ounces of water before exercise and 8 ounces of liquid for every 20 to 30 minutes of exercise will keep you well hydrated.

There are two people participating in any workout, and you'll need to take in enough salt and fluids for both of you. Drink water continually throughout the day as well as while you exercise, striving to drink eight 8-ounce glasses every day. The body's heart rate tends to creep up as it gets dehydrated and will stay lower when you are properly hydrated, so drinking plenty of fluid is an easy way to prevent overexertion.

Monitor hydration by checking your urine to make sure it's very clear and by weighing yourself before and after exercise. A loss of weight signifies a loss of fluid that needs to be consumed before you work out again, and 1 pound of weight loss equals 1 pint of fluid to replace. If you are dehydrated (dark yellow urine or loss of weight after a workout), don't work out again without fully rehydrating and checking your urine color for clarity. If you work out in the morning, keep a bottle of water next to your bed to drink if you wake up

## DOCTOR'S NOTE

**Salted or electrolyte drinks** help keep fluid in blood vessels. Remember, though, to consume these in moderation. It's best to alternate between plain and electrolyte waters. Your fluid balance from an exercise session can be measured by weighing yourself before and after your workout. Any loss of weight is body fluid, and 1 pound of weight is equal to about 1 pint of fluid.

during the night so you'll start the day well hydrated and prepared for a great morning workout.

If you're a coffee drinker, it's okay to have your morning cup, but keep in mind that caffeine is a diuretic and also crosses the placenta. While your fetus won't develop birth defects from caffeine, if you drink coffee or other caffeinated drinks while pregnant, your baby might be born with an attachment to caffeine and could go through the same cranky withdrawal that any coffee-loving adult would experience if giving it up. You might consider weaning yourself by diluting your full-caffeine coffee with decaffeinated, gradually replacing the caffeine with decaf altogether.

## How Do I Keep a Fit Mind?

The first trimester can be as much of an emotional whirlwind as a physical one. One minute you feel elated; the next minute you might panic with anxiety and apprehension. This is a big change for you in mind and body; don't feel guilt or shame over stress, anxiety, or depression. These are common emotions. Most women experience a wide range of feelings, and not all are blissful. It's okay.

*During the first 4 months of my pregnancy, I couldn't keep food down, lost weight, and was dehydrated. Exercise wasn't an option, which led to some pretty serious first-trimester blues. Everyone talks about the postpartum blues, but depression during pregnancy is common, too. It should be a happy time, everyone tells you, but when you can't lift your head off your pillow, it's anything but.*

CHRIS | YOGI AND MOM OF TWO BOYS

Having a baby is a wonderful, scary landmark in your life, and yes, it does shake up your identity. Balancing your job, your pregnancy, your partner, and an active lifestyle can be overwhelming, but you can apply the strength that has helped you overcome tough challenges, such as a marathon, to take each moment as it comes so that you can feel empowered during this phase. A daily 10-minute meditation may help ground you, and finding someone who will listen openly to the range of your feelings, such as a training partner, a close colleague, or another friend who's been through it, can also help.

## TENDING TO YOUR FIT SELF

If you've been an athlete prior to pregnancy, your fitness has probably become a core part of who you are. Maybe you got a tattoo to celebrate your Ironman. Maybe you have a regular group that runs a 5K race before coffee every week, or you love the rigors of your masters swim class. How you relate to your sport is your Fit Self. Not only does it let you eat more ice cream, but it's empowering, motivating, and one way you define your awesomeness. You are someone who is used to living a fit lifestyle, whether you're a recreational athlete or an aggressive competitor. An identity can form around your training regimen, connections with other active women, your athletic achievements, and the goals you've set, not to mention the miles in your log, the race medals you own, the meters you swim, and the readout on your bike's power meter. You're an athlete; it's a big part of how you define yourself.

And now you're essentially subletting your body, the temple of your Fit Self, to a tiny person who doesn't care that you wanted to run 40 miles a week and set a personal record at every distance this year while also trying out cyclocross. It is completely fair and typical to feel both elated and a little freaked out by what pregnancy means for your sense of self. So how do you keep your Fit Self and embrace this amazing new identity, your Mama Self, at the same time?

**Be active.** There was a time when exercise during pregnancy was frowned upon, but fortunately science (and countless mothers who came before you) have proven this notion wrong. Now that we know it's perfectly safe to continue running, swimming, and cycling, you shouldn't feel that you must lock up your Fit Self for 9 months. Your Fit Self is with you, at whatever level of activity you do. As you know, she's awfully hard to suppress, and really, why would you want to? Activity is your ally. It's perfectly safe to keep going with your workouts as long as you pay attention to your body's cues and keep your doctor in the loop. Workouts can reduce first-trimester symptoms and empower the athlete at your core. Even if it's just a brisk walk to buy that doughnut you can't get out of your head, pump those arms with determination to have your cruller.

**Be flexible.** Just because you feel so nauseated that you'd rather crawl into the darkest corner of your closet than go to the gym doesn't mean your Fit Self is resigned to sitting on the couch and doing nothing forever. There may well be days that you absolutely can't get out of bed to run, or when your hours at work do you in. That's perfectly okay. Everything is in flux, and feeling your lowest may mean you need rest. Modify your expectations and listen to your body's feedback, but at the same time, consider enlisting a friend to kick you into gear and to hold you accountable to some level of activity when a rest day becomes a rest month. Unless your doctor puts you on bed rest with a medical complication in the first trimester, feel free to be active several days per week. Or find a short race, such as a 5K, that has medals for finishers. It's amazing what a blingy medal will do for motivation and sense of accomplishment, and being around other athletes can keep you linked to the fitness community if you're feeling disengaged.

> *I felt much better keeping up with my regular running/strength training routine [during the first 12 weeks]. At times, [it was] not easy to get motivated, but I always felt better after.*
>
> LINN | MARATHONER, SOCCER PLAYER, AND MOM OF BRENDAN, MACKENZIE, CONNOR, AND JACK

*" I could not work out much. I had some serious morning sickness. I tried gentle walking and yoga on some days, but that was all I could manage the first trimester.*

CHRISTINE | MARATHONER, YOGI, AND MOTHER

## WHAT'S MINDFULNESS?

Mindfulness is the practice of devoting your awareness to the present moment by directing your full attention to repeated deep breathing. Research has shown that mindfulness meditation calms the mind, lowers stress and anxiety, and eases symptoms such as nausea and dizziness. It's not New Age voodoo. Studies using brain scans find that practicing mindfulness changes your neurological pathways for the better in the ultimate bridging of mind and body.

Set aside 10 to 20 minutes every day when you can be in a quiet place without distractions. Many people find morning works best to prepare for the day ahead, but some prefer to wind down at night this way to help them sleep. Sit on the floor, in a chair, or against the headboard of your bed, keeping your back straight. Take deep breaths, paying attention to each moment as you inhale and exhale. Your diaphragm should expand and distend your belly when you breathe in and contract when you breathe out. As you inhale, pay attention to the thoughts that pop up in your head, such as your lunch or e-mails you have to write. Don't force them out; just watch them come and go. Exhale any rigid self-discipline about how you think and feel about yourself and the changes going on in your life.

Experiment with these variations:

- Choose a mantra that is positive, calming, and empowering. It can be a phrase or just words that make you feel good. Let it pass slowly through your mind while you inhale or exhale. "Whole, strong, calm" is a simple mantra that can help center your Fit Self.

- Place your attention on different muscles and joints at intervals in your meditation. For example, start with your ankles, then move to your calves, then knees, quads, hips, glutes, abdomen, lungs, back, shoulders, and neck. Dedicate a few breaths to each area as you check in with it, and then work your way back down from head to toe.

**Try mindfulness meditation.** Muscle tone and cardio strength are great for your pregnant and postpartum body, but a fit mind is just as important to a healthy pregnancy. You have entered a new microcycle in your athlete life, a reorganizing of your Fit Self. She's not abandoning you, but you will need to revise your expectations and standards. That body you bent to your will, the one that would do whatever you told it to do? You're not the only one living in it now. Pregnancy is an exciting miracle, a gift, and a blessing. But for some, the physical adjustments can be a lot to wrap their heads around. You are going to gain weight, and yes, eventually, your profile will be convex. It's required by natural law. To keep calm through all of the changes, consider spending 10 minutes a day in a quiet meditation, either sitting or walking, when you can ground yourself in your knowledge of who you are and the strength you bring to being a mother.

## HOW CAN I INCLUDE MY PARTNER?

In your first trimester, your Fit Self needs your partner almost as much as you did to make the baby in the first place. Think of your partner like a spotter when you're lifting. Like a steady hand on your back, your partner is responsible for supporting you in both your activity and your rest. Here are some practical ways your partner can help you through the first trimester.

* Read this book together, or share particular passages that will help your partner support your active pregnancy. That way you'll have an advocate for your fit lifestyle when you inevitably talk to those with antiquated cautions about activity.
* Discuss expectations, fears, goals, and assumptions about what the pregnancy means for your activity level and athletic identity. Involve your partner to the extent that it feels helpful, and if you want to be left alone, that's cool, too. Speak up.
* Enlist your partner as a member of your fitness support crew, one who knows you and knows what will help you feel whole and sane. It might be a reminder that going for a swim reduces your dizziness along with the gentle nudge you need to get out the door. Or it might

be a reminder that it's okay to rest. And yes, your fitness crew is responsible for keeping pints of ice cream in the freezer.

* Seek out active fun with your partner. That does not mean suggesting your first skydiving adventure to prove that pregnant moms can do it all! But you can work out with a relay run at the track, a swim, going to the gym together, or something you haven't tried before, such as snowshoeing.

## CHOOSING AN OB-GYN

When selecting an OB-GYN, first, read as much as you can on the subject of fitness and pregnancy to stay educated. Bring your workout notes and questions to your appointment and be an advocate for yourself by reviewing your lifestyle with any prospective provider. If you're going to use a group practice, make sure all the doctors in that practice support exercise during a normal pregnancy so you don't wind up with contradictory messages when you have appointments with different doctors. Ask prospective doctors if they subscribe to the current ACOG protocol on exercise and pregnancy; if so, you will find allies to help you navigate your fitness plans.

Doctors who follow the exercise guidelines set by ACOG should affirm that a woman with an uncomplicated pregnancy can pursue virtually the same level of exercise or training as she did before pregnancy, with the same safeguards (such as hydration) that she observed before. The guidelines state that no research exists to indicate that you need to restrict your intensity of training, but you should use perceived exertion, or how you feel, to guide the intensity you maintain. Keep in mind that your doctor should be your crossing guard to fitness, not your detention monitor.

Find a doctor who has experience with athletes or, better yet, who is one. Many OBs depend on very conservative sports guidelines that are frequently updated, and it can be hard for them to keep up with new research. Doctors who are athletes (or who work with a lot of athletes) tend to be better-informed advocates for endurance sports and for more vigorous exercise in general, so don't be afraid to ask about a doctor's own fitness background when you shop around for one who will be a good match for you.

## WHAT DOES MY PROVIDER NEED TO KNOW ABOUT MY EXERCISE PLANS?

Have an early conversation with your provider about your prepregnancy fitness level, specific first-trimester symptoms, and an appropriate plan for exercise in the context of those symptoms. In these first weeks, morning sickness might inhibit you from rigorous training, so discuss your goals for training during this period when exercise can actually help counteract nausea and fatigue. If you have been relatively inactive prior to pregnancy, discuss the activity that will be right for your individual case so that you won't go for workouts that are too aggressive.

Another important point of discussion from the outset is how your exercise plan will play into your weight as the pregnancy progresses. Your training or fitness activity should not prevent your necessary weight gain. Your body needs to be able to support the fetus, which it can't do if you're working out too hard to gain weight. As a way of facilitating the discussion, before your first appointment, jot down your current daily activities or workouts as well as your fitness goals for the rest of the pregnancy. Your provider can then assess your expectations for a pregnancy fitness plan and reassure or caution you about how realistic that plan is.

Hoping to participate in your first triathlon at week 14? Thinking of running a half-marathon in your seventh month? Bring your current training notes, a list of target events and the week in which they occur, and a weeklong sample of your goal training plan (see Table 2.3) to your doctor to discuss the nutritional requirements for that plan. Don't forget that your plan should change during the pregnancy as your body and symptoms change, so this plan is a sample or starting point, as opposed to a strict regimen.

Ask your doctor for help linking up with other pregnant women so you can build a network of athletes. Other expectant women can be a great source of information and support as you enter this new phase of your life. The first trimester can feel like a 180-degree turn from your prepregnancy Fit Self if you're

---

### DOCTOR'S NOTE

**Review your BMI and current exercise routine** with your doctor to determine the right range for your minimum and maximum rates of perceived exertion.

**TABLE 2.3** Sample Workout Notes to Discuss with Your Doctor

**PREPREGNANCY ROUTINE**

| SUN | MON | TUES | WED | THURS | FRI | SAT |
|------|------|------|------|------|------|------|
| 10-mile run | Yoga | 60-min. spin class | 8-mile run | 30-min. swim | 5-mile run | 5-mile run |

**GOAL ROUTINE**

| SUN | MON | TUES | WED | THURS | FRI | SAT |
|------|------|------|------|------|------|------|
| 7-8-mile run or 10-12-mile run/walk | Yoga | 60-min. spin class | 5-mile run | 30-min. swim | 5-mile run | Yoga |

**TARGET EVENTS** **WEEK 10:** *10K race* ‖ **WEEK 14:** *Sprint triathlon* ‖ **WEEK 28:** *Half-marathon (run/walk)* ‖ **WEEK 20–40:** *Prenatal yoga (once per week)*

tired and not hitting workout highs as you did a month ago. Meeting other women who value fitness and are experiencing the same kind of change can be reassuring, and you'll also get some comic relief by finding friends going through other wild changes, such as sore and growing breasts and mood swings. These women can give you motivation and camaraderie to keep you moving when your initiative is low. Like your doctor, they are your fitness allies.

## How Do I Keep a Fit Body?

Your pregnancy is an exciting ultrarace, but your first trimester isn't always a peppy send-off. To hear many athlete moms tell their stories, the first 12 weeks are not unlike the exhaustion from *completing* an endurance race . . . except you're at the start of one. You might have taken that pregnancy test and resolved to be the fittest, healthiest pregnant woman ever to walk the earth, yet you find yourself dragging or struggling to work out.

*❝ My first-trimester fitness story? In theory: ambitious. In practice: meh, due to sleepiness, number of bathroom breaks, and worries about causing complications.*

KRISTIE | RUNNER AND CYCLIST, MOM-TO-BE

Most of your pep is directed toward helping your fetus grow, at the expense of your own energy. Many women feel like they're living in a tired fog, and if you're working, exercise can loom ominously as yet another exhausting commitment. Even devoted athletes often cut way back on training during the first trimester when their energy disappears. Other women simply feel fine, and those who spend months vomiting reserve the right to resent them. The point is: This is *your* pregnancy, so your body, not someone else's, must define your fitness plan.

> *Morning sickness and fatigue killed me, and by the time I started to feel better, I thought, "Oh, why bother now? You've been sitting on your can all this time, what's a couple more months? Go exercise your butt on over to the ice cream."* MARCY | DISTANCE RUNNER AND MOM OF KYRA AND KELSIE

During these first 12 weeks, listen to your body and be flexible about what it is asking you. Going to bed at 8:00 is fine, and scaling back the exertion and frequency of your workouts is reasonable. Your body has been hijacked by the miracle of life, and you may feel that you're no longer in the driver's seat. The good news is that women who kept up their fitness program in the first trimester attest that the boost they got in energy and mood from even modest activity helped get them through the sometimes bleary days of those three months. So go easy on yourself when you're low, but remember that activity is more like a sister than a frienemy.

Meaghan, a devoted runner and swimmer, remembers the shock of her first trimester. She was tired and nauseated, and even though she was determined to run every day, the motivation to get off the couch was just not there. "I needed a nap after runs that were supposed to be short and easy," she says. "Your systems

**DOCTOR'S NOTE**

If you experience more than six **painful contractions** in an hour or *any* vaginal bleeding or gush of fluid, call your doctor immediately.

are on overdrive, and even though I hadn't gained any weight, I was going slower because I felt so tired." She had some issues early on with bleeding, and, understandably, hypervigilance about a safe pregnancy derailed her commitment to working out. "I didn't want to risk anything."

> *You have to be willing to accept what your body has to give you.*
> MEAGHAN | TRIATHLETE AND MARATHONER, MOM OF CAITLYN

To keep a fitness routine when she felt lethargic and cautious, Meaghan and her doctor varied her workouts and relied on light, no-impact crosstraining when she started spotting or felt exhausted. Your doctor might insist that you take no exercise for two weeks if you're spotting, so always consult your provider about your individual case.

"Swimming was the best form of exercise. I did the elliptical, too, or I walked," Meaghan says. Communicating with her physician and rescaling her expectations were the keys to sticking with her fitness routine. What would once have been an easy run demanded greater energy, and she accepted those limitations as part of her own pregnancy story. By paying attention to her body and letting go of rigid expectations, she could keep some motivation when she felt lousy. Her nausea and dizziness dispelled within 10 minutes of starting any workout; that motivated her, too.

To stick to your workouts as much as possible, schedule your exercise in the morning. You'll have the least fatigue at that time of day, and many women say that exercise helped them reduce or eliminate nausea. Even though you feel tired, you tend to feel much better after working out, and just 20 to 30 minutes of activity each day can improve how you feel during the rest of the day and across the first 12 weeks.

## TRAINING SAFELY IN THE FIRST TRIMESTER

In the first trimester, most activities are safe for the growing fetus, as your uterus is protected during these early weeks by your pelvis. As long as you feel okay, maintaining as much of your regular exercise program as you can will set the stage for a healthier and happier condition later in pregnancy and during the postpartum period.

All women, however, whether new to or experienced with fitness, should be aware and cautious about any exercise that involves instability or a risk of falling. For example, trade that wobbly balancing work on a BOSU ball for more stable strength training. Be aware of the risks in an activity, and find alternatives that give you peace of mind, such as a spin bike instead of your road bike.

You simply need to give up some activities while you're pregnant—contact sports, for example. Skip any activities that you and your doctor agree could endanger your baby with hard contact or trauma from a fall. Here are some specific activities to avoid:

* Scuba diving
* Horseback riding
* Diving
* Inverted yoga poses

* Downhill skiing
* Training at high altitude (if you don't already live there)

---

### DANGER ZONE: SIGNS OF EXERCISE-INDUCED DISTRESS

- Pain in back or pelvis
- Exhaustion (more than fatigue)
- Dizziness
- Chest pain
- Hyperventilation or unusual breathlessness

- Severe headache
- Heart palpitations or dramatic slowing of heart rate
- Contractions that persist long after exercise
- Calf swelling
- Irregular heartbeat

When you work out, focus on exercise that makes you feel "good and tired," not wasted, which is tricky when you're starting off tired or used to pushing through the wall. Use the rating of perceived exertion (RPE) scale (see "Borg's Scale of Rate of Perceived Exertion," page 72) to measure the changes in exertion over the course of your workout and as the weeks go by. While you shouldn't be increasing the intensity of your workouts—and probably won't feel like it, anyway—you can continue to maintain your current level of exercise throughout pregnancy as long as you feel good doing it. Pay attention to warning signs of physical distress, and continue talking to your doctor about your workout habits.

*I typically felt a bit nauseous first thing in the morning but would run or swim anyway. I remember heart rate being higher than normal even at really relaxed efforts.... But working out nearly always made me feel better.*

MICHELLE | 10-TIME IRONMAN FINISHER AND COACH, MOM OF MOANA

## Heart Rate and Exertion

Because your blood vessels have enlarged but you don't have the blood volume to fill them yet, your heart rate can spike and your blood pressure can fall more easily during the first trimester. It's also true that exercise during pregnancy increases vascular volume above normal, and, as a result, your max heart rate decreases while your resting heart rate goes up. Because of this, OBs traditionally have relied on heart rate as a measure of overexertion in pregnancy, advising women to keep it under 140 beats per minute. But it is easy for your heart rate to be elevated when you aren't actually overtaxing yourself, and factors such as

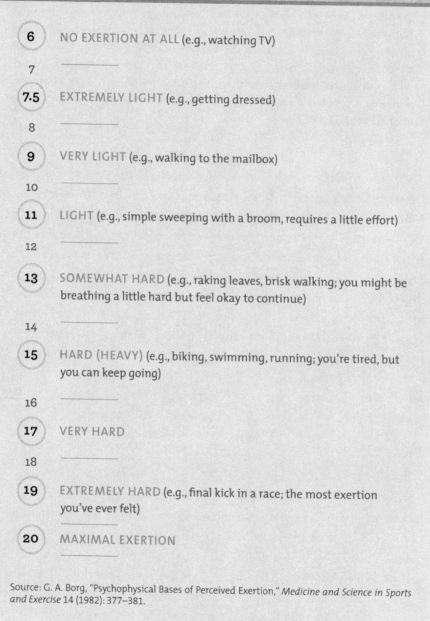

## BORG'S SCALE OF RATE OF PERCEIVED EXERTION

**6**   NO EXERTION AT ALL (e.g., watching TV)

7  ———

**7.5**   EXTREMELY LIGHT (e.g., getting dressed)

8  ———

**9**   VERY LIGHT (e.g., walking to the mailbox)

10  ———

**11**   LIGHT (e.g., simple sweeping with a broom, requires a little effort)

12  ———

**13**   SOMEWHAT HARD (e.g., raking leaves, brisk walking; you might be breathing a little hard but feel okay to continue)

14  ———

**15**   HARD (HEAVY) (e.g., biking, swimming, running; you're tired, but you can keep going)

16  ———

**17**   VERY HARD

18  ———

**19**   EXTREMELY HARD (e.g., final kick in a race; the most exertion you've ever felt)

———

**20**   MAXIMAL EXERTION

Source: G. A. Borg, "Psychophysical Bases of Perceived Exertion," *Medicine and Science in Sports and Exercise* 14 (1982): 377–381.

genetics, age, fitness history, hydration, type of exercise, and environment contribute to make heart rate an unreliable measure of strain—it simply varies too much from person to person.[5] Just watching the evening news can raise your heart rate, and that's not a very good workout.

Instead of using heart rate to direct workouts, it's more useful to focus on perceived exertion and a "talk test." Many doctors who are familiar with endurance sports recommend that active pregnant women use Borg's Rate of Perceived Exertion scale to gauge the safety and quality of a workout. You should be able to carry on a conversation during a moderate-intensity session and a three-word conversation during higher-intensity workouts. If you take a walk break or recovery interval during that higher-intensity workout, you should be able to say a three-word sentence, and if you can carry on a longer conversation, pick up the pace. An ability to debate the pros and cons of starting a 529 fund in your first trimester suggests that you could probably push the workout a bit harder. But if you can only eke out one word between gasps, ease off the effort.

## SAFETY SPECIFICS FOR THE FIRST TRIMESTER

- Spell out reasonable fitness goals, adjust your activity to your body's cues, and let go of disappointments or setbacks so that they don't consume you or discourage your activity.

- Focus on the quality of your sessions, not the numbers. This is not the time to train for your first marathon, but you don't have to give up your regular workout program altogether.

- Work out first thing in the morning if you can. It can help stave off nausea and dizziness, and you'll have more energy than you will after a day at work.

- Rest is integral to training and pregnancy. Be as disciplined with rest as you are with racing and training.

- Drink at least 8 ounces of water in the two hours before exercise, and drink water during your workout.

### "Moderate" Versus "Vigorous" Workouts

*Moderate* exercise consists of efforts that fall between 12 and 16, or "somewhat hard," on Borg's RPE scale.[6] Use the talk test to figure out your effort level: A moderate effort should find you requiring some effort to speak more than short sentences without a break in conversation. Types of activities in this category include walking at least 3 mph (but not power walking), water aerobics, and cycling slower than 10 mph. The elliptical can also count as moderate if you keep your exertion in the designated range, as can Pilates and yoga (but not hot yoga or power yoga).

*Vigorous* workouts place you in the 15 to 17 range, or "hard," on the RPE scale, meaning you require quite a bit of effort to speak. These activities include race walking, running, biking at least 10 mph, high-impact aerobics or step aerobics, hiking, and swimming. The elliptical can become a vigorous workout if your turnover exceeds 155 steps per minute or your heart rate is elevated enough to put you in the designated RPE zone.

Keep in mind that the line between *moderate* and *vigorous* is drawn by effort more than by the duration of your workout. For example, you can have a vigorous workout for 15 minutes and a moderate workout for 40. Also, remember that the reason you want to gauge exertion by effort rather than heart rate is that the same workout will feel moderately challenging on one day and exceptionally vigorous on another. Be willing to adjust your exertion during a workout so you don't overdo a session.

## FIRST-TRIMESTER SAFETY FOR FITNESS NEWBIES

Many women want to introduce a more active lifestyle during pregnancy to prevent too much weight gain, but they wonder, "How do I get moving?" Studies suggest that building an exercise habit up to five days of 40-minute sessions every week can help you with this goal. To start, your doctor will likely approve three to five days per week of light to moderate activity.

Walking, riding a stationary bike, using light weights and resistance bands, water aerobics, and swimming are great options for moderate workouts. You should not start running during pregnancy if you aren't already a runner. Talk to your doctor about the duration of your first workouts and what type of cardio exercise you can do. There is no danger of preterm labor from beginning a regular moderate fitness program when you're pregnant, and there are myriad benefits, both for you and your baby, of introducing a modest exercise routine.

While Borg's RPE scale (page 72) is recommended for women who were active prior to pregnancy, those who are new to fitness should consider getting a heart rate monitor as well to keep tabs on exertion because they may not be as familiar with their bodies' response to exercise intensity. Every woman is different, but knowing your resting and target heart rates will help you know you're exerting enough to reap a cardiovascular benefit while not pushing yourself too far. Ask your doctor about an upper limit (percentage of your maximum heart rate) that is suitable to your BMI. Generally speaking, your heart rate should reach 50 to 85 percent of your maximum, just as before pregnancy, as long as you feel well. According to the American Heart Association, for a rough estimate of your max heart rate, subtract your age from 220.

You want to increase your fitness base over time. Add 5 minutes to your workout every few days of exercise as you build your base to a goal of 45-minute sessions. This isn't like a New Year's resolution that wears off. You're making a great lifestyle commitment to be fit and healthy for your own sake and that of

> I was able to keep running through Week 6, but the Disney half I did at week 7 killed me, and I was done after that. The fatigue and nausea were too much to handle, and by the time they passed, I was feeling too big to run comfortably. Lots of walking on the treadmill and swimming.
>
> TARA | DISTANCE RUNNER AND MOM OF LUKE, BRIANNA, TABITHA, AND RUTH

your baby. A prenatal exercise class can be a good motivator and a more gentle introduction to working out. You want to maintain this healthy new lifestyle, so try different options to find a program that suits you.

### FIRST-TRIMESTER SAFETY FOR EXPERIENCED ATHLETES

If you're an experienced or competitive athlete, your body can sustain your pre-pregnancy level of activity because it's accustomed to more. There are few studies on competitive endurance training during pregnancy, but available research shows that experienced athletes can safely strive to maintain their volume and intensity as long as they don't experience signs of distress.[7] Your high levels of hormones in pregnancy mean your energy is being channeled to the blood vessels in the placenta, and your blood volume is doubling and consuming energy, so you're not going to post faster race times while you're pregnant, but it's still okay to engage in vigorous workouts as long as you listen to your body. Your higher resting oxygen need might actually boost ability in endurance activities in the first trimester. Remember that if you're going to maintain a level of activity that exceeds 2½ hours per week of moderate exercise, the safety of endurance sports can be compromised by the anemia of pregnancy, so pay attention to your iron intake.

## Sport Specifics: Guidelines for Run, Bike, and Swim Training

### FIRST-TRIMESTER RUNNING

When competitive mountain runner Nicole Hunt was pregnant with twins, she already had her hands full with her 3-year-old son, a coaching business, and an accomplished racing career with the world mountain running team. At 10 weeks, she ran a 10K at an easy pace and could manage 50-mile weeks because her pre-pregnancy fitness had been established at a volume of 70 miles per week. Still, during her first trimester, she was hit by fatigue. "For a few weeks I was surviving on watermelon, pistachios, and 1 pint of Ben and Jerry's ice cream (yes, 1 pint per day!!)," Nicole posted on her blog. When she came out of "the first-trimester funk," she inched back toward 65 miles. She listened to her body and adjusted her running to her first-trimester lows. You don't have to be a racer at Nicole's level or mileage to appreciate that even a pro has to heed the cues of her body and do what feels right.

*There were many days during weeks 7–12 that I was so tired during the day that I fell asleep on the couch reading a book. . . . It was a chore just to walk up stairs or keep my eyes open.*　　NICOLE | COACH, TRAIL RACER, AND MOM OF THREE

Running during pregnancy might seem like hell on earth when you're nauseated, but it's perfectly safe and may even reduce the symptoms of morning sickness. Don't take up running if you've never done it before, but recreational and competitive runners can safely keep it going. Continue running the mileage you can safely handle without the warning signs listed in "Danger Zone: Signs of Exercise-Induced Distress" on page 70.

Warning, runners: Be prepared to see slower splits on your track workouts, and don't get bummed about the numbers. Remember, you're running for two, and the baby gets credit for those extra seconds on your intervals. Speed work and interval training are perfectly fine during pregnancy as long as you're willing to be flexible about changing up what you do based on how you feel that day. Be willing to curb a tempo run or a speed workout if something doesn't feel right or you experience any of the warning signs listed above. For example, if you feel

TRAINING TIP　Use random pickups in effort level to adjust your run to how you feel. Try 6 to 10 random fartleks of 30 seconds to 2 minutes during which you increase your effort to a 15 or 16 on the RPE scale. Be flexible, and adapt to your body's cues.

good at the start of a track workout but find yourself dizzy midway through, switch to walking for 5 to 10 minutes to see if your dizziness goes away. If you still feel sick, call it a day and don't try to push through. Save the pushing for the finish line in 9 months.

A great option for intervals is to do a fartlek run, which lets you play with pace (*fartlek* is Swedish for "speed play") in a flexible format based on exertion and how you feel. Your easier periods between each pickup should be longer than the fartlek itself, giving you plenty of time to ease off the higher level of exertion before the next one. If you work some pickups into your run on a random basis, the longer stretches will function as your easy-run recoveries, and you'll get the endorphins from the short, faster intervals. Simply do as many as you feel like doing. If you're out for a run and decide you're just not feeling it that day, let the fartlek intervals go, enjoy the air, and appreciate the level of effort you can make.

## FIRST-TRIMESTER CYCLING

Because your pelvis encases and protects the uterus during the first trimester, it's safe to ride a bike up to 12 weeks because your uterus is still below the pelvic brim. Talk to your doctor about your own individual risks for cycling, and keep in

### TRAINING TIP

Keep water or a sports drink with you while you cycle, and be well hydrated before you start.

Use a bike with wider tires (a mountain bike or hybrid) for more stability.

Replace clipless pedals and toe straps with standard pedals.

Ride in small groups or with a friend.

Stay off triathlon bikes for better maneuverability.

Bring your cell phone and identification on rides.

Tell someone where and when you're riding.

mind that women carrying multiple fetuses, diabetics, and women with high blood pressure are at a higher risk for falling. Similarly, consider how far you can ride on a bike (versus the farthest you could run, for example). If you feel off and need to cut a workout short, you won't want to be 8 miles from home without a way to get back. Set up your rides to have a Plan B for finishing a workout early and getting a ride home.

Take precautions to avoid falls and crashes. Avoid rides in large groups as well as pacelines, fast hill descents, and racing. Think about your priorities and how you define a fit pregnancy. Remember, you can have a fit pregnancy with several months away from single-track speed. Alternative workouts that work your quads, calves, hamstrings, glutes, and cardio capacity (e.g., elliptical, arc trainer, or stationary spin bike) will help you retain your cycling fitness while you're pregnant.

### FIRST-TRIMESTER SWIMMING

Many active women swear by swimming and water running during pregnancy to maintain fitness in a very safe and comfortable environment through all 40 weeks. Whether laps, water running, or water aerobics, swimming is one of the best fitness activities for moms-to-be. The weightless conditions offer great buoyancy for a pregnant body, and other advantages include:

* Centripetal change in blood volume
* High resistance with reduced impact on weight-bearing joints
* Thermoregulation because body temperature dissipates into the water
* Zero concern for falls
* No problems with balance

> **TRAINING TIP**  A group exercise class, like water aerobics, can make your time in the pool more fun and is great for building a network of motivation.

You can work out in the pool as long as you feel comfortable. Take recovery breaks to assess your level of exertion with the talk test, using the fartlek method from running. Using a talk test, you should be able to speak full sentences without pausing to catch your breath. You can randomly increase and decrease your swim effort based on how you feel and when you need a break to tread water or rest at the wall.

If you're an experienced swimmer, you can safely keep your swim workouts and flip turns at whatever level feels good as long as you don't experience dizziness or other warning signs listed on page 70. If you're new to the pool but work out regularly in other sports such as running, build your swimming or water-jogging time gradually by incorporating it into other workouts, such as following a 20-minute treadmill session with a 10-minute water run. Shift the balance over time so that you're in the pool longer. If you're a new athlete, start with a water aerobics class that will be less aggressive and more varied than putting in laps.

For water running, it's best to use a deep-water pool where your feet won't touch the bottom because you can get a nonimpact, high-resistance workout that builds more leg strength than a workout in a shallow-water pool in which you push off the bottom. You will need a flotation belt to keep part of your torso above the water, and you should make sure you're leaning forward slightly as you run. Your gait will need to be exaggerated because of the water's natural resistance. Try to keep good running form, with arms pumping hard to move you forward. Don't expect speed; the pace of water running is altogether different than the pace you'd expect from running on a track. Your pace will feel like slow motion, so it goes without saying that you need to measure your workout in laps or time. If you can't find a deep-water pool, you can still get a great, faster-pace run in a shallow one where your feet push off the bottom. Look for a water running group, or convince a few friends to join you for a workout to get some company in the pool.

## First-Trimester Strength and Flexibility

Now you know you can keep your fitness routine—run, bike, swim—throughout the first trimester to the extent that you feel good in body and mind and take steps to stay hydrated and mindful of your body's cues. Run what's rewarding, but don't run yourself ragged. Bike what's satisfying, but weigh your risks and resist driving the watts past fatigue and into exhaustion. Embrace your inner mermaid.

Light weights and prenatal strength and flexibility exercises lay the groundwork for a fit pregnancy with less back pain and a potentially easier delivery. Strength training during the first trimester will help you manage exertion levels later in the pregnancy and prevent injury when the pressure on your joints increases and makes weight-bearing exercise harder. (See suggested exercises at the end of this chapter.) It's a good idea to maintain musculoskeletal fitness with both resistance training and flexibility exercises by using low weights (less than 5 pounds) or resistance bands and going for multiple repetitions (14 to 20).

Because your pelvis is shielding your uterus when it sits lower during the first trimester and your blood flow is being channeled to your fetus, you are free to lift weights on your back for the first 12 weeks. The same is true for any stretches or strength work you do while lying on your back.

Resistance bands are great for pregnancy strength building and appropriate for every level of fitness without risk of strain. They're also an inexpensive

### BENEFITS OF STRENGTH AND FLEXIBILITY TRAINING IN PREGNANCY

- Less back pain
- Muscle and joint strength to prevent athletic injury or pregnancy strains from relaxed ligaments
- Builds deep ab and back muscles
- Helps reduce postpartum pain
- Boosts your mood

## STRENGTH TRAINING GUIDELINES

**Competitive athletes** (racers and high-volume endurance athletes):
2 to 3 sets of 12 to 15 reps, 2 to 3 times per week

**Recreational athletes** (social athletes, noncompetitive midpack exercisers):
2 sets of 10 to 15 reps, 2 times per week

**Newbie athletes:** 1 to 2 sets of 8 to 10 reps, 1 to 2 times per week

way to build muscle and train at home instead of going to a gym. The elasticity of the bands varies (differentiated by color), so as your strength improves, you can upgrade to a higher level of tautness.

Keep the reps slow to elongate your muscles and build strength, as opposed to reps with a quick or short, jerky motion. Exhale as you perform the exerting step of each exercise (as opposed to the recovery motion).

The following series of exercises will help build all-around muscle strength and flexibility.

### PLIÉ LATERAL SHUFFLE

Abductors, Hips

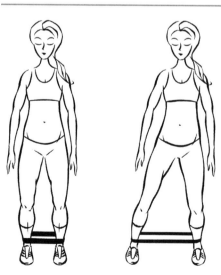

*With feet parallel and knees bent, step sideways. Open and close your steps while keeping the resistance band taut. Complete a set of reps to the right before returning to the left to finish the set.*

## SEATED ROW

Lats, Biceps

With legs in front of you and the band pulled tight around your feet, cross, wrap, and grip the ends of the band. Pull the band back with bent, raised elbows and straight back.

## SUPINE CRUNCH

Abs

Wrap the band around a stable point in front of you and grip the ends. Hold the band taut while lifting upper back and head, but without using the band to pull yourself up Keep arms still and strong.

## SEATED BACK TWIST

Core

While sitting with knees bent, twist gently to one side, hold for 30 seconds, and repeat on the other side.

## LYING LEG STRETCH

Quads,
Hip
Flexors

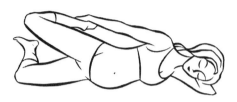

*While lying on side with legs bent, reach around take hold of ankle of top leg. Very gently pull leg back until you feel a modest stretch in the quads. Hold for 30 seconds, and repeat on the other side.*

## STANDING FORWARD FOLD

Calves,
Hamstrings

*Stand with legs hip width apart and one foot planted about 12 inches in front of the other. With straight spine, slowly bend forward and rest hands on shins, feet, or floor. Hold for 30 seconds before returning slowly to an upright position. Repeat on the other side.*

## Gear to Get You Going

In the first trimester, your appearance and gear needs might not change dramatically, but this is a great time to prepare for the coming months.

* Look for a *sports bra* with wide straps and a flat band under the cups, and then buy it in a few sizes.
* Buy *clothing* that wicks sweat and allows your skin to breathe.
* Opt for *shorts* with liner briefs rather than compression shorts, which can constrict, chafe, and trap moisture.

* If you plan to try water running, buy a *flotation belt* to give you buoyancy when you run and make sure the belt is expandable.
* *Flippers* or *fins* help build leg strength while water running or swimming. You can buy fins that are smaller and specific to running in a pool, such as Zoomers, which build more ankle strength than barefoot running in water.
* Consider getting your *bike* adjusted by someone at a specialty store who knows women's cycling and mechanics.
* *Resistance bands* are a great tool for strength training, with a lot of options for various muscle groups. Exercise series are available online and on DVD.
* Buy an *ID bracelet, anklet,* or *shoe tag* to wear while running, walking, or cycling. Make sure it has all the vital information: name, emergency contact, allergies, and an indication that you're pregnant.
* Always wear *reflective material,* a safety vest, and a flashing light when exercising outdoors at dusk or dawn.

## Chapter Summary

This trimester kicks off with all the adrenaline you'd get on any starting line, but soon it might feel like the fatigue you have at the end of any race or hard workout. If you're tired, nauseated, and dragging, don't worry. Legions of active, fit women have felt the same way in the first 12 weeks of pregnancy. The key to coping with the symptoms of the first trimester is to use exercise to offset nausea, boost energy, release stress, and lay the groundwork for a fitness routine that will act as a supportive friend in the coming months. You have a lot of options for staying fit, and listening to your body's feedback during workouts will help you maintain a safe, happy, and healthy start to pregnancy.

If you've felt low and lethargic during this initial period, the second trimester often feels like a runner's high, that delicious flow state of euphoria. The middle stage of pregnancy can be that endorphin rush you love as an athlete. Get ready to find your rhythm.

## TO REVIEW . . . THE DOCTOR'S NOTES

✱ Don't expect to set new time records in the first trimester. While you likely haven't gained weight, these early weeks are marked by specific physiological changes, such as shortness of breath and fatigue, that will typically keep you from feeling or setting your personal best.

✱ Keep well hydrated with fluids that have electrolytes and carbs.

✱ Your growing baby requires no extra calories in the first trimester, and pregnancy isn't a license to overeat. Strive for a healthy balance, as excessive weight gain increases the likelihood of pregnancy complications and childhood obesity.

✱ Severe nausea in the first trimester can indicate twins or an abnormal pregnancy, so seek medical attention if you're so debilitated that you can't keep food or liquids down or feel you can't function during the day.

✱ Call your health care provider immediately if you notice bleeding or any symptoms of a urinary tract infection (UTI), such as burning or pain when you urinate. A UTI can lead to a dangerous kidney infection if left untreated.

✱ Exercise is often a good antidote for nausea. Even getting outside for a short, brisk walk can help beat morning sickness.

✱ Exercise that starts in the first trimester may decrease the risk of preeclampsia later in pregnancy, so this is the time to commit to a regular fitness program.

✱ Bring an exercise log to your first doctor visit so you can consult about your current habits and exercise goals for the pregnancy.

# 3

## Wonder Woman, Activate Your Second Trimester

FOR MANY WOMEN, the start of the second trimester feels like coming out of a hard uphill trudge through a fog. Your body finally understands what it's doing, and your hormones enter a period of feeling in the zone, as if you've shifted gears and every effort seems easier. If the first trimester acts as the base-building phase of the endurance event that is your pregnancy, the second trimester can feel like the midpoint in a race when all systems are go and you're fired up with zest and strength. Your interest in fitness—and probably your sex drive, too—might surge for the next few months as your energy picks up. In fact, many women experience the expectant woman's equivalent of a runner's high. This is the time to take advantage of your energy and positive outlook and to empower your health with activity oriented toward strength and wellness for you and your baby.

With any luck, you're starting to feel like your former self, like you're ready to roll with more activity in your day. However, as you begin to "show," you might hear more unsolicited input about your level of exercise from other people, including people you don't even know. Until recently, many people didn't consider sport or exercise an option for moms-to-be because conventional thinking held that women's bodies aren't capable of multitasking motherhood and sport. *What kind of selfish woman would work out when she's pregnant?* Fortunately, as you enter the best trimester for working out, *you* know the real deal. The idea that pregnant women's bodies and babies are best served by sitting and watching the world go by is as outdated as the orange polyester maternity muumuu. It turns out that exercise is as important as your pregnancy multivitamin. An athletic woman who's expecting might be a little top-heavy, but that warm glow has as much to do with her endorphins as with progesterone.

This chapter will guide you through fitness in the second trimester. You'll find important information such as:

* What's happening to my body?
* Special issues and complications
* How do I fuel my second trimester?
* How do I keep a fit mind in weeks 13 through 27?
* How do I keep a fit body?
* Gear for the middle months

## What's Happening to My Body?

Hormones increase at a fast rate during the first trimester; they pretty much sprint off the start. Once your hormones reach a sustained level, you've created the extra 2 liters of blood to fill your expanded blood vessels, and your body settles in. Between 10 and 20 weeks, the easing of nausea occurs in part because your blood volume increases as a result of increased production of blood plasma and erythrocytes, reaching 1,500 milliliters (ml). Carrying multiple fetuses can result in an even greater increase in blood volume.

Most women emerge from the first 12 weeks with an overwhelming desire to move, and they feel at their best for training and exercise in the second trimester. Your body is better adjusted to the hormonal typhoon of the early weeks, and your baby's major organs have formed, so the extreme demands on your energy have eased up a little. Less dramatic change means you'll start to feel better, something like settling into your zone. As a result, nausea usually subsides and you enter a "glow period." Energy typically returns, as does interest in food, sex, and being places other than your couch and bathroom. And while you aren't going to set any personal bests as you move and sweat in these middle months, you can get back to feeling energized, not depleted, by the activity.

**TABLE 3.1  Second-Trimester Changes for Your Baby and Your Body**

## YOUR BABY

| FOURTH MONTH | FIFTH MONTH | SIXTH MONTH |
|---|---|---|
| Baby grows to about 4.5–6 in. and weighs 4 oz. | Baby grows to about 9 in. and weighs 10 oz. | Baby grows to about 12 in. and weighs 2 lbs. |
| Facial features and eyebrows form. | Body is covered in an oily substance, "vernix caseosa," to prevent infection and keep skin from peeling. | Skin is wrinkled and red, with veins visible through translucent skin. |
| Digits separate and nails develop. Some start thumb sucking. | Organs and muscles are formed, and fat is developing. | Body looks like an infant (head/body ratio is more proportionate). |
| Arms and legs become mobile. | Baby turns and flips. | Eyelids can open. |
| Intestines shift into place, and bones harden. | Baby's sex is visible on ultrasound. | Baby continues to gain fat to keep warm. |
| Baby responds to sound and stimuli from the outside (if you poke your belly, baby will move). | Baby follows regular cycles of sleep and waking. | White blood cells develop to fight infection. |
| Baby covered in fine hair called lanugo. | Fingerprints are formed. | Kicks and thumps with shoulders, fists, and feet. |
| Heartbeat audible with ultrasound. | | Hiccups can be felt. |
| | | Heartbeat sometimes audible by stethoscope or an ear to your belly, depending on baby's position. |

## YOUR BODY

| FOURTH MONTH | FIFTH MONTH | SIXTH MONTH |
|---|---|---|
| Uterus expands upward to abdomen and weighs up to 8.75 oz. | Cramping, or tiny contractions that come before Braxton Hicks contractions later in pregnancy | Leg cramps, felt largely in the calves, often overnight |
| Belly bump appears, and skin and muscles start to stretch. | Belly button "pops out." | Numbness or tingling in fingers and hands |
| Constipation is possible. | Stomach may be itchy due to stretching skin. | Abdominal muscles separate. |
| Down syndrome screening ("quad marker" test) is possible. | Nipples are more sensitive and can secrete colostrum. | Leaking urine possible |
| Amniocentesis is an option (for women over 35). | Vision can worsen. | Shooting pain in lower back, abs, and outer thighs due to pressure on nerves from your uterus, the baby, or relaxed pelvic joints |
| Baby's movement ("quickening") can be felt. | | Varicose veins can appear. |
| Blood volume increases and can cause nosebleeds. | | Glucose test for gestational diabetes performed |
| Leg veins might be more visible. | | |

## UTERINE SHIFT

After the first 12 weeks, the uterus expands and shifts from a pelvic organ to an abdominal organ for the rest of the pregnancy. It's as if your uterus is traveling with an abdominal work visa. As the uterus gets bigger, bladder capacity gets smaller because the bladder sits on top of the lower part of the uterus. In addition to pressure on the bladder, constipation can become an issue because your increase in progesterone slows down the movement of your digestive tract in order to give the fetus more time to absorb nutrients. Exercise can help food to move through your system, as does drinking enough water and eating raw fruits and vegetables that are high in fiber.

## POSTURAL CHANGES

The uterine shift during this trimester causes a change in your center of gravity, giving you more of a forward tilt and potentially causing lower back pain. The change can result in a new curve in your spine (kyphosis) that can lead to motor weakness.[1] By your fifth or sixth month, you'll experience a progressive inward curve of the spine (lordosis, or swayback) because your pelvis is tilting forward.[2] As a result, you will also experience shortened hip flexors and piriformis muscles. These postural changes develop to compensate for your growing uterus and usually go away after birth. Strength work during pregnancy will help your back before, during, and after delivery. Plank and side-plank yoga poses will fortify your core and back and help prevent pain from motor weakness, muscle contraction, and posture changes.

TRAINING TIP  Back pain occurs for up to 50 percent of pregnant women, making core stability exercises key to a solid and strong back while you're expecting, as well as an easier labor and delivery. You can develop excellent back and ab strength with standing core exercises that can be performed comfortably into the seventh month of pregnancy. Try the sequence on pages 92–93 for safe, stabilizing core work that won't disrupt your balance as your body changes.

## ABDOMINAL CHANGES

In concert with changes in your back, your ab muscles will separate in the sixth month as your uterus expands further. Once the ab muscles separate, you'll be able to feel the gap if you run your hand down the middle of your torso. Avoid

TRAINING TIP  To strengthen your back and abdominal muscles, do plank pose every day. Start with two sets of 20 to 30 seconds each for the **basic plank** and the **side plank** on both sides, working your way to 2 to 3 sets of 60 to 90 seconds for each position. Keep your spine as straight as possible, thinking of a straight line running from the crown of your head to your heels. Resist the urge to push your rear out and back. Planks might become difficult after week 20, when you can try the standing core exercises (see pages 92–93).

If necessary, make the planks easier to adapt to your changing weight. To make a side plank less difficult, lie on your side and instead of lifting onto the side of your lower foot, keep your lower knee on the mat, with that leg bent behind you. To make a basic plank easier, put your weight on your knees instead of your feet or open your legs wider and hold yourself up on your palms instead of your forearms.

SIDE PLANK

BASIC PLANK

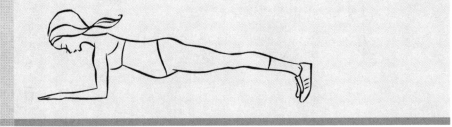

sit-ups from the beginning of the second trimester (the abs separate before you can feel it with your fingers). Don't lie flat on your back when lifting weights or exercising because the weight of the uterus on the big vessels that bring blood back to the heart will decrease blood flow. When you exercise, you need to increase the blood flow to the heart. However, planks and standing core exercises will strengthen your back when crunches become a bad idea.

## OBLIQUE TILTS

1–3 sets of
12–15 reps

*Stand with your feet slightly wider than hip width apart. Raise your arms straight over your head. Without pushing your hip out to the side, tilt your torso to the right for 4 seconds, engaging your back and ab muscles to keep your spine vertically straight and strong. Slowly lift your torso back to return to the center, again using your abs to pull you back up. Repeat to the left side.*

2ND
TRIMESTER

## FORWARD BEND WITH SQUAT

1–3 sets of 12–15 reps

*Stand with your feet hip width apart. For extra stability, hold on to a counter, chair, or table. With arms extended outward from your sides, slowly bend forward from the waist until your torso is parallel to the ground, about 4 seconds. Then bend your knees for 3 seconds while your torso is parallel to the floor. To finish, straighten your legs as you raise your torso back to its upright posture. You can perform this exercise without the squat if you wish. And, as your midsection grows, you need not bend until parallel to the floor; just keep your spine straight and bend as far forward as your body allows.*

## FLUID SECRETION

Women in the second trimester tend to sweat more readily than they did prior to pregnancy because their core body temperature can increase by a degree. Many women also begin to experience congestion and postnasal drip, with some expectant moms saying they feel as if they have a cold. The hormones that cause your sinuses to fill might also increase salivation and affect your gums, making them red and more sensitive. Getting a dental cleaning in the second trimester can help prevent pregnancy-induced gingivitis (bleeding gums).

Although it's more likely to begin in the third trimester, don't be alarmed if you start to secrete colostrum in the fifth month, when your breasts swell and begin to prepare for nursing. Colostrum is the thick, highly nutritious substance a baby will suck in the days before your milk comes in after delivery. It's never too early to invest in a supply of cotton nursing pads, which you can slip into a sports bra if you want to conceal leaks during a workout.

Many women also begin to experience a white vaginal discharge during the second trimester, which increases over the course of pregnancy. The hormones and increased blood circulation that help you deliver a baby also create that substance, and you might find you have to change underwear throughout the day (or wear liners). If you get a yeast infection, consult your doctor before applying medicated creams. The same applies to taking anything for congestion.

## LOOSENING JOINTS

The second trimester marks the point at which most women experience looser joints, though the degree varies from woman to woman. At about 12 weeks, most women's pubic symphysis (the joint that connects the right and left pubic bones) widens by 10 mm to prepare for delivery. The round ligaments that attach your pelvis to your uterus stretch, becoming more responsive to sudden changes in position, such as getting up from a chair or twisting. A round ligament strain from getting out of bed or standing up from your desk can cause pain in the side abdomen or back. Use the leg exercises at the end of this chapter to strengthen your hips and prevent strain.

## SPECIAL ISSUES AND COMPLICATIONS

### Carpal Tunnel Syndrome

Some women develop the repetitive stress injury known as carpal tunnel syndrome in the second trimester as a result of retaining fluids. The same way your feet might be swelling out of your shoes and your rings are getting tight on your fingers, the swelling in your wrists puts pressure on your nerves, which can cause tingling and numbness in your hands. It can worsen at night, when the

**TRAINING TIP**  Feeling pain in your wrists? Try this yoga-derived stretch to release tension and pain. Don't force palms to touch; just gently push fingertips against each other if your hands barely meet. If you can't get your fingertips to touch, you can still get a mild stretch by doing it in front of you.

fluid that causes swelling in your lower half during the day redistributes throughout your body.

A few tools can help you to alleviate the pain: An ergonomic keyboard can shift your arm position to adjust your wrists and decrease discomfort, as can raising your desk chair so your wrists are lower than your elbows. Wrist braces are also available, and wrapping your wrist with an ice pack can also reduce swelling. Gentle yoga is a way to improve wrist and hand strength, which can prevent carpal tunnel pain. While it's painful and annoying, particularly when you need to type, pregnancy-induced carpal tunnel syndrome usually disappears in the weeks after the birth when the swelling decreases and your nerves aren't compressed anymore.

## Leg Cramping

Beginning in the second trimester, many women experience strong cramping in their legs, in particular at night. They are the kind of cramps that athletes sometimes experience late in a race due to dehydration, salt deficiencies, or low potassium. Cramping is also sometimes attributed to imbalances in calcium, phosphorous, and magnesium. In pregnant women, cramping can occur from holding an inactive position for too long—for instance, when you are sleeping or sitting at your desk—leading to low circulation in your leg muscles. When your uterus puts pressure on major blood vessels that go to your legs, you experience reduced blood flow to those muscle groups, causing the cramping.

To combat cramping at the office, try doing 15 to 20 calf raises a few times per day while seated at work by flexing your feet and pushing the balls of your feet against the floor and lifting your heels. If you find yourself standing for long periods, calf raises will keep the blood moving in your lower legs, where cramping is

What are some ways to treat leg cramps?

- Get up and walk, heel striking to stretch out the calf.

- Gently pull the toes of the cramping leg into a flexed-foot position, with the knee as straight as possible. If you can't reach your feet, use a towel or resistance band around your foot and grip both ends.

- Stretch your calves for 30 to 60 seconds per side by standing on a step and dropping your heels off the back.

- Try 2 sets of 10 to 15 wall push-ups, making sure you are inclined enough to feel a gentle stretch in your calves.

### DOCTOR'S NOTE

To avoid **dizziness** during a workout, make sure you're well nourished and not hungry when you start. Eat a snack that contains both carbs and protein about an hour before you exercise. Almond butter on whole-grain toast or a cup of granola with milk are two quick options.

The movement of regular exercise can help prevent **hemorrhoids** by reducing swelling and, as a result, decreasing the pressure on your veins.

most common. For cramping in bed at night, do what athletes do best: Get up and move. Walking around is the best way to fix a cramp, although groaning and swearing while you do it definitely helps.

## Dizziness

It's not uncommon for the first trimester's dizzy spells to continue into the second trimester. In the first 12 weeks, you felt light-headed because your blood volume hadn't yet caught up with the expansion in your blood vessels. That's now been corrected, but there are times when the weight of the uterus might settle onto blood vessels, causing dizziness, particularly when you stand up quickly or dismount from a bike. Grab hold of a wall or stable surface to regain balance, then walk for a minute. If possible, lie down on your left side or sit with your head between your legs. And remember to stand up slowly. If you get dizzy during a run or other workout, it's fine to continue after the feeling passes, but if you continue to feel dizzy, call it a day and find some fluids.

## Hemorrhoids

The increase in blood volume causes swelling in the large veins in the rectum, which means that many women experience the discomfort of hemorrhoids in the second half of pregnancy. The constipation that's common during pregnancy can exacerbate the problem. If possible, avoid sitting for long stretches of time in order to relieve the pressure on the veins around your rectum. Take walking breaks at work, and lie down at home to change your weight distribution. To prevent hemorrhoids, make sure your diet contains enough fiber (see page 105) and that you're drinking water consistently during the day, about 8 to 10 8-oz. glasses.

Several treatments can alleviate the pain of hemorrhoids. Sitting in a bath of warm water offers a lot of relief, as can sitting on an ice pack several times a day to reduce swelling. You can also apply witch hazel, available over the counter, with a sterile cotton pad to your rectum. Using premoistened wipes is advised if you find dry toilet paper itchy and scratchy. You can also buy hemorrhoid creams, though these treat only symptoms, not the underlying problem. The good news is that hemorrhoids typically go away after delivery.

## Placenta Previa

The placenta sits low in the first trimester, but it normally shifts upward as your pregnancy progresses and your uterus grows. When it continues to sit low and covers the cervix, which is the opening to the uterus, placenta previa occurs. About 1 in 200 women experiences this complication, which is more common among women carrying multiple fetuses. Previa is also more common among those with larger placentas; many previous pregnancies; or scarring on the uterus due to a prior surgery, such as a C-section.

Mostly occurring at the end of the second trimester, previa's primary symptom is vaginal bleeding, sometimes accompanied by cramping in the uterus. The bleeding can become severe and might stop on its own, only to start again a few days later. It is possible to develop previa without bleeding, however, and your provider will be able to diagnose it during your ultrasound. If you're diagnosed with placenta previa, you will be advised to limit your activity and will be put on pelvic rest (including no sex). In cases where women lose a lot of blood, a provider might require a hospitalized bed rest or delivery, which is the ultimate treatment.

While some cases of second-trimester placenta previa fix themselves, the majority of women with placenta previa deliver via C-section because the placenta, which is made mostly of blood vessels, will start to hemorrhage with labor if it's covering all or part of the cervix. Vaginal delivery poses a risk of maternal or infant death due to severe bleeding. Call your provider right away if you're experiencing any vaginal bleeding.

## Preeclampsia

High blood pressure that develops after the 20th week is known as gestational hypertension, and it can lead to preeclampsia. This condition is diagnosed from a combination of high blood pressure in a woman with a prior normal blood pressure reading, the presence of protein in the mother's urine, abnormal liver-function tests, and/or decreased blood platelets. Those with chronic hypertension are at increased risk for developing preeclampsia in the second half of pregnancy. Untreated, preeclampsia can be lethal for both the mother and baby, but gestational hypertension and preeclampsia go away after delivery. Sometimes called "toxemia," the condition is diagnosed anytime beyond 24 weeks. Symptoms can include:

* Persistent headache
* Pain in the right upper side from a swollen liver
* Weight gain
* Dark spots (floaters) in your field of vision.

Your doctor will routinely check your blood pressure, and a spike in your blood pressure higher than 140/90 in the second trimester can point to preeclampsia. Keep in mind that a single blood-pressure test that reads high is not enough to diagnose it. If a second reading performed about six hours later also shows high blood pressure, it's likely your doctor will decide that you have preeclampsia. Take the diagnosis seriously. Left untreated, this condition can cause maternal and fetal death. Fortunately, modern medical treatments mean very few women in the United States die from preeclampsia.

If preeclampsia is diagnosed, your doctor will require regular blood tests to check your liver and kidney function. You'll also have to undergo regular urine tests, which will measure your protein levels and determine the severity of your condition, over a 24-hour period after the initial blood-pressure reading. In addition, it's common for a woman with preeclampsia to have additional ultrasounds to assess fetal development as well as a nonstress test, which gauges your baby's oxygen supply by measuring its heart rate over time. If the fetal heart rate

## WHO'S AT RISK FOR PREECLAMPSIA?

Some factors can put you at higher risk for the diagnosis:

- Obesity
- Carrying twins or more than two fetuses
- First pregnancy
- Age under 20
- Age over 35

- History of lupus
- History of kidney disease
- Diabetes (both gestational and nongestational)
- Blood-vessel problem

increases at least 15 bpm for at least 15 seconds twice in a 20-minute period, the baby is doing just fine.

Rest won't cure preeclampsia, but it can mean more time with the baby in utero, delaying a preterm delivery. The only true treatment for preeclampsia is delivery, although you can lower blood pressure with medications, such as anti-hypertensives, prescribed by your doctor. When ignored, preeclampsia and high blood pressure put women at risk for seizures, placental abruption, stroke, severe bleeding, and death.

In addition to blood-pressure medication, your doctor might require bed rest. Specifically, you might be advised to lie primarily on your left side. Your activity will be highly limited, and your doctor might want to increase your office visits to measure your blood pressure, dip your urine for protein, check your liver function and blood tests, and question you for symptoms.

While many experts believe that exercise can prevent preeclampsia by keeping your blood pressure down, it's no guarantee because doctors don't know exactly what causes preeclampsia. Even highly fit women and athletes can develop high blood pressure and preeclampsia. This is another good reason to heed the cues of your body and give it rest when you're tired or experiencing stress. If exercise helps your stress level and doesn't drive you to exhaustion, it's healthy. If your training contributes to feeling pressure and fatigue, scale back on the volume and intensity of your sessions and consider alternative forms of fitness.

## How Do I Fuel My Second Trimester?

Beginning around week 12, a woman who is a normal weight before pregnancy will want to be gaining about a pound per week, even though her desire to eat constantly might dissipate a little after the first trimester. Gaining about 1 pound per week—as opposed to giving yourself over to a carnival of calories—will mediate the force on your joints when you exercise. Believe it or not, a 20 percent weight gain can increase the force on a joint by up to 100 percent during a workout. Gaining a safe and healthy amount of pregnancy weight can prevent hemorrhoids, back pain, varicose veins, stretch marks, and shortness of breath as you get into the third trimester. Table 3.2 shows the U.S. Department of Agriculture (USDA) recommendations for second-trimester nutrition.

Of course, you need to fuel yourself to stay fit, maintain your energy, and grow a baby. Remember that the baby will take what it needs from you and will continue to grocery shop from your stores as long as you breast-feed, leaving you in need of good fats and calories to take care of your body. Your weight gain will probably fluctuate from week to week, but your provider will monitor you to keep you in a zone of healthy weight for your BMI. If you're carrying twins, you'll need to gain more, though not double the weight gain recommended for a single fetus.

## TABLE 3.2 Nutritional Guidelines for the Second Trimester

*These USDA recommendations for a 28-year-old woman with a moderate exercise plan of 30 to 60 minutes per day are based on prepregnancy weight and are meant to be general guidelines. You can use the Choose My Plate feature on the USDA web site (www.choosemy plate.gov) to customize the plan to your weight and height. Please consult your provider for nutritional guidelines that are specific to your exercise volume, dietary needs, and desired weight gain throughout pregnancy.*

|  | 5'4", 115 LBS. | 5'4", 140 LBS.<br>5'9", 135 LBS. | 5'9", 170 LBS. |
|---|---|---|---|
| CALORIES/DAY | 2,400 | 2,600 | 2,800 |
| Vegetables | 3 cups | 3½ cups | 3½ cups |
| Fruits | 2 cups | 2 cups | 2½ cups |
| Grains | 8 oz. | 9 oz. | 10 oz. |
| Dairy | 3 cups | 3 cups | 3 cups |
| Protein | 6½ oz. | 6½ oz. | 7 oz. |
| Oils | 7 tsp. | 8 tsp. | 8 tsp. |

Source: USDA Daily Food Plan for the Second Trimester, 2012.

Women who are a normal weight can achieve the pound-per-week goal by eating 300 extra calories per day starting in the second trimester. However, the number of calories you require ultimately depends on how much energy you're expending every day, particularly in workouts. This is another reason that you should review your training or exercise routine with your provider on a regular basis. Because your activity might well change from what you did in the first trimester, you'll need to confer about how many calories per day you'll need to replace what you burn and gain enough weight to support the baby.

In the same way that you would before you were expecting, be sure that you're consuming sufficient carbs to keep you going with adequate energy for fitness, work, baby, and the other demands in your life. Chapter 2 reviewed the benefits of whole-grain carbs versus foods with simple carbohydrates and listed several options that provide a high whole-grain carb content.

You metabolize carbs faster when pregnant, whether active or at rest, and have lower glycogen reserves, which can result in lower blood glucose. This situation predisposes pregnant women to hypoglycemia. The carbs you get later in pregnancy are used to give the fetus glucose and amino acids for neurological

## HOW MUCH WEIGHT IS RIGHT TO GAIN?

### PRENATAL WEIGHT GAIN GRID IN POUNDS

Use the BMI calculator to determine your weight gain category and which grid line you should follow. The weight gain lines indicate the **minimum** weight gain for your category. Gain **below** these lines is considered inadequate.

···· Underweight Prepregnancy ‖ BMI: <19.8 ‖ Wt. gain: 28–40 lbs.
— Normal Prepregnancy ‖ BMI: 19.8–26.0 ‖ Wt. gain: 25–35 lbs.
— Overweight Prepregnancy ‖ BMI: 26.1–29.0 ‖ Wt. gain: 15–25 lbs.

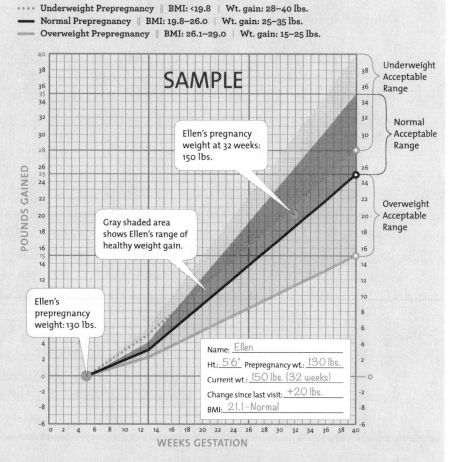

**How to Plot Your Weight:** Start by entering your weight before pregnancy (pregravid) on the zero pounds line. The line across the bottom of the grid is the weeks of pregnancy. The number of pounds gained is found on each side of the grid. From the pregravid (zero pounds) line, count the squares above or below to mark your pounds gained or lost so far. Each square is one pound.

Source: Based on Colorado Department of Public Health and Environment chart.

Note: Go to **http://healthy-baby.org/weightgaingrid.htm** to find a blank copy of the chart that may be used to fill in your own information.

Here are some tips to make sure you're steadily **gaining a healthy amount of weight**:

✳ Eat several smaller meals more frequently throughout the day.

✳ Always eat a breakfast with carbs and protein, such as peanut butter on a bagel or an egg on an English muffin.

✳ Make sure snack foods are high in good fats, not empty calories that don't keep you full. Trade potato chips for pita and hummus. Opt for high-protein nuts or yogurt with granola instead of pretzels or muffins.

✳ Quit a soda habit and switch to water or vegetable juices, such as carrot or tomato.

development while also supplying you with fatty acids, ketones, and glycerol. Studies have found that exercise can actually induce near-hypoglycemic states in workouts of 45 to 60 minutes at 60 percent of $VO_2$max.[3] You'll metabolize carbs on a par with the intensity of activity during exercise, particularly in non-weight-bearing workouts. In short, kick those low-carb diets to the curb and try to eat 200 to 225 grams per day of carbs from a variety of foods, including fruits, vegetables, legumes, and grains.

Because constipation becomes more likely in the second trimester, it's a good idea to eat foods that are very high in fiber. In addition, gestational diabetes is more rare among women with diets high in fiber.[4] Fiber is most readily available in plants and plant-based foods, which is great news for vegetarians, though whole grains and legumes are also a good source. You should strive to eat about 25 grams of fiber every day, which isn't hard if you eat a lot of raw fruits and veg-

**DOCTOR'S NOTE**

Your growing baby needs approximately **33 grams of carbohydrate nutrition** from you every day to achieve optimal brain development. That means your diet should be 40 percent carbs, or between 200 and 225 grams each day.

½  cup 100 percent bran cereal (8.8 grams)
½  cup black beans (7.5 grams)
1  medium baked sweet potato with skin (4.8 grams)
½  cup white beans (4.5 grams)
1  whole-wheat English muffin (4.4 grams)
1  raw pear (4.3 grams)
2  figs (4 grams)
1  cup strawberries (4 grams)

etables, especially the skin. Although you can get fiber from supplements, it's best to boost your intake through food because you tend to get more that way, and high-fiber supplements can inhibit your body's ability to absorb other nutrients.

Iron continues to be key for women in the second trimester because blood volume outpaces red-blood-cell volume, posing a risk for anemia. As many as 50 percent of pregnant women do not get enough iron, which is critical for preventing fatigue and feeling weak and is known to stave off depression. It also acts as a key player in tissue repair, which is a major issue for athletes who want to continue training while they're expecting. As mentioned in Chapter 2, you'll find iron in meat, but it's also plentiful in nonanimal sources such as beans, raisins, and enriched cereals such as Total.

Vitamin C is another key nutrient during the second trimester because it helps your body to absorb the iron that you need. It's also useful for fighting infection and boosting your immune system. In keeping with the three-servings rule you're applying to iron and calcium, shoot for three daily servings of vitamin C, which you can easily find in fruits, vegetables, and juices. It's best to eat these raw, as heat will cook out a significant amount of the vitamins.

## DOCTOR'S NOTE

**Caffeine** can inhibit your body's ability to absorb iron. Eat your servings of iron 1 to 3 hours before or after consuming anything with caffeine.

| ½ | medium kiwi | 1½ | cup grapes |
|---|---|---|---|
| ⅓ | cup strawberries | ½ | medium green bell peppers |
| ½ | medium grapefruit | 1 | medium tomato |
| ⅛ | small cantaloupe | ½ | cup vegetable juice |
| ½ | cup orange juice | ½ | medium mango |

While your baby depends on these vitamins and nutrients in order to grow, too, fetal development depends heavily on your hydration. Your fluid intake will help to build your baby's cells, transport nutrients to the placenta, and excrete waste. In addition, staying hydrated will help you retain less fluid, reducing the swelling that comes with the second trimester. Strive for 2 quarts of water every day, but keep in mind that you'll get credit toward your daily fluid requirement from fruits, soups, and any additional decaffeinated drinks—however, steer clear of sugary sodas. As a reminder, you know you're hydrated if your urine is clear.

## How Do I Keep a Fit Mind?

The second trimester can bring feelings of exuberance and energy and the conviction that you might be Wonder Woman in an empire-waist top. This isn't a symptom of pregnancy-induced psychosis; you're fully saturated in the glow period. Let those feelings propel you in your training and your relationships to other people and your changing body. As you get bigger, fitness and exercise can serve as a physical talisman, a feeling of strength and independence that you can hold on to while everything about you feels as if it's changing rapidly.

### TENDING TO YOUR FIT SELF

As your baby develops in the second trimester, there may be times when you catch your reflection in a mirror and wonder just whose body you're seeing. The second-trimester changes can feel like a wonderful but strange identity crisis. So how do you hold on to your Fit Self when your appearance seems to change by the minute?

**Opt out of fat thoughts.** If you're an athlete or live an active life, you are probably so engaged with your own body on a daily basis that you notice every niggling twitch and change it goes through. Pregnancy can turn those observations into billboards. You might feel like your body is public domain, like people feel free to touch it and comment on how you look, especially as you begin to show. *You're carrying high. You're carrying low. You're carrying in front* (obvious, but people say it). *You're carrying in back* (uncouth, but people say it). It is easy to become self-conscious. Keep the self-criticism in check with the knowledge that this kind of evaluation by others is part of our culture's "pregnancy talk," and the shape you take is insignificant relative to the great shape you're in by maintaining a fit pregnancy. Opt out of any fat thoughts by reminding yourself of the incredible process your body is performing. You're making a human being! Ground yourself in the miracle of what your body can do.

Weight gain is a by-product of pregnancy, not an assessment of who you are. By prioritizing fitness throughout your pregnancy, you will drop the weight quickly when returning to activity postpartum. Staying active over the next 9 months is about staying healthy and sane, not staying slim. The power you get from being an athlete can help shield you from fat thoughts and other people's comments.

**Keep moving.** Activity is the best treatment for any mental lows. We tend to stay stagnant in mind when we aren't active in body. Continuing a fitness program, even if you're modifying the volume or intensity, can be a powerful force in offsetting any stress from a changing body. Activity will benefit the health and fitness of your pregnant body, not to mention a mind unsettled by body image.

**Express yourself.** Along with renewed feelings of zest and that delicious flow state of the second trimester, many women feel a renewed interest in sex. Sex is perfectly safe for you and your baby during a normal pregnancy (see the cautions on page 98 for those with placenta previa), and it can help you feel more at home in your changing body. Your sexual expression is a great source of empowerment and a way to own your body. You don't have to pose naked for a magazine to make a statement about your comfort in your own skin, but encouraging yourself to feel sexual and to flaunt your beautiful body is a great way to feel empowered and boost your self-esteem as your shape changes.

As you become more visibly pregnant, you'll likely be dealing with how others perceive (or misperceive) pregnancy and exercise. Be prepared to hear unsolicited advice, even from complete strangers—and even when you're in the middle of a workout. This is a good opportunity for you to cultivate a thick skin while you're building muscle and cardio fitness. Your doctor or midwife should be on board with your workout plans and will help you assess your own case to decide the type, frequency, and intensity of your workouts as you enter the trimester when you probably feel most capable of exercise. It helps that you know it's safe, and while you might not want to educate people with stats and the guidelines from ACOG, you can shrug off criticism by replying with Wonder Woman grace, "Research and my doctor agree that it's safe and healthy."

The critics you might meet provide a great opportunity for being a strong, self-possessed mother. Motherhood is laced with other people's ideas about your choices and parenting style, and for better or worse, it starts before the baby is even born. Take some faith and strength from the countless women who believe in a fit pregnancy—and who are now raising healthy, active, and happy kids. These are your sisters, and they have your back . . . and belly.

## TALKING TO YOUR PROVIDER

No matter what level of intensity or volume your training takes—beginner, recreational, competitive—you'll need to involve your practitioner in a regular schedule of monitoring your physiological response to exercise and the fetal response starting in the second trimester. You can chart several key data points and bring the information to your appointment for discussion with your doctor or midwife:

* Weight before and after exercise to assess hydration and fluid loss
* Temperature measured before and after exercise as well as at the point of highest exertion in a sample workout. An ear thermometer is most accurate
* Sensations before, during, and after exercise, on a scale of 1 to 5, of hunger, weakness, fatigue, and mental state
* RPE for different types of exercise
* Weight gain and expansion of your belly by the week
* If you're a rigorous athlete training at high intensity, work out at your peak intensity in a sports medicine laboratory environment so that fetal heart rate and activity can be monitored

Exercise specialist and OB-GYN James Clapp recommends that women new to exercise should discuss their notes on this information with their provider every four weeks, and competitive athletes should be monitored biweekly. Those who fall between these two ends of the spectrum should be assessed every three to four weeks. He also notes that, if possible, women should have their blood glucose tested after a workout.

If the assessment of your fetal responses and physiological symptoms (temperature, weight) is all clear but you feel low and fatigued, you'll still need to modify your training regimen. Discuss options for making some changes in your routine with your provider. Here are some key points of change to cover and possibly modify:

* Duration (exercise in shorter sessions)
* Frequency (take a rest day between workouts)
* Type of cardio workout (more or fewer intervals, switching activities)

* Type of strength training (different muscle groups, number of reps, types of exercises)
* Gear and equipment (shoes, kickboard, heart rate monitor)

## How Do I Keep a Fit Body?

If morning sickness led you to scale back your fitness activities in the first trimester, rebuild your activity with slow, gradual increases in the time you spend working out, adding anywhere from 5 to 10 minutes every other workout and one day of exercise per week. Your boost in activity grows a healthy baby, even though the placenta is doing a lot of the babysitting in midpregnancy. It provides oxygen and nutrients to the developing baby and mediates your body's use of exercise and your baby's growth. A baby in utero will typically experience a higher heart rate in response to your exercise, but medical research indicates that the increase in heart rate (up to but not higher than 180 beats per minute) shows that the baby is adjusting to a decrease in oxygen availability, not suffering damage from oxygen deficiency.

While regular weight-bearing exercise can increase placental volume during early and midpregnancy, research has yet to find any adverse impact on the pregnancy or health of the fetus. The placenta's strength and functioning benefit from your fitness, which supports its capability to support your baby. To put it simply, midpregnancy workouts are good for everyone.

Starting or continuing your fitness program in the second trimester will help to offset the potential pain from loose ligaments and lower-back stress as well as maintain your muscle tone, posture, cardio fitness, and ab strength. Obvi-

### DOCTOR'S NOTE

Women who **increased moderate exercise** volume (treadmill or stair climber) from 20 minutes, 3 to 5 times per week, at week 20 to 60 minutes, 5 times per week, in week 24 had lighter babies with less fat mass. Differences in birth weights were attributed to the difference in the volume of weight-bearing exercise in the last 5 months of pregnancy.[5]

ously, staying active also helps you avoid unnecessary weight gain during the second trimester, which will help you feel better mentally and physically and create a strong, healthy, lean baby and mother.

Although the expansion of your chest when your diaphragm moves during the second trimester increases the amount of oxygen you can consume (to a capacity of 300 ml), you have higher resting oxygen needs. On top of that (or below, rather), your larger uterus is pushing on your diaphragm, which means you have less available oxygen during aerobic exercise, making breathing harder. You'll probably take more breaths relative to your prepregnancy self, even during a light workout, and your anaerobic exercise ability (meant for speed and building muscle mass) will drop because you have a decrease in your pulmonary reserve.

Along the same lines, you will start perceiving an increase in the workload of a session that felt mild before, and your performance output will probably decrease. While some women find themselves able to increase activity compared with the first trimester, those who have exercised throughout the first trimester might find that they need to decrease the length of their workouts as they gain weight (even with the Wonder Woman frame of mind). Everyone will be different. As your baby and belly grow, reducing the distance or time of a particular type of workout is a normal outcome of listening to your body.

Don't lose heart, though. Remember that pregnancy is a phase in your athletic life, not a changing of the tides. It should be of some comfort that researchers have found that if you regularly engage in aerobic training, your exercise capacity can still increase during pregnancy, relative to that of sedentary women. During these weeks, you can get creative and substitute an alternative workout that offers great training with less demand for a more rigorous one. Thirty minutes of pool running, for example, offers great strength and aerobic benefit when your 30-minute road run demands too much cardio effort and uncomfortable impact. Another option is breaking your workout into double sessions: either two shorter (15- to 20-minute) workouts in the day or switching between types of exercise every 10 to 15 minutes in one session to target different muscle groups that will augment the aerobic demand.

Starting in the second trimester, you'll want to focus more on the overall duration of a workout and the feelings of exuberance and wellness that training gives you. Shift your mind-set from hitting mileage targets or split times to striving to feel invigorated by a workout of a duration that leaves you tired but not exhausted. Allie, mom to an active three-year-old boy, has been a strong runner since college, loving the sport from the first day. Under the guidance of a coach, Allie considers herself "excessively competitive," training hard to hit rigorous goals such as breaking 18 minutes in the 5K and 3:10 in the marathon. In her words: "I can't run on the treadmill at the gym without seeing what pace the guy next to me is running." She says pregnancy was an opportunity to run for pure fun.

## TRAINING SAFELY IN THE SECOND TRIMESTER

Because you're reorienting yourself toward achieving a "wellness workout," monitor your body's response to training throughout each session and stop if you experience any of the warning signs listed on page 70 of Chapter 2. Don't ignore your body's cues in order to get a longer workout, and remember to maintain your body's stasis by drinking water when thirsty during a workout and paying attention to your rate of perceived exertion. Sometimes exercise can lead to contractions, and while they typically go away shortly after a workout ends, a competitive athlete with a history of preterm labor should scale back high-volume, high-intensity activity (from 16–19 to 13–16 RPE) starting in the second trimester as a safeguard.

### Rest

In order to continue a training program that feels invigorating but not excessive, it's important to maintain the same kind of rest-exertion schedule that any athlete needs to avoid overtraining. Your body won't be able to do what it needs to do without rest between bouts of activity. The standard way to accomplish a rest-activity cycle is to alternate harder workouts with rest days or easy sessions. For example, the day after a run or spin (a higher level of exertion), take a moderate yoga class or do the elliptical at a low level of resistance.

Pregnancy isn't a sickness or an affliction, but it's nonetheless important to honor a new need for time off your feet. Elevate your legs when you can. Calf, ankle, and foot exercises are especially good for taking care of lower legs stressed by the greater difficulty of mobility while you're expecting, particularly if you're experiencing cramping at night. The wall push-ups mentioned on page 96 are

> **TRAINING TIP** Along with the wall push-ups (page 96) and resistance-band exercise (pages 82–83), here is an easy and effective exercise to aid your recovery from stress on your lower legs. Sit with one leg crossed over the other and roll the upper ankle clockwise and counterclockwise to loosen the muscles in your calf. Do 2 to 3 sets of 12 to 15 reps per side.

great for stretching your lower legs. For strength building, sit and hold a taut towel or resistance band under the balls of your feet and slowly alternate between pointing and flexing your feet across the band.

## Temperature Control

In the second trimester, new weight means you'll sweat more easily, particularly because your core body temperature rises about 1 degree during pregnancy. Because your metabolism is slowing down, you will get hot earlier in your workouts than before you were pregnant. There's limited research on the effects of increased core temperatures in pregnant women (scientists tend to rely on animal studies), but no studies have found a relationship between hyperthermia in pregnant women and adverse fetal outcomes.

To help you work out safely as you gain weight, sweat is your internal thermostat's way of cooling you off, albeit making you sopping wet with a different kind of glow. A pregnant body is an amazing temperature regulator, and one way it maintains a stable core temperature is through sweat. It's not sexy, but it keeps your baby in a safe zone. If you maintain safeguards on your exertion by keeping

**FITNESS Rx**

Use ice baths for your feet to aid recovery from a workout and to reduce swelling.

it at a 12–14 on Borg's RPE scale for a moderate session and 15–16 for a vigorous session and drinking water when thirsty, you'll be fine, and everyone in your body's ecosystem will benefit from your exercise. Doctors believe that the pregnant body alters its thermal response to exercise and allows women to adapt, balancing temperature throughout pregnancy with your new ability to release extra heat.

Because you might sweat more easily, the key factor is to stay hydrated, especially if you're working out in a hotter climate or you're pregnant over the summer. Many women have maintained a fitness program in hot environments when they're expecting, but be sensible about exercise in the heat of a summer day and choose mornings or evenings for outdoor exercise. Forget the electric diaper pail, and invest in water bottles. Although your body will adapt its core temperature to the pregnancy, pay attention to symptoms of overheating (dizziness, mental fog, headache, muscle cramping, nausea), and look for temperature-controlled exercise options. Try to work out in a thermoneutral space (air conditioned, or at least not hot and humid); go for a swim or water run; and pay attention to feeling feverish, versus warm.

Athletes in cold regions or trying to maintain winter training have a lower risk of dehydration or exhaustion from overheating, but don't assume that cold air means you don't need water. Carry fluids with you when you undertake any winter activity, and be sure to layer when you get dressed. All of those stretchy clothes you're buying will easily accommodate multiple layers.

*My early weeks of pregnancy were in January and February here in upstate New York, so it was cold and not ideal pregnancy running conditions. I carried my cell phone with me on every run, and a little piece of paper that said I was pregnant and listed my OB's number.* FELICE | RUNNER AND MOM TO CONAL

## SAFETY SPECIFICS IN THE SECOND TRIMESTER

Some key points to ensure you are working out safely during your second trimester:

- Exercise to the point that you feel invigorated (e.g., that endorphin rush), followed by fatigue, and stop well before you're exhausted and tottering.

- Drink water when thirsty throughout a workout.

- Discontinue abdominal/core work while lying on your back.

- If you feel dizzy when working out, stop immediately, drink water, sit with your head between your legs, and let your heart rate drop. If the dizziness persists when you restart the workout, call it a day.

- Relaxin can make your joints and ligaments very loose, causing a risk of strains during yoga, stretching, and high-impact cardio exercise. Stretch gently, and be careful not to overstride when you run.

- You might feel more energized and healthy than during the first trimester, but be careful not to increase your workout duration or exertion too much too soon. Lengthen run, bike, and swim workouts by 5 minutes every three sessions rather than by distance, and don't strive to outperform your prepregnancy fitness level.

## Injury Prevention

When you're pregnant, your joints are especially sensitive to how you work out, making you more susceptible to impact-related injuries from running and strains that can come from overstretching. A hormone called relaxin is released to loosen your hip joints and prepare you for labor with hypermobility. Here are a few ways to prevent strains from exercising with looser joints and ligaments:

* Be gentle with your yoga poses and stay away from hot yoga, which can raise your temperature dangerously high and can lead you to overstretch because the room heated to 90 to 100 degrees will loosen your muscles.

* Strive to train at a level that is either on a par with or modified from what you did before pregnancy.
* Resist adhering to a rigid daily mileage goal if you're feeling exhausted or experiencing joint or muscle pain.

## Sport Specifics: Guidelines for Run, Bike, and Swim Training

### SECOND-TRIMESTER RUNNING

Maybe you had to lie low for the first 12 weeks due to sickness or low energy. Now is your time to rebuild a run program with gradual, incremental increases in the run part of a run/walk ratio. Because the second trimester usually marks a turnaround in your energy and vitality, it is the perfect time to find your feet again.

Athletes know that running is a highly efficient way to burn calories from fat. However, because running is such an efficient calorie burner, you need to focus on getting enough fuel for the two of you. Remember, you have to replace the calories you're burning and consume enough to grow a baby. This means that refueling during longer runs is even more important than before you were pregnant. Be careful taking sports gels as fuel because your body absorbs them at a slower rate than other carbs. Consider replacing a gel with a small organic energy bar that's high in carbs and protein. If you do take gels, sports beans, or chews during a workout, always drink water to help you metabolize the carbs.

**DOCTOR'S NOTE**

**Aerobic exercise,** such as running at a conversational pace, acts as a training program to improve your baby's strength for dealing with a period of decreased oxygen and blood flow to the uterus. Increased heart rate and reduced movement are a normal fetal response to your workout, and both should return to normal within minutes of finishing your session. These fetal reactions actually benefit your baby's physiological ability to cope with anything taxing, such as a difficult labor.

## FITNESS $R_X$

If you were a runner prior to pregnancy who was slowed by morning sickness during the first trimester, here's a simple formula for building back a run program:

- Start with 20 to 30 minutes three times per week.

- Begin each session with a 5-minute brisk walk.

- Alternate 2 to 4 minutes running with 1 to 2 minutes walking for each session of the first week.

- Increase the run portion by 2 to 4 minutes every other workout after the first week, changing the recovery walks so that each walk break amounts to 50 to 100 percent of the time spent running.

- Add 5 minutes to the workout duration every three sessions without exceeding the length of the workouts you achieved at your prepregnancy fitness level.

Listen to your body, and don't push past the feeling of being tired. This program isn't for speed or distance training. It's about increasing cardiovascular fitness and general wellness. Stop if you feel any of the warning signs listed on page 70.

While running is generally very safe, your general risk of falling during exercise increases due to changes in your center of gravity as well as an increase in relaxin and estrogen, particularly if your workout demands balance. This means that abrupt stop-and-go drills, such as plyometrics, CrossFit exercises, and tennis can lead to injury because of difficulty stopping. Some runners even have trouble stopping a run once they are up to pace. Slow down to a conversational pace overall, and start each run with a walk or slow jog to find your balance before you pick up the pace.

Give yourself a broad range of time or distance for the run before you start so that you can adapt to how you feel once you're moving. Instead of a strict 5 miles or 45 minutes, tell yourself you're going to try for 3 to 5 miles or 35 to 45 minutes, and allow yourself recovery periods during a run. Whereas the first trimester was ideal for fartleks that let you increase and decrease effort randomly, an interval workout is ideal in the second trimester because it obligates

## FITNESS Rx

Interval runs at a track or on a treadmill are great options for midpregnancy because they enforce walking breaks while giving you a solid workout. Remember to warm up with a 5-minute brisk walk. Try these interval options:

### Treadmill ups and downs

- 2 to 4 minutes running at 14 RPE on a 2.5 percent incline
- 1 to 2 minutes walking at 12 RPE on a 1 percent incline
- Repeat three to four times
- 2 to 4 minutes running at 14 RPE on a 1 percent incline
- 1 to 2 minutes walking at 12 RPE on a 2.5 percent incline
- Repeat three to four times

### Half-time intervals

- Run ¼ mile or 3 minutes
- Walk ⅛ mile or 90 seconds
- Run ½ mile or 5 minutes
- Walk ¼ mile or 2½ minutes
- Repeat two to four times

### Quarters and eighths

- 4 to 6 × 400 meters (¼ mile) run at 14–16 RPE with 1- or 2-minute walks between each
- 6 to 8 × 200 meters (⅛ mile) run at 14–16 RPE with 1-minute walks between each
- 4 to 6 × 400 meters (¼ mile) run at 14–16 RPE with 1- or 2-minute walks between each

## THE TREADMILL IS YOUR FRIEND

The second trimester is a good time to run on the treadmill, especially if you're worried about traffic or being stuck and exhausted away from home with a return run ahead of you.

A treadmill run can also precede a pool run, where you'll get a great non-impact workout. A treadmill lets you run flat, which helps when those small hills you once charged up look like Everest. It also gives you:

- A temperature-controlled environment
- A cup holder
- A preset incline to take the impact off your joints from downhills on roads
- Proximity to a bathroom
- A heart rate monitor
- A handrail for balance

you to take recovery periods when your athlete's mind wants you to push. Use the structure of a track or an interval workout to keep you motivated and feeling like a runner when you're discouraged by the slower pace or need for a walking rest. As running starts to become more of a challenge, run your intervals with walk breaks, as opposed to jogging recoveries.

Don't worry—walking doesn't mean you have to hand in your VIP athlete card or resign from your running club. It makes you a smarter runner who is maximizing her run by inserting recovery periods rather than bailing on a run early due to fatigue. This is just a reframing of training and doesn't have to differ in structure, even when you're running for two.

TRAINING TIP  To prevent being stuck miles from home if you need to cut a run short, measure a short loop of about a mile and run repeats. You'll never be that far from home.

Some women who are dedicated distance runners might be wondering if they can complete a longer event, such as a marathon, when they're pregnant. If you were running 50 to 70 miles per week when you got pregnant and are in excellent shape with extensive marathon experience, your doctor might be okay with you completing a walk/jog marathon in your 13th week. But a runner of any level who is pregnant will want to rescale her time goals for that event and eliminate speed work that can lead to injury—and she shouldn't try to increase her weekly base mileage now that she is pregnant. As with any fitness plan, discuss your interests and routine with your health care provider, and if you aren't satisfied with the answer, seek other opinions from medical practitioners who know your particular situation. Listen to what your body tells you about how it feels.

## SECOND-TRIMESTER CYCLING

Although balance and your changing center of gravity can be risks for cycling while pregnant, there are no hard-and-fast obstetric rules that prohibit a woman from riding when she's expecting, as long as it's a normal pregnancy without complications. Your muscles will reap the maximal benefit from cycling without the risk of impact-related injuries because the bike supports your (increasing) body weight.

That said, be sure to discuss your thoughts about cycling outdoors—in particular mountain biking—with your provider. Most doctors will advise that you stop cycling outside after the first trimester, and you do need to feel some concern about falling, as a fall at this stage could be dangerous to the placenta and fetus. Your pelvis no longer protects your uterus after about 12 weeks, so the danger to your abdomen from a fall is a serious consideration. That means that mountain biking will be particularly risky because roots, rocks, and a technical surface increase the likelihood of an accident. If you're determined to keep at it, consider walking your bike down hills when you're in the woods.

**DOCTOR'S NOTE**

A woman who has **placenta previa** should not bike, as bouncing on an uneven surface could cause bleeding.

Many women continue cycling, even participating in triathlon and other bike events, while others decide it's a risk they do not want to take. You'll have to make that choice for your own comfort level, knowing that the decision to stop has no bearing on how serious an athlete you are. Regardless of your choice, you shouldn't *start* an outdoor cycling routine after the first trimester because your balance is now compromised, and getting on (and staying on) a bike could be difficult if you haven't been doing it regularly. If you're intent on riding outside, a paved rail trail is perfect—no cars, and the paths are usually wide—as long as the path isn't swarmed with kids, whose movements can be as unpredictable as a puppy's.

As with running, you can create an interval bike workout very easily on bike paths because they're usually flat, allowing you to cycle for a period of time at a harder effort that alternates with coasting for a recovery period. Follow the exertion-rest pattern described earlier for running by making your easy or coasting segments 50 to 100 percent of the time spent on higher-intensity spin segments. Keep your efforts at 14–16 RPE, with recovery intervals at 10–12 RPE.

So that your bike fits your expectant body as comfortably as possible, consider a fitting that will adjust it to your changes in posture and weight distribution. As your belly grows, your weight distribution affects your range of motion and how you perform it. The more upright you can sit, the easier you will breathe. Here are some adjustments you (or a bike fitter) can make to improve the comfort of your ride:

FITNESS Rx

A wider saddle may be more comfortable than your regular one as your pregnancy progresses.

* Raise your handlebars to accommodate any difficulty bending forward and to help lift your chest for better breathing. An adjustable stem is a great idea for your body's progressive changes in the next 6 months.
* Adjust seat height and position and pedals to correspond with the change in your handlebars. Lowering the seat will shift your weight more into the saddle and less over the shaft of the bike. This will shift your pelvis to a more comfortable angle for pedaling.
* Move the pedals as needed to keep your knees from opening too far.

Because you want to avoid being stuck far from home if you get tired or a tire goes flat, opt for a double loop or a multiloop circuit that ends at home. Similarly, try to pick a route that passes by friends' houses in case you need help. Although the breeze makes it easier to stay cool while cycling than while running, you can still overheat when you ride, especially if you don't want to shift your balance by using one hand to grab your water. A great option is a hydration pack that you wear on your back, which allows you to drink through a tube more easily than fussing with a water bottle.

If you decide you want to spin, but you're nervous about traffic or falling, you can put your bike on a trainer to give you stability and a safe distance from cars. Another great option for cycling if you don't want to deal with balance or traffic outdoors is to find a CompuTrainer center, where you bring your own bike and a coach sets you up at a designated wattage for your individual level. The workout is then customized to you and eliminates the one-size-fits-all workout of a spin class. Just be sure to tell the instructor that you're pregnant, and be willing to adjust the target wattage based on how you feel during the session. A CompuTrainer center lets you ride on a stable bike in a temperature-regulated

## FITNESS R$\chi$

Frequently adjusting your hold on the handlebars can release tension in your back that often develops from gripping them in one position for an extended ride.

space, with a skilled cycling expert to adjust your level of difficulty and bike fit. In addition, you'll be able to end a workout midway through without being miles from home if your fatigue builds too much or your range of motion is restricted by a baby that settles onto your round ligaments. It's a great option for athletes of all levels—novice to competitive—and lets you ride with stability while watching a simulated outdoor course.

Intervals are also feasible on a stationary bike or CompuTrainer if you spin in repeats that frequently and regularly change your effort. As with any other cardio, use RPE (see the bike workout RPE recommendations on page 122) and the talk test to determine whether you're working too hard. You shouldn't be too breathless to speak. If you're cycling intervals in a warm studio or on a trainer in your home gym without air conditioning, pay attention to your temperature. You might want to carry a basal thermometer with you to make sure your core body temperature is in a safe zone. While intervals are a great way to change up your effort in a regulated fashion, don't spin for an hour because that's how long the class lasts or until you're about to fall off a stationary bike. Working out so hard that you feel exhausted and light-headed defeats the purpose of a fit pregnancy.

TRAINING TIP   Many maternity suits are more appropriate for wading than for swimming. Try an online search to find a maternity suit that will work for swimming. Consider wearing a sports bra under your suit for more support, and if you're more modest, you can swim in lined light-weight shorts and a lined tank.

## TRAINING TIPS FOR NEW SWIMMERS

Swimming and pool walking or running are ideal forms of exercise for expecting women. However, as with any new exercise, check with your health care provider about starting a swim program during pregnancy.

- Use a kickboard when swimming or wrap a pool noodle around yourself for a workout at a lower intensity.

- Exercise at a "conversational effort": You should be able to speak without getting breathless.

- Warm up with a low-intensity effort, using sidestroke for a few laps at the start of your swim. Then build intensity progressively every 3 to 4 laps over the 20 to 40 minutes that you're in the pool, changing strokes to increase or decrease the challenge.

## SECOND-TRIMESTER SWIMMING

Swimming is an excellent exercise choice throughout pregnancy, particularly as it doesn't involve some of the challenges that other sports present as your belly grows, such as balance issues and high impact. The cool-water conditions are easy on your body during a workout, so no need to modify your swims as you get bigger in the second trimester. Balance is also not an issue, and your hypermobile joints aren't endangered by swimming because it's a nonimpact workout buoyed by water.

If you're new to swimming, maintain a "start low and go slow" principle: Begin with three swims per week of 20 to 40 minutes. Research shows that women with

**TRAINING TIP** When water running in the second trimester, bring your knees as far toward your chest as you can lift them when your abdomen has grown. You'll still get the benefit from the use of your muscles in the motion of running, even though you cannot lift your knees as high.

## FITNESS $R_X$

You can create many variations of interval workouts in the water, combining running, swimming, and repeated strength exercises. See Chapter 2 for more on water-running technique. After a 5-minute sidestroke warm-up, here are some options for a 25-meter pool workout:

### Upper-lower workout

- Swim 100 meters of breast stroke
- Hold on to the wall and do 1 set of 6 straight-leg raises to the side with each leg
- Swim 100 meters of breast stroke
- Hold on to the wall and do 1 set of 6 bent-knee raises to the front with each leg (as if you're marching)
- Repeat 2 to 4 times

### Runner's high

- "Run" 50 meters in the pool
- Tread water for 20 to 30 seconds

little or no swimming experience can reap aerobic benefits with no adverse effects on body or baby when beginning a swim program in the second trimester.[6]

Breast stroke is a good stroke choice in the second trimester, as it doesn't require you to rotate your torso, demanding less exertion and helping your back. Your growing abdomen has rounded your shoulders and tilted your pelvis, putting your back out of its normal alignment, but swimming offsets your altered alignment. Avoid backstroke to improve fetal position. You'll also have to give up the butterfly as your baby and belly grow, making it very taxing on your heart to hoist your torso up and forward. Flip turns continue to be perfectly safe. As with run and bike workouts, swim until you're fatigued, not exhausted, and create systematic, timed breaks of 1 to 3 minutes between laps, as needed, to set up a regulated interval workout.

- "Run" 75 meters
- Tread water for 30 to 40 seconds
- "Run" 150 meters
- Tread water for 60 seconds
- Repeat

### The trifecta

- "Run" 25 meters, pumping your arms and striding long in a running motion (without feet touching the bottom, if possible)
- Breast stroke 25 meters
- Freestyle 25 meters
- 2-minute rest at the wall
- Repeat 4 to 6 times
- Tread water for 5 to 8 minutes

## Second-Trimester Strength and Flexibility

You're in the prime of pregnancy during the second trimester, so it's a great time to maximize your strength training to benefit yourself and your baby. Exercises that strengthen the joints for your major muscle groups (shown on pages 82–84) can reduce the risk of injuries related to the force of impact you might experience from workouts. Leg strength (quads, hips, hamstrings, and calves), in particular, can offset impact-related stress on your joints.

Beginning in the second trimester (at about 12 weeks), you can't do ab work or lift weights when lying on your back because lying supine decreases the blood flow back to your heart, leading to lower cardiac output. Simply put, you're asking your heart to work hard while not priming it with enough blood. There are great alternatives to strength training on your back, however, and as your sense

**Swimming and pool jogging** can reduce the swelling that comes from pregnancy because the water pressure forces the movement of fluids in your circulatory system. The best way to counteract bloating is by treading water in the deep end.

of balance changes and your weight increases, you might find that supported strength training gives you peace of mind while also assisting muscle tone.

The sequence in this section can be performed with the aid of a stable surface, such as a chair or table, or with TRX straps at a gym or at home. TRX is ideal for building leg and upper-body strength by using your own weight as resistance and tasking several muscle groups at once. Because women are advised to stick to light weights for lifting during pregnancy, you might want to turn to either TRX or stabilized strength work for a boost in challenge. You'll use your own body weight as resistance and will be able to achieve total-body strengthening and stretching when you are advised against lying on your back and sit-ups become impossible. When performed properly, the exercises help you keep your back muscles engaged and straight when it's very easy to hunch over with your nose pointed toward that belly. While some leg exercises can make you feel tippy as your movement challenges your center of gravity, performing squats and lunges with the help of TRX or a hand on a chair can stabilize your equilibrium.

Perfect for all fitness levels, these exercises can be adapted to the number of reps and sets that keeps you in the "comfortably challenged" zone, starting at 8 reps and not exceeding 20. Aim for 1 to 3 sets per exercise. Make sure the line from the top of your head to your heel is straight as you perform each exercise. This requires engaging your core muscles to resist collapsing or arching your back.

## PUSH-UPS

1–3 sets of
8–20 reps

*Perform the push-ups by lowering
yourself (with a straight spine)
toward a stable countertop. If using
TRX, grip the straps with straight
arms, then tilt and lower yourself
forward into a push-up position
so that forearms and biceps are
perpendicular. Remember, you're
still standing and simply lowering
yourself forward with a straight back
so that your arms reach this
90-degree position.*

## CROSS-OVER LUNGES

1–3 sets of
8–20 reps

*These lunges can be performed with
the same technique as the squats,
holding on to the ends of a straight
and taut strap while lowering into
your lunges to a count of 4.*

**SQUATS**

1–3 sets of
8–20 reps

*Perform these squats by wrapping a resistance band or a necktie around the handle of a closed door so that the band is taut and you can grip each end. Keeping the lengths of the band straight, lower yourself into a squat, counting to 4. You can achieve the same effect with TRX straps.*

2ND

T R I M E S T E R

## Gear for the Middle Months

As your body starts to grow in new shapes and directions, finding the right gear will help you adjust to the "new you" more comfortably. Here is a list to get you started:

* *Compression socks.* These tight knee socks improve blood flow and can help support swollen legs and veins. When combined with shorts, they make quite a fashion statement, but you won't care because they offer needed relief to sore lower legs.

* *Shorts, capris, and tights* with thick, soft, and nonbinding support bands at the waist. Look for natural fibers because the skin on your stomach can be easily irritated and start to itch during this trimester.

* *Wicking socks.* Thinner, natural fibers, such as bamboo, offer the best action for wicking moisture and can help with shoes that start to feel constricting due to swelling.

* *Stability shoes.* Your feet are likely to grow and swell, and you want all athletic shoes to be up to one size bigger than your street shoes. During the second trimester, it's common for arches to fall and for fluid to collect in ankles and feet, stressing out your base of support. Look for shoes with more stability and a wider platform (save the minimalist shoes for a postpregnancy treat) for crosstraining and

running, and buy them at the end of the day, when your feet are most swollen.

* *Orthotics.* Over-the-counter shoe inserts can provide much relief by way of some added cushioning and arch support.

* *Pedicure* at a clean and reputable salon. You can call it health care, even if insurance doesn't cover it.

* *Moisturizer.* Due to dry skin, it's common for a pregnant woman's abdomen to itch beginning in the second trimester. Lotion or moisturizer with aloe can prevent the dryness with a cooling sensation.

* *Petroleum jelly or antichafing stick.* Lubrication in your delicate places—armpits and crotch—will help with chafing that can come from tighter-fitting workout gear or any rubbing of skin on skin as you gain weight.

## Chapter Summary

After some lows in the first 12 weeks, the second trimester reintroduces you to yourself: energized and active. Your baby's organs are formed, and your body is now fine-tuning fetal development. With solid nutrition and hydration and applying the exuberance of this glow period to a modified but invigorating fitness program, you're a Wonder Woman of wellness. This is the ideal time to work out with interval training and stretches that will prevent cramping; build mind-body strength; and empower you with a safe, mindful level of intensity. Remember, labor and pushing during delivery can go faster if you've developed strong legs and a powerful core. As your body and baby continue to grow in the home stretch that is the third trimester, you'll be well equipped by second-trimester fitness to finish this race strong.

✳ Call your provider for any bleeding, gush of fluid, or more than six painful contractions in an hour.

✳ Eat fiber-rich foods to prevent constipation, and continue to take prenatal vitamins.

✳ Be aware that your center of gravity makes you a fall risk due to larger breast and uterus size, so consider switching from outdoor biking to indoor spinning.

✳ Drink water before, during, and after exercise, hydrating to meet your thirst.

✳ Do not perform any exercise while lying on your back after the 13th week, as blood flow is restricted in this position.

✳ Exercise with interval workouts that enforce rest or recovery periods to prevent exhaustion and give you a high-quality session.

✳ This is the best time in your pregnancy to be active. Live it up!

# 4 Your Third Trimester

*The Push to the Finish Line*

THIS IS THE HOME STRETCH, an idea that really takes on new meaning in the third trimester. Weeks 28 to 40 are not unlike the last push to the finish line in a distance race: You can see the clock and the banner, and you can feel the excitement build, but it probably seems as if you're taking an unreasonable amount of time to get to the line, where you finally get the medal. Whether you've loved pregnancy or spent months counting down to the end of it, no doubt by now you're ready to complete this event and cradle your prize. The third trimester is the time to start preparations for that amazing moment and the final push to get you there. It's also the time to prioritize your physical comfort, to accept what your body has to give you when you exercise, and to make your way through the day focused on your body's and your baby's wellness with a calm mind.

This chapter will guide you through fitness in the last 12 weeks of pregnancy, setting the stage for a safe and smooth birth experience. By reading this chapter, you'll find answers to:

## What's Happening to My Body?

In the third trimester, your body might be starting to feel more and more like a continent with a population of two. Even though you may have felt like a super-powered Wonder Woman in the second trimester, you may now find yourself waking up tired and moving with a good deal more discomfort through the day. Because the baby has grown so big, it can keep you awake as you seek to find your comfort zone. This is the ultimate in mother-baby bonding: two of you uncomfortable in *your* skin as you go through the final weeks before you finally meet face-to-face. Yes, it can be a challenge to get comfortable, but now is the time to keep your eyes on the prize. You're both so close to the very best day of your lives.

During the third trimester, your health care provider will continue to check your baby's size and heart rate, and your appointments will increase in frequency. You will probably schedule appointments every other week by the eighth month. By the final month, you'll be seeing your provider weekly, and at each appointment, he or she will likely conduct a vaginal exam to assess the baby's descent into position for delivery. If your baby is breech (bottom down), you might receive an ultrasound to confirm the baby's position and possibly a procedure to turn the baby, known as an external cephalic version. Your provider will check the baby's heartbeat and measure the distance from the top of your uterus

FITNESS ℞

To keep your back and chest comfortable while exercising in the third trimester, try doubling up on bras to reduce bouncing and strain.

3RD TRIMESTER

**TABLE 4.1** Third-Trimester Changes for Your Baby and Your Body

## YOUR BABY

| SEVENTH MONTH | EIGHTH MONTH | NINTH MONTH |
|---|---|---|
| Baby grows to about 14 in. with weight at 2–4 lbs. | Baby grows to 15–18 in. and weighs up to 5 lbs. | Baby grows to about 18–21 inches and weighs 7–9 lbs. |
| Fatty tissue develops. | Extra stores of fat continue to develop. | Baby can turn head. |
| Eyelashes grow. | Baby's bone marrow responsible for red-blood-cell count. | Grasping reflex develops. |
| Lanugo (fine hair covering body) starts to disappear. | Fingernails are fully grown. | Kidneys are fully functioning, allowing baby to urinate into amniotic fluid. |
| Testes form in boys. | Hair on head grows. | Eyes can blink and close. |
| Hearing is developed, and baby can hear your voice as well as your heartbeat. | Baby can see and hear, with irises that dilate in response to light. | Lungs are completely developed. |
| Baby could survive if born prematurely. | Baby kicks more. | Fetal position changes for birth by lowering into your pelvis. |
| Baby moves often, responding to outside stimuli (sound, light). | Baby sleeps with regular REM cycles. | Umbilical cord is 2 feet long. |
| Space is limited in uterus, which causes squirming. | Most organs are formed, with lungs last to fully develop. | |

## YOUR BODY

| SEVENTH MONTH | EIGHTH MONTH | NINTH MONTH |
|---|---|---|
| Uterus expands further upward, with its top about 4–5 inches above your navel. | Baby's weight limits your ease of mobility, giving you that waddling motion. | Uterus about 6 inches above navel. |
| Glucose screening determines presence or absence of gestational diabetes. | Doctor's appointments increase in frequency, to weekly or biweekly. | Leg cramps continue, mostly in the calves at night. |
| Braxton Hicks contractions are typical (practice for birth). | Hot flashes common as baby's temperature radiates to increase yours. | Uterus fills pelvis and abdomen, pressing on other organs. |
| Breasts often begin to leak colostrum. | Libido can diminish. | Swelling (edema) in hands, feet, and legs increases. |
| Frequent need to urinate as uterus pushes down on your bladder. | | Varicose veins and stretch marks can appear. |
| Easily fatigued, with need for increased sleep. | | Doctor tests for Group B strep bacteria. |
| Blood pressure can drop when baby's weight presses on the vein that sends blood to your heart. | | Hair may grow on arms and legs due to hormone increases. |
| Sciatic pain possible. | | When baby turns downward, you get kicks in the ribs. |
| | | Sleep can be difficult. |
| | | Doctor performs internal exams to check for dilating, effacement, and softening of cervix. |

to your pubic bone to ascertain the baby's growth rate. He or she will also conduct a pelvic exam to check your progress and the status of your cervix.

Some providers want to test for the following during the third trimester:

* Anemia (a blood test) if you have a history of anemia
* Sexually transmitted diseases, e.g., syphilis, chlamydia, gonorrhea, or HIV, if you are deemed at risk
* Placenta status (ultrasound) if you had previa earlier in pregnancy

At this time, you should review with your provider all symptoms and your current level and type of activity to make sure it's compatible with the stage and status of your pregnancy. During your visits, be sure to discuss methods of pain management and hospital policies. You might be a swimmer who envisioned a water birth only to find out your provider or birth center won't perform one.

## BLADDER PRESSURE

As the baby descends into position, you may experience a more frequent and urgent need to urinate. While getting out of bed repeatedly to use the bathroom is a good rehearsal for night life with a newborn, it often contributes to the fatigue of the third trimester. The pressure can also exacerbate the tendency to leak when you laugh or sneeze, but Kegel exercises (see page 168) can strengthen your pelvic floor to reduce that problem. Contact your provider if you experience the symptoms of a UTI, such as fever, burning when you urinate, or backache, because a urinary tract or bladder infection can mean danger to your kidneys or cause other pregnancy complications.

## BREAST CHANGES

In the third trimester, your breasts continue to grow and may have gained as much as 2 pounds of tissue. They fill with colostrum, the viscous, yellowish substance that a nursing baby eats before your milk comes in. High in protein, low in fat, and rich in antibodies, colostrum offers easily digestible nutrients that an infant requires to begin life with a healthy start. You might never look at vanilla sports gel the same way again, but colostrum will serve a similar purpose for your new baby: fuel for energy that builds strength.

In the last several weeks of your pregnancy, it's common for the colostrum to leak, so you may want to use the nursing pads you bought in the second trimester more regularly. Just slip them into your bra, and they will absorb any leaky fluid. You can buy disposable pads that you replace when saturated or washable pads that you reuse.

During the third trimester, your nipples develop more elasticity and begin to secrete oils to make nursing more comfortable. Tiny bumps on your areolas that produce this lubricant are called Montgomery's tubercles and become more noticeable toward the end of pregnancy. While those elastic nipples and oil-rich tubercles aren't the most seductive qualities of your larger breasts, you'll come to appreciate these assets if you choose to breast-feed. Don't get freaked out when your breasts leak, secrete, and change during the third trimester; they're testing for the launch of the biggest job of their life.

## BREATHING

Because your uterus applies pressure to all of your internal organs, including your diaphragm and lungs, it can be more difficult to breathe in the third trimester, causing shortness of breath, particularly when you're trying to exercise. If you're carrying multiple fetuses or carrying your baby high, you might have even more difficulty breathing. Many women begin to breathe more easily a few weeks prior to delivery—just as they're probably getting more anxious. As the baby descends into position toward the end of your pregnancy, the uterus ceases to press against your lungs and diaphragm, allowing more normal breathing.

Try to stand and sit up straight to relieve the compression of your diaphragm, and use pillows (see "Gear," page 166) to prop up your torso to reduce the pressure on your lungs. In addition, consider the available lung capacity when you exercise, taking the standard shortness of breath into account when you work out. Don't push yourself as hard as you might want to, and focus on the quality of the activity—how good you feel—as opposed to any metrics. As soon as you deliver, your breathing will improve, which makes oohing and ahing over your new baby much easier.

## PRACTICE CONTRACTIONS

Just as your body benefits from a warm-up before a race or hard workout, it warms up for delivery with practice contractions known as Braxton Hicks. These

### DOCTOR'S NOTE

A **full bladder** is thought to be one cause of Braxton Hicks, as are sex and dehydration, which can occur when you exercise. To ease or prevent the discomfort of Braxton Hicks contractions, try any of the following:

❋ Increase your fluids. Remember to drink plenty of water. A good rule of thumb is 8 × 8: 8 ounces of water 8 times per day.

❋ Change your position or activity. If you've been sitting for a while, get up and walk. Or lie down if you've been on your feet.

❋ Rock in a rocking chair or on an inflated exercise ball.

❋ Take a warm bath for 10 to 15 minutes.

❋ Eat a snack or a small meal.

❋ Get a lower-back massage.

When they occur close to your delivery date, Braxton Hicks contractions are sometimes called "false labor," and while these contractions can contribute to effacement and the softening of the cervix that accompanies labor, they won't cause you to go into labor. If you are actually in labor, the contractions increase in intensity and begin to occur closer together and with more regularity. What was once just mildly uncomfortable becomes painful. If your contractions build in pain and recur with predictable regularity, contact your provider right away.

contractions typically come in the form of a low-grade cramping sensation that starts and ends unpredictably. During a Braxton Hicks moment, the muscles of your uterus will contract for 30 to 60 seconds, but the cramping feeling can last longer. The contractions are usually more uncomfortable than painful and will ease gradually. Just as your breasts are testing their system for go time, your uterus is readying itself for opening night, too. Braxton Hicks contractions also give you the chance to practice labor breathing and other techniques for relaxation during delivery (see Chapter 5).

## RELAXIN

The hormone relaxin increases just prior to labor, after having decreased a lot since its initial surge in your first trimester. Relaxin assists your pelvic movement to help your body accommodate a growing baby, stretch your ab muscles, and give more laxity to your pelvic-floor muscles. As you progress into the last weeks of the third trimester, avoid overstretching to prevent strains or slight muscle tears as a result of relaxin's influence on your flexibility. Listen to your body and use stretching and yoga for relaxation and stress release; a prenatal yoga class with your expectant peers is a great option for stretching that won't be overly aggressive.

## RH IMMUNOGLOBULIN

At 28 weeks, if you are Rh negative and the baby's father isn't, your doctor will give you a shot of Rh immunoglobulin that will block you from making antibodies against the fetus's red blood cells if it is Rh positive. After delivery, the baby's blood type will be tested, and if it is Rh positive, you'll receive another shot of Rh immunoglobulin. Being Rh negative, you are part of the minority of the population that won't have a specific protein on your red blood cells.

### DOCTOR'S NOTE

You can **reduce swelling** by reclining as much as possible, or at least propping up your feet if you're deskbound all day. Elevating your feet on a pillow while you sleep will also help to decrease the swelling in your lower legs.

## SWELLING

It is common for your ankles, wrists, and legs to swell more in the third trimester. This condition, known as edema, occurs because your uterus has grown so large that it puts pressure on the vein that pumps blood into your extremities. You might be retaining more water, which constricts blood vessels and makes your face appear puffy, especially when you get up in the morning. And you may need to remove rings that start to pinch your fingers. The swelling and weight gain can intensify how you perceive your appearance in the third trimester, but just remind yourself that the ends more than justify the means. Drink water throughout the day, and focus on the meaning of it all, which far outweighs any fluid you may be retaining.

## VARICOSE AND SPIDER VEINS

As blood circulation increases in the third trimester, you might notice the appearance of red splotches with spidering lines on your face and neck or blue varicose veins on the legs, in particular if you are fair-skinned. These veins are sometimes painful as they swell but can be effectively treated with compression socks (see "Gear" on page 130). These very tight socks work to reduce swelling in the lower legs and work even better if you can elevate your feet while wearing them. Staying active during your third trimester can also prevent varicose veins from developing. If you sit at work during the day, enforce breaks to get up and walk for a few minutes every 40 minutes, which you might have to do to find a bathroom anyway.

**Spider veins tend to fade quickly** after delivery, whereas **varicose veins take a bit longer,** usually disappearing within a few months of giving birth.

## SPECIAL ISSUES AND COMPLICATIONS

### Bed Rest

Even though time spent lounging in bed with books and magazines might sound like a dream vacation, bed rest can be frustrating, particularly for active women. There are several reasons a doctor might prescribe bed rest in the third trimester:

* Bleeding
* Preterm labor (before 37 weeks)
* Intrauterine growth restriction
* High blood pressure; rest reduces the demand on your heart
* Relieving pressure on an "incompetent" cervix (i.e., risk for dilating too early)

* Multiple babies
* Placenta previa or other issues with the placenta
* Preeclampsia

Depending on the level of risk that activity poses to your pregnancy and what your individual issues are, a bed-rest requirement can mean a lot of different things. More serious conditions might prohibit you from leaving the bed or couch or demand that you lie on your left side (even to eat), using a bedpan and sponge baths for hygiene. A less serious condition might allow some activity, mainly just ruling out exertion, heavy lifting, or prolonged periods on your feet.

## PRESERVING YOUR SANITY DURING BED REST

- Maintain communication with friends and family with visits, Skype, e-mail, texts, or phone calls. Don't isolate yourself or limit your human connection to reality TV.

- Develop a new skill that you can do lying down, such as knitting, blogging, beading, or scrapbooking.

- Put important supplies in arm's reach: phone, laptop, tissues, book, snacks, water bottle, the remote, and a blanket or extra pillow.

- Remember how you wanted to learn a foreign language? Now's your chance to do it.

- Don't be shy about asking for help when it comes to cooking, child care, errands, and lawn maintenance.

- Stock up on all those baby supplies you'll soon need, using online shopping.

- Set fitness and life goals for the first year after birth: Pick some races or events as well as classes you can take with your baby.

- Watch movies and play games with your other kids to keep your connection with them.

- Read that trilogy you've heard everyone talking about or a few of those classics you've never had the time for.

Because there is variation to the definition of "bed rest," ask your provider for specifics on what you can and can't do.

Bed rest can lead to aching muscles and joints, and it's normal to feel at your wits' end when your activity is severely restricted, especially if it takes you away from work or your other kids. It can be exasperating and even depressing, but most doctors won't require it unless absolutely necessary, so it's important to take it seriously. If your provider tells you that bed rest is necessary, allow yourself to accept help from friends, family, your partner, and your older children. Sometimes it takes a village to raise a child in the womb, too.

## Group B Strep

A provider will routinely test you for Group B strep in the third trimester, often between the 35th and 37th week. Group B strep is a bacteria that lives in your vagina or rectum, and while it won't make you sick, it can place your infant at risk for infection when he or she passes through the birth canal. A baby who contracts Group B during delivery will typically become sick in the first six days of life with GBS disease, a dangerous disorder that affects breathing, kidney and gastrointestinal function, and blood pressure as well as causing pneumonia or meningitis.

Because the screening and treatment of women who test positive for Group B has improved, fewer babies are at risk for this condition: approximately 1 of every 2,000 babies. About 25 percent of women carry Group B, and although it is somewhat rare, testing is routine because the consequences to an infant are considered very dangerous. As a result, women are routinely tested for Group B toward the end of pregnancy, and mothers who test positive will receive antibiotics during labor to greatly reduce the infant's risk of infection.

## Gestational Diabetes

At 24 to 28 weeks, your doctor will test you for gestational diabetes. If you experienced gestational diabetes in a previous pregnancy, your doctor might test you earlier than the 20th week. The oral test for gestational diabetes involves drinking a sweetened liquid, which contains glucose that your body absorbs quickly. The sugared fluid will cause your blood-sugar levels to spike within an hour, at which point your doctor will draw blood to measure how you metabolize the sugar.

Unlike Type 2 Diabetes in nonpregnant populations, **gestational diabetes** has nothing to do with your fitness level or diet, although some new research indicates that exercise can help prevent gestational diabetes.[1] Keep in mind, though, that an active pregnancy doesn't mean you can't develop it.

Gestational diabetes afflicts 2 to 5 percent of women. It is a function of genetics and is not based on your weight or activity; it can certainly afflict endurance athletes. This is because a pregnancy changes your energy use and makes your muscles and fat somewhat insulin resistant, regardless of how much you weigh. To ensure that the fetus can access adequate nutrients for growth, your carbohydrates take the fast lane to your uterus, reducing your body's personal stores of sugars (glucose). Starting in the second trimester, a pregnant woman becomes a mild diabetic as her increase in insulin resistance allows the baby to consume the bulk of those sugars. However, an oversupply of glucose in your bloodstream can be a side effect of the insulin resistance. Most women simply start producing more insulin to process that glucose.

Gestational diabetes occurs when your body simply can't make enough insulin (or can't make use of the insulin you have) to process the glucose in your bloodstream. Untreated, it can lead to macrosomic (large) babies, nerve damage to the baby, shoulder dystocia (the baby's shoulders can't pass through the birth canal after the head has delivered), obesity in adolescence, and increased risk of the need for a C-section. Babies of moms with gestational diabetes often experience a significant drop in blood sugars after birth, when they're no longer receiving the overabundance of their mother's glucose. This can lead to seizures in the baby after delivery. However, if you have gestational diabetes and you keep your sugars normal, your risks are equal to those of a woman without gestational diabetes.

Treatment consists of self-monitoring your blood sugar levels four times per day around meals. Your doctor will also want to measure the ketones in your urine, which will show whether or not your diabetes is under control. If diagnosed with gestational diabetes, you'll need to follow a specific diet to regulate your glucose. Avoid electrolyte drinks that are high in calories, and be careful with any high-carb fuels, such as Gu, that are metabolized very slowly.

If so advised, you might need to restrict your weight gain and alter your exercise plan in response to your pre- and postexercise insulin tests. You should continue to work out with cardio and strength training, but you will want to involve your doctor closely in your exercise plan. Research shows that exercise can increase glucose level at 8 weeks, but on average, this increase doesn't result in a change in insulin level and has no adverse effect on mom or baby.[2] Still, there will be individual variation when it comes to your body's production and use of insulin when you exercise, as your body is processing glucose for energy. As long as you monitor your insulin and test your glucose regularly before, during, and after workouts, exercise is good for you and your baby and can be helpful for managing gestational diabetes, which will go away as soon as the placenta is delivered after childbirth because the placenta secretes the hormone that causes insulin resistance.

What and how often to eat are detailed later in this chapter, although, again, talk with your provider about the appropriate diet plan to keep both you and your baby healthy.

## Sciatica and Back Pain

In the third trimester, muscle weakness related to your constantly changing posture, combined with an expanding abdomen compressing the joints of your spine, frequently leads to back pain. If the pain shoots down your leg along the sciatic nerve, you can develop a painful feeling of pins and needles all the way down to your foot. Known as sciatica, this sensation can make it difficult to walk, which you might already feel looks more and more like shuffling due to your changing center of gravity. Trying to walk with sciatica in your third trimester can make you feel like a penguin with a peg leg. It is also quite painful and is made worse by bending and lifting.

To treat back pain and relieve pressure on the sciatic nerve, try lower-back stretches that elongate your muscles. They will stretch out your hamstrings and hip joints, relieve pressure on your lower back, and tone your perineal muscles. In addition to these exercises, you can also head off back pain with the squats (page 130) and TRX upper-body exercises (page 129) found in Chapter 3.

## CAT STRETCH

8–20 reps

*Position yourself on hands and knees. Keeping the motion slow and constant, tighten the muscles in your abdomen and arch your back, stretching the length of your spine. Return to the original position with your back straight and parallel to the ground. This is a great exercise to do before you sleep, and you can repeat this motion as many times as feels good to you, making sure you move slowly and gradually through the straight- and arched-back postures.*

### FETAL-KICK COUNTS

According to the American Pregnancy Association, a good way to monitor your baby's well-being is to conduct "fetal kick counts" at about 28 weeks (24 weeks in pregnancies with complications). Many babies will be more active at night—when you're trying to sleep—and more calm during the day, so assess kicks on a daily basis while also paying attention to how many kicks per hour you feel over the course of a few days, at different times of day. You want to note 6 kicks in 1 hour, at least once per day. ACOG recommends that you note how long it takes your baby to perform 10 movements at the time of day when your baby is most active: kicks, jabs, twists, rolls, or turning. You should feel 10 movements in 2 hours.

Decreased fetal movement can be a sign of distress, and although fetal-kick counting might not prevent a stillbirth, decreased fetal movement is associated with increased risk for stillbirth. A log of your baby's movements will help you monitor the baseline of your baby's activity and wellness.

## How Do I Fuel My Third Trimester?

By this stage in your pregnancy, your diet should center on maintaining the healthy balance of nutrients you cultivated in the first two trimesters. The nutrition advice from Chapters 2 and 3 is intended to ensure that you get enough protein, iron, vitamin C, and complex carbohydrates for energy and bone strength. Continue to eat this healthy balance in the last three months. Table 4.2 shows the U.S. Department of Agriculture (USDA) recommendations for third-trimester nutrition.

You might be inclined to make minor adjustments to prevent discomforts common toward the end of pregnancy, such as heartburn and retaining water. Although many women experience heartburn earlier in pregnancy, it can worsen in the third trimester, when your surge in hormones relaxes the muscle between the stomach and esophagus, which lets stomach acid creep into the throat. To reduce heartburn, try to neutralize your stomach acid by avoiding spicy foods or those with vinegar or citrus. In addition, continue to eat several smaller meals during the day, and don't eat dinner right before you go to bed at night.

Because the third trimester brings on swelling as a result of water retention, eating a lot of salty food will exacerbate your body's tendency to retain

### DOCTOR'S NOTE

You can lower your risk of **heartburn** by sleeping propped on pillows. Stay away from sodas and hard candy to lower your risk.

## TABLE 4.2 Nutritional Guidelines for the Third Trimester

*These USDA\* recommendations for a 28-year-old woman with a moderate exercise plan of 30 to 60 minutes per day are based on prepregnancy weight and are meant to be general guidelines. You can use the Choose My Plate feature on the USDA website (www.choosemy plate.gov) to customize your plan to your weight and height. Consult your provider for nutritional guidelines that are specific to your exercise volume, dietary needs, age, and desired weight gain throughout pregnancy.*

| | 5'4", 115 LBS. | 5'4", 140 LBS. | 5'9", 135 LBS. | 5'9", 170 LBS. |
|---|---|---|---|---|
| **CALORIES/DAY** | 2,600 | 2,600 | 2,800 | 3,000 |
| Vegetables | 3½ cups | 3½ cups | 3½ cups | 4 cups |
| Fruits | 2 cups | 2 cups | 2½ cups | 2½ cups |
| Grains | 9 oz. | 9 oz. | 10 oz. | 10 oz. |
| Dairy | 3 cups | 3 cups | 3 cups | 3 cups |
| Protein | 6½ oz. | 6½ oz. | 7 oz. | 7 oz. |
| Oils | 8 tsp. | 8 tsp. | 8 tsp. | 10 tsp. |

Source: USDA Daily Food Plan for the third trimester, 2012.

fluids, so look for low-sodium options. You can also lower water retention by avoiding sodas, coffee, gluten, or foods with wheat. And while it might seem counterintuitive, staying hydrated by drinking a lot of water will actually reduce your water retention.

While it's a smart idea to boost your diet with omega-3 fatty acids throughout pregnancy, it becomes even more important in the third trimester because infant brain development depends on the flow of omega-3s provided by the mother in the third trimester and first six weeks of life. Not only are they valuable for fetal eye and brain development, but omega-3 fatty acids are known to reduce the risk of premature birth. Omega-3s are readily found in fish oil that you can take as a supplement, and you can also boost your omega-3 intake with

Processed and packaged foods tend to be higher in sodium. To **shop for a low-salt diet,** buy the bulk of your groceries from the perimeter of the store, where the freshest items are displayed.

## DOCTOR'S NOTE

Low-mercury, good omega-3 seafood options (two 6-ounce servings per week)[3] include:

**700 mg per serving of**

- ✳ Halibut
- ✳ Salmon
- ✳ Rainbow trout
- ✳ Canned light tuna

**Between 150 and 700 mg per serving of**

- ✳ Catfish
- ✳ Oysters
- ✳ Flounder
- ✳ Scallops
- ✳ Shrimp
- ✳ Cod

vegetable oil or by eating two servings of low-mercury fish per week. Wild salmon, avocado, nuts and nut butters, and extra-virgin olive oil in your diet will mean you don't need omega-3 supplements. If you aren't breast-feeding, infant formulas now contain omega-3s to boost neural growth.

Along with complex carbs, sufficient calcium is key to a fit pregnancy, especially if you're planning to breast-feed. Your pregnant body will leach calcium from your bones to support the growth of the baby through your milk, so it's common for a new mom to find herself low on calcium. Get into the habit of increased calcium consumption during the third trimester. During pregnancy, you should aim for 3 servings of high-calcium foods every day, totaling 1,000 to 1,300 mg.

Athletes, in particular, need adequate calcium to maintain strong bones so they can reduce the risk of bone-related injury such as stress fractures. Keep in mind that calcium interferes with your body's ability to absorb iron, making it a good idea to avoid eating your high-calcium foods with iron-rich foods.

Pregnant and breast-feeding women should **aim for 200 to 300 mg of omega-3 fatty acids** every day.

| | |
|---|---|
| 1 cup yogurt (240–400 mg) | ½ cup cooked kale (90–100 mg) |
| 1 cup milk (290–300 mg) | 3 ounces wild salmon (170–210 mg) |
| 1 ounce Swiss cheese (250–270 mg) | 8 ounces juice (500 mg), calcium- |
| 4 ounces tofu (145–155 mg) | fortified |
| 1 cup broccoli (160–180 mg) | |

## How Do I Keep a Fit Mind?

In the third trimester, the butterflies in your stomach are flapping hard. Not only have the flutters of the second trimester turned to penalty kicks, but it's common to feel nervous about the impending birthday party. At this point in pregnancy, you might feel a mix of excitement and anxiety about your baby's arrival. Trepidation is normal—this is a major transition—so don't feel guilt or shame over any panic or anxiety. This is particularly true for first-time moms, for whom this can feel like the SAT and an Ironman rolled into one. Look to other women you trust and who won't increase your fear—they will be your mentors and cheerleaders leading up to the big event.

### JITTERS AND NERVES

Many women begin to feel nervous about the birth itself, and dreams (or nightmares) about childbirth are typical. Anxiety can be exacerbated by fatigue, whether it's because you're waking up from vivid dreams or just for another trip to the bathroom. Rest as much as you can throughout the day, knowing at the same time that staying physically active can actually reduce feelings of fatigue as long as you work out for wellness and don't overexert (see "Training Safely in the Third Trimester" later in this chapter).

Remind yourself that this is the most common endurance event in the human race, and you have the added experience of your athletic training to help you through it—mentally and physically. No one is better equipped than an athlete to tough out labor and delivery, even if you'll cross the finish line cooing to a baby in your arms instead of pumping your fists in the air.

3RD TRIMESTER

## CONTROLLING BLOOD SUGAR FOR GESTATIONAL DIABETES

As discussed earlier in this chapter, gestational diabetics must watch their sugar intake and need to base their diets on whole-grain carbs that aren't loaded with refined sugars. High blood sugar can be dangerous to both you and your baby, so it's a good idea to consult with a dietitian who will advise you on the optimal balance of protein, carbs, and fats for your body and condition as well as the best timing for your food intake throughout the day. In general, you should aim to eat every 2½ to 3 hours, pretty much measuring your carbs by the fistful: the right serving size of carbs for a gestational diabetic is about 1 cup (250 ml or 15 grams), which roughly corresponds to the size of your fist. As a general guideline, a woman with gestational diabetes will need to eat about 12 servings per day, 2 to 3 for a meal and 1 to 2 for a snack. Of course, you need to talk to your provider about your specific case and the right individual diet for you.

If you have gestational diabetes, try to combine lean protein and fiber with carbs every time you eat because protein will help you feel full, not to mention boost your energy and help with controlling your blood sugar. While eating a consistent level of carbs throughout the day is recommended, high levels of carbohydrate at breakfast can spike your blood sugar.

One way to reduce jitters and nerves is to get an idea of what to expect on labor day and beyond. Touring the hospital where you will give birth, choosing a pediatrician for your new baby, and finalizing your maternity-leave arrangements at work are all proactive ways to calm your nerves and give you a sense of control.

## Touring the Hospital

Many hospitals offer tours of their birth centers so that you'll be able to see the rooms and facilities and ask questions about the big day. This is a great opportunity to get a sense of what to expect, which can ease some anxiety about the unknown. Take the tour with your birth partner or spouse, and don't be shy about bringing a list of questions to ask. Here are some suggestions for questions that will help you prepare for your stay at the hospital:

* Do labor and birth take place in the same room? Do I move to a recovery room?
* Are there restrictions on the number of people in the room for the birth? Can my other children be there?
* What kind of fetal monitoring is used during labor—occasional or constant?
* Are there restrictions on my mobility during labor? Can I get up and walk around?
* Does the hospital offer breast-feeding instruction to new mothers?
* What other classes or instruction may be available to new parents?
* What is the nursery's practice for using formula if I'm asleep and the baby is hungry?
* What are the visiting hours?
* Can my spouse sleep in my room overnight?
* Do I get a private recovery room?
* Can I bring my own food and drinks?
* What security measures does the hospital take with new babies?
* Is this a teaching hospital, and will medical students be observing any of my treatment?
* Will my baby stay in the nursery or in my room?
* Does the hospital have an on-site newborn intensive care unit (NICU)?
* Is there any follow-up care from the hospital after I go home?
* Do you have staff that can check the safe installation of my car seat?

If you don't get to all of your questions, be sure to ask your doctor during one of your routine visits. You'll find more discussion of the birth process in Chapter 5, including information on pain relief, C-sections, and episiotomies. Be sure to also ask your doctor for his or her specific thoughts on those topics. In particular, you may want to ask some of the following questions:

* Are there restrictions on birth positions I can use during delivery?
* What is your practice for use of an IV during labor and delivery? Is an IV routine?
* What are your beliefs about pain interventions during labor?

* What happens if I decide I want an epidural?
* How often do you use episiotomy and/or forceps?

## Choosing a Pediatrician

It's important to start "shopping" for a pediatrician by 34 weeks so that you can find one who is a good match for your parenting style and personality. Ask friends whom you trust for their pediatricians' names, and then arrange an appointment with the doctor to ask questions about his or her medical beliefs and to determine whether your personalities are a good fit. You can ask some preliminary questions of the staff on the phone to get a sense of whether or not you want to follow up with a short interview of the doctor in person. After the call, you might use the website Healthgrades (www.healthgrades.com) to learn more about the doctor's education and specializations. When you go to the office, make a mental note of how long you wait for the doctor, how clean the space seems, and whether or not there are separate sick and well areas for patients. Also pay attention to whether the doctor welcomes your questions or you feel rushed through the conversation.

Important preliminary questions include:

* What are the office hours and days of service?
* Which hospital is affiliated with the practice?
* Is it a group practice, and will my baby see the same provider every time?
* Does the practice use nurse-practitioners for routine visits?
* Does the practice take my insurance?
* How many years has the practice existed?
* How many years has the doctor been in practice and at this location?
* Who covers service when my doctor isn't on call?
* What are the areas of specialty of each doctor in the practice?

Key questions to ask the doctor include:

* Do you have children of your own? What are their ages?
* Do you have any degrees or training in other areas of child development?

* Are you available to work with children on behavioral issues, or just for medical care?
* What is your general thinking on breast- versus bottle-feeding?
* What do you think is the best way to create a sleep schedule for a baby?
* How do you feel about prescribing antibiotics for children, and on what basis do you prescribe them?
* What is your perspective on immunizations?
* What books do you recommend to new parents?

## Work and Maternity Leave

On top of the excitement and anxiety that increase as your delivery date nears, you may need to complete tasks at work before you take maternity leave. This deadline effect can contribute to stress and the risk of high blood pressure in the final months and weeks, so do what you can to start the process of wrapping up projects as early as possible. Because of this and other causes of anxiety, staying active for wellness is even more important in the third trimester because it gives you a time-out to decompress and release stress.

Women with routine pregnancies (that is, those who don't have medical complications) can usually continue working up to their due dates, although the anxious attention of their coworkers might make them want to telecommute. If working from home is an option, it can reduce your stress level in the final weeks and help you transition to long periods of time at home.

Don't plan to bring folders of work to deal with in the hospital; there might be a lot of downtime, but it's unrealistic to think of your room as a mobile office. Tie up loose ends as much as you can when maternity leave approaches, and then try your best to leave it behind.

A childbirth class or a support group for expectant mothers is a helpful resource for handling third-trimester anxiety, and the women you meet in one of these groups can be indispensable for managing life with a newborn.

## TALKING TO YOUR PARTNER

Most likely, any jittery nerves you have are balanced by equal parts excitement and eagerness. As the days go by, it is common to feel an increased bond with a baby who's beginning to develop a personality. Together with your partner, you'll start to set up the nursery for your little boy or girl; the desire to make improvements at home is colloquially known as "nesting." Involving your partner in this process, as well as the decisions on buying a stroller, car seat, and other major gear, is a great way to stay connected when you're both overwhelmed by details for getting ready.

It's also wise to make sure the two of you share dates that have nothing to do with the baby. In no time at all, much of your relationship will be consumed with infant care, and these last few weeks are a precious opportunity for you and your partner to enjoy each other's company over leisurely meals, walks, and whatever else you enjoy doing together. See all the movies in the theater, get tickets for your favorite team, and consider indulging in an evening at a restaurant where you'd never take a baby.

## TENDING TO YOUR FIT SELF

Staying in touch with your Fit Self can be a challenge during the third trimester, when you feel large and unwieldy. It may feel as if you're waddling through each day. Here are a few tips to help you with this challenge.

**Refuse to compare yourself to anyone else.** That woman who ran a marathon on her due date? She had her own pregnancy story, and it probably won't be yours. Your pregnancy journey is your own, and it changes from day to day. Remind yourself, daily if necessary, that you have focused on keeping yourself fit in mind and body, and reject the idea that you have to be fit with someone else's mind and body. The 10-minute meditation described on page 63 in Chapter 2 will help to ground you in your own body, your own experience of this ultimate training cycle. Let yourself write your own story. Do what makes you feel whole, and don't worry about anyone else.

**Practice balance.** The key to keeping your sanity is looking for balance between obligations, such as work, and aspects of life that help you feel good, such as time outside. Focus on the things you can control, such as the ways you can nourish your mind and body, and let go of things you can't, such as other people's reactions to your fitness activities or how you look. Turn to your "vices of wellness." Vices of wellness are the activities that you love but might not have had very much time to enjoy, such as baking bread, Sudoku, yoga, or strolling the farmer's market. They might seem like luxuries, but that's the reason to work them into these last months and weeks when you feel stressed or out of touch with your own needs and interests. Toward the end of pregnancy, you can feel as if every conversation and thought focuses on the baby. This feeling combined with possible third-trimester physical discomforts means time for your own pleasures will be a positive diversion that nourishes your independent identity.

## How Do I Keep a Fit Body?

By the third trimester, when your mobility is limited and you fatigue easily, even from modest activity, fitness is helpful primarily as stress release. For the most part, the shape and size of your body will serve to prevent you from overdoing your exertion, and even though your relaxin levels decrease during the third trimester, you still want to be mindful of taxing muscles, joints, and ligaments that are working harder in all of your activities. With that precaution in mind, you can still safely log a 30-minute moderate workout at least 4 days per week in order to maintain your good base of physical fitness and mental health. If you feel exhausted, scale back to 3 days per week and shorter durations of exercise. If your doctor determines that you have a reason (such as high blood pressure) to restrict activity, ask

*" I didn't do any races or hard workouts. But I did work out just as regularly as I had before I was pregnant. I just had to slow down, as I couldn't walk as fast when it got later in my pregnancy. I walked right up until my due date.*

TAMMY | CHAMPION RACEWALKER AND MOM OF CALVIN AND MICHELLE

for specifics regarding the type, intensity, and duration of what will be safe for you to do. With a healthy and routine pregnancy, it's perfectly fine (and healthy) to keep your cardio exercise routine going right up to the day you deliver. In fact, walking and motion can help your labor to progress after you begin contractions.

## TRAINING SAFELY IN THE THIRD TRIMESTER

In the third trimester, it's common to believe every change in sensations indicates labor has started. Your apprehension or eagerness for the big day has a lot to do with your extra attentiveness about everything you feel, but a healthy vigilance is important. Critical signs that you should contact your provider include:

* Decrease in fetal movement
* Temperature higher than 100.5
* Severe headache
* Blurred vision
* Leg cramp that doesn't go away when walking or stretching
* Breathing difficulty, nagging cough, or coughing blood
* Flu symptoms
* Depression or anxiety that leads to panic
* Painful abdominal cramping that occurs regularly or with increased frequency
* Vomiting or extreme nausea
* Vaginal bleeding
* Dizziness
* Pain or burning when urinating

Listening to your body's cues will give you assurance that you're staying safe and healthy. Continue to pay attention to Borg's RPE scale (page 72) and

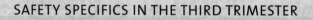

## SAFETY SPECIFICS IN THE THIRD TRIMESTER

- Use the handles on an elliptical to steady yourself, as keeping your balance becomes difficult.

- While your level of exertion might stay the same, your movement should be slower when running, walking, spinning, or using the elliptical.

- Carry a handheld water bottle during all workouts so that you have hydration ready when you're thirsty.

- Require yourself to take regular rest intervals or water breaks during any workout.

- Discontinue a workout if you feel contractions that increase in intensity and become closer together.

- Running a marathon or half-marathon at term (37 weeks) is not advised. Just because you *can* does not mean it's a good idea. If you go into labor, the proper personnel won't be readily available, and race congestion will delay your transport to the hospital.

- Adhere to any prescription of bed rest and follow your doctor's instructions for any limits on your activity.

3RD

TRIMESTER

remember that the effort/recovery pattern that has guided your workouts is even more important now that you tire more easily. The rest intervals of walking or standing between run, bike, or swim intervals of exertion might get longer or slower, which is to be expected now. Recovery periods are a good opportunity to

**TRAINING TIP** In the third trimester, aim to maximize your run effort at a 15 on Borg's RPE scale; it should be a challenge to speak more than a couple of sentences without effort. You'll likely reach a 15 sooner in the workout and at a lower level of effort than earlier in pregnancy, so pay attention and don't be attached to prior baselines.

rehydrate, lower your heart rate, and recharge yourself mentally when a third-trimester workout might feel dispiriting. Enforced, systematic rest intervals are the best antidote to feeling like you're bonking.

## Sport Specifics: Guidelines for Run, Bike, and Swim Training

### THIRD-TRIMESTER RUNNING

By the third trimester, the thought of running can feel like a cruel joke to a lot of women, but some want to continue running as long as possible, and it's perfectly safe to do so. As long as you're comfortable, hydrated, and careful not to overexert, you can feel confident going for a run. One way to stay comfortable is to pay particular attention to what you wear when you work out. While it might feel like a tent, a loose shirt made of moisture-wicking fabric will go a long way toward keeping you cool and comfortable, not to mention less likely to suffer from chafing of fabric against sensitive skin. As in previous trimesters, carry a water bottle with you on any run to help prevent overheating and dehydration. Electrolyte drinks and coconut water are still great hydration go-tos and will keep you from sweating out too much salt. However, sports drinks tend to be high in sugar, so don't drink them exclusively.

While running in the third trimester is safe, you don't want to start running in your seventh month if you haven't been running during the pregnancy thus far. Women who run longer distances well into their third trimester are typically seasoned athletes who logged high-volume mileage prior to pregnancy and were able to run throughout their first and second trimesters. That said, there is no hard-and-fast definition of what is too hard or too fast, since every woman's preg-

*I ran about 40 miles a week on the treadmill (lived abroad at that time in my life in an unsafe area) up to my sixth month, when I developed low-back pain. At that point I switched to the elliptical and continued to run 40 miles a week on it, plus swimming a ton during the last month. . . . I am positive that exercise not only kept me sane during pregnancy but was also instrumental in my quick postbaby recovery.* ANA-MARIA | RUNNER AND MOM OF PETRU

nancy story, fitness level, and base of experience are different. That's why you need to focus on your own rate of exertion, comfort, and sense of wellness during a run rather than a specific time or number of miles as the definition of what is reasonable or acceptable.

While wellness is a smart third-trimester running goal, participating in a race can be a great experience for staying connected to the running community and helping you feel invigorated. Avoid a race in extreme heat or cold, and be sure to clear the event with your provider, who knows your specific condition and

**TRAINING TIP** You might read about women in their third trimesters who train for distance races they'll complete shortly after giving birth. Chances are, they're carefully and frequently monitored by their doctors while training, but even so, it's crucial that you don't feel bound to a training calendar or scheduled regimen in the last few months of pregnancy. Your body's cues should guide your workouts more than your self-discipline or ultimate race goal.

For example, Kara Goucher, elite American marathoner and mother, had ambitious plans for racing after delivery, but a stress fracture in her second trimester compelled her to change her thinking. In her third trimester, Goucher relied on the elliptical machine for her harder training and ran only to get time outside and keep her muscle memory.

If you're scheduled to run 10 miles, but you feel depleted, tired, or simply "off" at the midpoint, listen to your body. Take a 5-minute break to rest, hydrate, and walk. If you don't feel better when you start running again, call it a day. Remember, wellness and health are the real goal, and you want to feel more process-oriented than goal-driven during this phase of your athletic career. Even Goucher, a self-described routine-driven athlete, was willing to change her plan when her body needed her to stop.

circumstances. Also, leave your watch at home. Make it about love of sport, recreational running, and the fun of a race. People will be impressed to see you with a bib number on that belly, and just remind yourself that those who give raised eyebrows haven't consulted your doctor.

### THIRD-TRIMESTER BIKING

If you've been biking throughout pregnancy, it's fine to continue in the last trimester, particularly because it's a smoother, less demanding activity than running and you won't feel any jarring from the impact of a heavier footfall. Your weight is supported by the bike, which is more forgiving on the joints in your hips and knees and allows your cardiovascular system to benefit from the exercise without taxing your joints. In addition, your feet might be swelling and achy much of the time, and cycling won't stress them out to the same extent that running can.

Keep in mind that your balance will continue to feel less reliable as your belly grows and changes your posture and center of gravity. Because of that, the time is right to make the switch to a stationary bike or an indoor bike that's on a trainer, if you haven't already. A recumbent bike is another good option because the seat is wider and your back is supported so you don't arch forward and strain it. If you'd like to continue cycling outdoors, ride slowly at first to establish your balance.

**Don't begin cycling in the third trimester** if you haven't been biking throughout the previous trimesters, as your unfamiliarity with your body's center of gravity on a bike could lead to a fall.

Ruxandra Looft, a longtime recreational cyclist and writer of the popular blog *Simply Bike*, decided to ride her bike throughout her pregnancy. "Although being pregnant meant slowing down, riding shorter distances, and being more mindful of my body, it never meant changing my lifestyle completely or opting out of things I loved to do before the pregnancy," she wrote. At the beginning of her third trimester, Ruxandra was able to ride about 10 miles with breaks. By her 35th week, she biked 5 miles at a time because of the summer heat. "I wanted to make sure that I didn't push my body too much and didn't risk overheating and dehydration," she explained. She continued riding until her 38th week, when breathing during a ride felt too strenuous. A perfect example of fitness for wellness, Ruxandra stopped riding when it wasn't fun anymore. "My body knew when it was time to quit, and I respected its wishes." For the final weeks of pregnancy, Ruxandra stuck to swimming.

As in your prior months of riding, choose low-traffic routes on a smooth surface and ride only in daylight. If you'd like to go off road, remember that an accident or fall of any kind could be dangerous, so weigh the risk against the ride and discuss your choices for cycling with your provider. As you make your decision to ride or take a break from the bike, keep in mind that you might need to adjust your seat height again as your body changes, and try to go with a lower resistance to prevent a slipped disc or ligament issue.

### THIRD-TRIMESTER SWIMMING

Deanna, a triathlete, mom of three, and coach, ran through her first trimester before deciding she'd prefer to swim while pregnant. She'd considered herself a runner, but her newfound love of the water tapped a passion for swimming that has only grown in the years since having her babies. She now coaches triathletes of all levels and believes that transitioning from running to swimming is a great option when expecting, even if you haven't been a swimmer before.

Deanna doesn't recommend a one-size-fits all approach for workouts in the third trimester, explaining that you can't just jump into the pool and churn out lap after lap if your body is not used to swimming. Each woman has to listen to the needs of her own body, she advises, adding that this is how you'd want to

Forgo the **backstroke** after week 16, as the weight of your uterus on the vena cava can restrict blood flow to the placenta.

train when you aren't expecting. "If I was coaching a pregnant woman, I wouldn't treat them any differently than my regular athletes. If you aren't feeling well, you go easier, either way."

When talking about swimming as the best workout for the third trimester, Deanna acknowledged, "The hardest part is putting on the bathing suit. Once you're in the water, you're back in your old body." As in your earlier months of pregnancy, swimming and water running are ideal forms of exercise into the third trimester. Deanna recommends doing online research for good stroke technique or consulting with a swim coach in a session on form. "If you use the right technique and listen to your body, you can be safe doing it. Look at these things as opportunities. This is an opportunity to try something else and to get good at it."

With your joints now more flexible, the water supports them while providing resistance to tone your muscles. The water also provides buoyancy to your growing belly and keeps your core temperature cool while you exercise. In addition, there are no balance concerns when you're swimming or water running, unlike with biking and running.

While it's safe to switch to swimming if you haven't already been swimming in the first and second trimesters, be careful with your level of effort so that you don't strain muscles from overworking them in a new or unfamiliar way. You can switch from road running to water running without any concern about trying a new activity because the motion of the run stays the same while removing impact concerns. There are countless workout variations that will help a runner or other type of high-impact exerciser transition to pool sessions by adapting running intervals to the pool. To get you started, try these three workouts after a

 *The only thing I could handle was swimming. It was nice to feel so light.*

WENDY | TRIATHLETE AND MOM OF MILES AND EVELYN

5-minute warm-up of treading water with both arms and legs to get your limbs ready for exercise.

### PYRAMID RUN INTERVALS

*Run laps in the pool using the technique from Chapter 2, but measure the intervals in time instead of numbers of laps. Start with a 5-minute run, then take a rest for 1 to 2 minutes by gently treading water with your arms and legs. Decrease your running intervals to 4 minutes, 3 minutes, and 2 minutes. After a 2-minute rest, perform the intervals and rests in the opposite order: 2, 3, 4, and 5 minutes of water running. Keep your RPE at 14–16.*

### 8-BY-2 INTERVALS

*Run or swim in 2-lap increments of a 25-meter pool, taking a 1-minute rest at the wall between each pair of laps. Then switch to an 8 x 1 lap series with a 1-minute rest at the wall between laps. Keep your RPE at 4–16.*

### 10-MINUTE KICKS

*Swim 3 sets of 10-minute intervals. Swim 2 laps with a kickboard, then 2 laps using both arms and legs and no kickboard, alternating for the whole set. Take a 3-minute rest at the wall between each set.*

\* \* \*

In the third trimester, while the crawl and sidestroke are fine, the breaststroke will likely be the most comfortable and beneficial choice because your belly hangs below you and the arm and leg motions are great for strengthening your back, chest, glutes, and hips. When you give in to rounding over your shoulders as it becomes harder to stand up straight, this stroke is especially good because it lengthens your chest and shortens back muscles that tend to overstretch during pregnancy. The breaststroke counteracts that posture with a gentle arching of the back and doesn't require that you twist your torso.

Take care not to arch your back too drastically when lifting yourself out of the water as you stroke, as this contraction of the lumbar region can strain your lower back. Consider using a snorkel while doing the breaststroke so that you don't have to lift your torso so far. In addition, working your legs too aggressively can prompt round-ligament pain or strain because the pubic bone is beginning to separate in preparation for labor, making your hip joints and ligaments very loose and prone to overstretching. Even with these issues, the breaststroke is

## FITNESS $R_X$

Treading water is a great way to work your core muscles. Or try leg curls and leg and knee lifts while holding on to the wall. There are great strengthening options you can perform in water. Hold on to the wall with the hand of the side that isn't performing the exercise, or support yourself with a pool noodle by wrapping it around you. Perform 2 to 3 sets of 12 to 15 reps per side.

Hamstring curls (for glutes, piriformis, and hamstrings):

- With the knee of your working leg in line with the knee of your standing leg, lift one leg and pull the heel slowly back toward your butt. Lower to starting position.

Side leg lifts (for abductors and glutes):

- Without tipping your torso to the side, raise one leg to the side, about 6-8 inches off the ground. Hold for 3 seconds. Slowly return to standing.

Front knee raises (for quads):

- With legs hip width apart, slowly march in place, raising your knees as high as your belly will allow, holding each raised knee for 2 seconds before returning it to the ground.

one of your best options for third-trimester exercise, and taking these few precautions will help you benefit from it.

Swimming in a chlorinated pool poses no risk to you or the baby as long as the pool chemicals are monitored. That said, an indoor, chlorinated pool can produce fumes, so if you have the option, opt for outdoor water, where you have the ventilation of fresh air, not to mention the dose of vitamin D from the sun. Just remember to wear waterproof sunscreen to protect your sensitive skin.

Indoors or out, swimming or pool running is ideal for regulating your temperature during a workout (see Chapter 2 for tips on water running). Keep in mind, however, that even though your body temperature stays cool and safe while you're swimming, a swim cap can trap heat and increase your core temperature. Also, you can still get dehydrated, so don't forget to drink at least 8 ounces of water before and after your time in the pool. And when you see that bubbly, relaxing hot tub next to the pool, walk on by. Any pool or tub that's heated to a temperature higher than your body temperature can be dangerous.

## Gear for the Last 12 Weeks and Beyond

### PILLOWS

Stocking up on pillows of different densities can make a big difference in your comfort in the final weeks. You might find that you need a pillow to support your belly if you sleep on your side, as well as a lumbar pillow for sitting. It's a good idea to invest in a few for different positions, including a nursing pillow, which looks like a large version of the neck-support pillow you'd use on a plane. At the end of the pregnancy and in the early weeks of new motherhood, it's amazing what comfort will do for your mind and body.

### BELLY BAND

When your baby settles lower into position for delivery, your belly settles lower, too, and you might feel as if you're trying to walk with a bowling ball between your legs. A belly support band can help to lift that weight and support your lower back, relieving some of the pressure in your pelvis. While it hardly has the sex appeal of a garter belt or the slimming functionality of Spanx, the band can reduce pain in your legs, glutes, back, and abs. Your clothes will conceal it nicely, and as an added benefit, it makes a great resistance band for postpartum strength training exercises.

## FITNESS BALL

This large, inflated ball is a great companion to your late-pregnancy fitness program, and not because you might feel like its twin. The ball allows you to strengthen your oblique ab muscles and legs without putting strain on your hips, pelvis, knees, or back. If you can sit on a ball at work—or as much as possible when you sit during the day—you'll be working your core muscles by virtue of the balance you need to stabilize yourself. It's the easiest sit-up you'll ever do. When your back begins to get sore, it's time to switch to a stable seat with more support for your back.

There are several beneficial exercises you can do with a big belly and a big ball. These will help to strengthen your core, pelvic floor, quads, and hamstrings as well as stretch key muscle groups that tend to suffer toward the end of pregnancy. The stabilizing nature of using the ball also makes it an ideal tool for Kegel exercises, which will help with bladder control during the third trimester and beyond, when you might feel the need for a bathroom every five minutes. Just be careful of your balance on the ball, using it in front of a wall to touch if you have a moment when you need stability.

### PICKING YOUR BALL

Stability balls come in different sizes for users of various heights, so be sure to check the package before you buy one. There are even balls specific to pregnancy that can be found online. If you're not sure which ball to choose, go for the one that can support the most weight, about 250 pounds. While you may not test that limit, you will feel confident it can support you plus your baby. The instructions will also advise you on how to inflate it properly and avoid a puncture.

Not only is the ball great for stretching and toning in the third trimester, it's also useful for easing pain during labor, particularly in your back. Many hospitals and birth centers will have a ball that you can use when labor builds in discomfort. It might seem like a toy, but its therapeutic use during labor can give it a serious value.

## WARM-UP ROTATIONS

*Start with a gentle warm-up to get your body used to balancing on the ball. While sitting on the ball with your legs open wide and feet touching the floor, rock your hips from side to side for about 1 minute, rolling the ball slightly underneath you. Next, move your hips in a clockwise rotation so that the ball moves in a circle under you, repeating the circle 10 to 15 times before switching to a counterclockwise rotation. Then switch to a figure-eight rotation so that you alternate between clockwise and counterclockwise circles, repeating 15 times.*

## KEGELS

*Sit on the ball with your legs open and feet on the floor 12 to 18 inches apart. As you exhale, count to 5 and slowly tighten your vaginal muscles and try to contract your pelvic floor by pulling it up and toward your belly button. Keep your torso—back, neck, shoulders—relaxed as you perform this contraction, tightening only the vaginal muscles. As you inhale, relax before performing another contraction on the exhalation. Repeat this sequence 20 to 25 times per day.*

## AB CONTRACTION

*Sitting on the ball with your back straight, legs wide, and feet on the floor, inhale through your nose for 5 seconds, feeling your rib cage expand. As you exhale through the mouth, tighten your ab muscles to a count of 5. Hold the contraction for 3 seconds before inhaling again. Repeat this exercise 20 to 25 times per day. If you prefer, you can put one hand on your stomach as you inhale, making sure you aren't pulling upward and are instead tightening the abs on the exhale and pulling the muscles in toward the spine.*

## QUAD-CORE STRENGTHENER

1–2 sets of 10–20 reps

*Stand with the ball between your lower back and a wall, knees slightly bent and hip width apart. Lengthen your torso as you press against the ball. As you inhale deeply, envision pulling your belly button toward your back. Hold for 3 seconds before exhaling.*

## CHILD'S POSE

1–4 sets of 30 sec.

*Come down onto the floor, kneeling on one leg at a time. With your legs open to hip width, shift your weight back so that you're sitting with your heels under your butt, making sure your legs are wide enough for your belly to have space for you to lean forward. Hold the ball between your hands in front of you. On the exhale, slowly curve your spine and push the ball forward on the floor so that you can lean over onto your thighs (or as close as you can get to them). Push your weight back toward the tailbone so that you can relax your neck and chest. Hold this stretch for 30 seconds before slowly returning to a seated position. Repeat the stretch by rolling the ball toward the right and left as you lean forward so that you can stretch your obliques and back in all directions.*

## Chapter Summary

Way to go! You started this chapter in the throes of the third trimester and finished it ready to show everyone in the delivery room what you're made of. Your body and your baby continued to develop, and getting into the right frame of mind—fitness for wellness—eased you through the discomforts and nerves of the third trimester. If you follow balanced nutrition and exercise for wellness, the final 12 weeks of pregnancy can place you in top shape for beginning motherhood on the right, less swollen, foot. And if you employ the skills that athletes use for optimal performance, labor and delivery will become a less stressful rite of passage to life as a fit mother. The next chapter will guide you through the labor experience, giving you an inside track on the mental and physical demands of becoming a mom.

### TO REVIEW ... THE DOCTOR'S NOTES

❋ Swimming and spinning are the easiest forms of cardio for your joints as your weight increases.

❋ Expect your stamina to decrease from the first and second trimesters; lower intensities will elicit more fatigue than ever before. Don't worry— just like pregnancy, it's temporary.

❋ Call your health care provider immediately if you experience any bleeding, a gush of fluid, or painful contractions.

❋ Choose your pediatrician by 34 weeks.

❋ Tour the hospital and be sure to review any questions that come up during your tour with your provider.

❋ You should feel your baby move every day, and be sure to conduct fetal kick counts. You're looking for 6 kicks in an hour, once each day.

# Delivering Your Personal Best

*Labor and Childbirth*

**PREGNANCY IS A LITTLE LIKE** training for a race without knowing the course or distance. Because every woman's pregnancy and birth experience will vary, it's easy to feel trepidation when you hear the details from friends and family about what happened to them. As with many new challenges—whether it's your first day at a new job, the morning of a big race, or your baby's birth—anxiety stems from the unknown. Fortunately, as with training for a big race, childbirth isn't entirely an unknown, and you're blessed to have access to some of the best care and knowledge about birth in the modern world. This chapter will help to settle your nerves by preparing you for what to expect from labor and delivery and how to apply an athletic mind to successfully enduring the pain of birth. There's no cool T-shirt, unless you count the hospital gown, but the medal is one of a kind.

In this chapter, you'll read about:

* Tapping your mental toughness during labor and delivery
* Breathing and visualization techniques for labor
* Optimal fetal positioning exercises for birth
* What to expect from labor and delivery
* Gear: what to pack for the birth

With your fit pregnancy and your strong mental game, you'll cross the finish line with a heart—and arms—full of joy.

## Mental Toughness: Bringing Your A-Game to the Birth

Your fitness training will help more than just your body when it comes to labor and delivery. As one ultrarunning mom puts it, "We are used to pain. It's our currency." Athlete moms often say that their experience in sport sharpened their mental toughness and ability to cope with pain over a long period of time. They talk about an ability to apply a competitive race mentality to the labor game and endure with the grit it takes to succeed in overcoming the hardest workout ever. In the most basic sense, your experience with the exhausting sort of physical discomfort that you get during workouts and races is good training for getting through the pain of childbirth.

Crissy, a mom of two, has been a lifelong runner, having been raised by a mom who was a running devotee at a time when few women participated in sports. As a result, Crissy grew up with a deep intrinsic value for sports and has applied her athlete experience throughout her life. Reflecting on how running prepared her for childbirth, she said, "I think running teaches us that we can endure more pain, and for longer periods of time than we may have previously thought. Also, that pain or discomfort doesn't always mean something is wrong and should be feared. I think it's a big benefit to experience that before giving birth."

From a sports perspective, the vaginal birth process is not entirely unlike a track workout. Now expecting her second baby, runner Steph likened contractions to putting in laps: "While in labor, I kept telling myself that each contraction was shorter than a 400 (heck of a lot of 400s, though)," adding that being an athlete gave her as much mental training for birth as it did for her physical fitness.

## Breathing and Visualization for Labor

Like Steph, when competitive triathlete and coach Michelle Simmons was in labor, she channeled her inner Ironwoman toward perceiving contractions as an interval workout with recovery periods. She didn't use Lamaze or hypnosis;

instead, she visualized speed work. She thought of every contraction as a tough interval of hard running, during which she dug deep and focused on finding a regular, meditative breathing rhythm to get her through it. Every rest period was her recovery before the next interval began. Breaking the labor into segments helped her manage the pain in small cycles, which is especially useful when you don't know how long the workout will take. Michelle even muses that the interval workout in labor is easier for athletes because the pain diffuses in the periods between contractions.

> *I thought of it as a track workout but easier, because in labor when the contractions stopped, the pain went away completely, like a light switch, versus sometimes at the track it takes a while before your breathing calms down and you feel recovered between intervals.*
>
> MICHELLE | 10-TIME IRONMAN FINISHER, COACH, AND MOM OF MOANA

Perceiving each contraction as a high-intensity interval that would always include a rest period minimizes a feeling of being overwhelmed and exhausted by the prospect of countless contractions. By applying the concept of focus on the present interval, Michelle avoided feeling intimidated by the big picture of the delivery and the anticipation of the pain of pushing.

Along the same lines, the Lamaze method of breathing, found to be helpful for pain management, mimics the ideal breathing of a hard-effort race or workout. Finding a regular, consistent rhythm of breath that reaches deeply into the diaphragm on the inhalation helps you relax and focus while it increases the oxygen directed to your bloodstream. It releases a mind that's trapped in pain as much as possible by regulating your breathing in a steady pattern that will lower your exertion, whether in a race or in the birth room.

Your experience as an athlete will make a big difference in your familiarity with using your breath because it helps you manage moments of discouragement by calming your anxiety and helping you to push through. As devoted runner Nancy describes, "I learned from being at the back of the pack not to get discouraged too quickly. You just have more self-control with breathing and keeping calm through pain. What I found out is that I am no back-of-the-packer when it comes to labor."

While breathing techniques can be helpful for putting you "in the moment" so you don't get overwhelmed by the task ahead of you, some women find it useful to transcend the discomfort by psychologically stepping outside the moment. This is where an athlete's experience with the late stages of endurance training and long workouts can come into play. Kara Haas, champion runner and mom to Ella, believes that her experience with pushing through the wall of exhaustion in distance running helped her endure a long childbirth experience. As she puts it, "After 26 hours of sunny-side-up natural labor, I would have to go with the ability of marathon runners to go 'outside themselves'—kind of existential, but it worked for me in both childbirth and the marathon." Fixing your gaze on parts of the room or focusing your attention on the words of your birth partner are two possible ways to go "outside yourself" to push through the wall of birth.

As in a race, having a mantra can be a blessing during labor. You might feel like screaming your partner's name in rage, but there are other cathartic options for helping you manage pain. Pick something short and empowering, with a rhythm that you like to hear in your head. You might not be able to actually speak the words because it disrupts the cadence and physical release of rhythmic breathing such as Lamaze, but repeating it in your mind can center you and keep you calm. Repeating a three-syllable phrase such as "Almost there" in your mind has an especially meditative rhythm. A patterned breathing technique with a mental mantra provides a twofold approach for multitasking moms-to-be to stay focused but relaxed (as much as possible), mindful and managing the moment.

Visualization is also a great athletic tool to practice before labor and to carry with you into the delivery room. Many of the best athletes use mental images to center themselves before competition, and the rest of us can benefit from this tool, too. Visualization not only gives a competitive edge it provides confidence and mindfulness when you're about to be put to the test. In its most basic sense, visualization gives you a mental picture of what you want to happen when you're about to perform. This doesn't just mean a picture in your head.

**TRAINING TIP** Consider taking a birthing class where you'll learn breathing techniques, such as those taught in Lamaze (though this old-school method is taught less and less). To find a class, ask your provider or the hospital or birth center where you'll be having your baby. Here are a few tips to practice in advance at home or to use when labor commences:

When a contraction starts, take a cleansing breath: Inhale very deeply through your nose, then release with a long exhale through your mouth.

Find a comfortable number of seconds to assign to a slow inhale and exhale that will help you manage pain by relaxing your breath, about 3 to 5 seconds for each.

Try a patterned breath of short and long breaths that you repeat like a mantra. The hee-hee-hoo rhythm is a pattern that most people are familiar with, but you can find one that suits you. The focus here is on the exhale, so inhalations should be brief and light, emphasizing the exhalations with the hee and hoo.

Combine your breathing with focus on a point across from you in the room. During a contraction, use a cleansing breath to center your eyes on this spot, then begin your patterned or slow breathing.

Try using a technique inspired by *ujjayi* breath, which is the basis for many yoga disciplines because it helps to calm you and to deliver more oxygen to your bloodstream. To begin, drop and relax your jaw so that you aren't grinding your teeth. Inhale deeply through your nose, directing the air through the back of the nasal passage as if you're snoring. This creates a deep, oceanic sound. Exhale very slowly through your mouth for the same number of seconds. Traditional *ujjayi* would have you exhale through your nose, but you might find that too constricting during labor.

*Exercise taught me how to stay strong with my body, to feel but not hold on to the pain, to visualize a finish line in heart and head until I could see it with my eyes.*　　　　HELEN | MARATHONER AND MOM OF SAM AND GUS

Visualization should also include how you want your body to feel and what sounds and thoughts will help you calm yourself and focus.

To help ease your anxiety about what labor and delivery will be like, try visualizing a softly lit room; a sound machine with the ocean playing to relax you; and a confident, calm demeanor in total control to help you endure contractions. The more you can practice your optimal birth scene, the more likely you are to be able to tap into it in the moment it happens, so rehearse your visualization on a daily basis, ideally when you practice your breathing technique. If you tour the hospital or birth center, ask if you can play music during labor and to what degree you can choose the lighting so that, when the time comes, you can do your best to re-create those conditions.

## Optimal Fetal Positioning

Chapters 2 and 3 provided strength training exercises using resistance bands and TRX straps to help you tone and build lean muscle mass. In the third trimester, you're exercising for wellness, and the exercises on the fitness ball will boost your core and leg strength. Now is also a great time to start thinking about your baby's position in the uterus, which some birth specialists believe you can help along.

Labor and delivery are generally shorter for babies who are head down, with the back of the head at your belly, or the occiput anterior position. The pressure of the back of the head on your cervix pushes it into a wider opening to increase hormone production and assist delivery, and when a baby in the occiput anterior position moves through the cervix, the smallest part of its head goes first. Think about pulling on a turtleneck while looking down versus at the ceiling, and you'll get why the occiput anterior position, or baby looking down, is ideal.

Babies typically settle into the head-down position in the final few weeks of pregnancy, and the head finds its place closer to the birth canal. A baby who presents feet or rear first is known as breech; this position occurs in about 1 of every 25 births, according to the American Pregnancy Association. Breech position is most common after the first pregnancy, or with twins or more than two babies. It is also more common in cases where the amniotic sac has too little or too much fluid, or in an atypically shaped uterus. Women with a history of premature births also tend to experience breech presentations more frequently, as do those with placenta previa.

Your provider will be able to detect whether the baby is presenting breech in the final weeks of pregnancy by performing an external exam to assess its position: pressing on your abdomen to find the head, back, and buttocks. If a breech position is suspected, the doctor might require an ultrasound to confirm the baby's presentation. Talk to your provider about the options for turning the baby, which usually takes place at 37 weeks. If a baby stays breech, it is safest to deliver by C-section.

## Labor and Delivery

Your talents as an athlete truly come into play during labor and delivery, which are among the most physically demanding challenges a woman will face. During labor, you'll use your ability to distract yourself from pain with the breathing and visualization techniques explained earlier, and you'll use your body's muscles—especially your abs—to push your baby out. The mental strategies you've acquired as an athlete don't influence just the final push; your inner strength can also be helpful for controlling discomfort in the early stages of labor.

**DOCTOR'S NOTE**

As opposed to "false labor," **contractions** that occur regularly and gradually move closer together and cause cervical change indicate you've gone into labor.

Consistent uterine contractions that increase in intensity are the clearest signal that you're in labor. When your contractions start, you'll be able to tap your athlete's mind for logging data by timing the duration of each one and the time between them. Don't be surprised if 20 to 30 minutes elapse between contractions in the early stages of labor. When they fall about 5 minutes apart, call your provider for instructions on when to go to the hospital or birth center.

When your doctor decides your contractions are close enough together that it's time for you to go to the hospital, a labor nurse will admit you. Once admitted,

## OPTIMAL FETAL POSITIONING EXERCISES

Many birth specialists agree that when done consistently, exercises derived from yoga and Pilates can turn the baby for optimal fetal positioning. Although more old-fashioned folks have suggested that you scrub the kitchen floor to put the baby in an anterior position, we're more progressive in the 21st century. These exercises might not put a shine in your linoleum, but they're much better for your dignity.

Emerging research shows that, when practiced routinely, a few minutes in a hands-and-knees position (the Pelvic Tilt exercise) reduces late-pregnancy back pain and may encourage a baby into the occiput anterior position.[1] Starting at 32 weeks, perform each exercise twice a day when the baby is moving to encourage him or her into the best position for labor and delivery. They're simple, and you can do them on the floor in front of the TV or while your other children play next to you.

### PELVIC TILT

*Get on all fours and tuck your rear down while lifting your lower back toward the ceiling and lowering your chin to your chest (see Cat Stretch, page 146). Then look straight ahead while straightening your spine so that it is parallel to the floor and ceiling. Repeat this motion slowly up to 40 times while the baby is active. Don't strain your back by forcing it into a concave position instead of simply straightening the spine.*

women who are Group B strep–positive or those who know they want an epidural will be placed on an IV drip. Two straps will be gently placed around your abdomen; one picks up the baby's heart rate, and the other detects your contractions. This monitoring shows whether the baby is safely tolerating the contractions.

As long as the fetal heart rate is reassuring, you'll likely be encouraged to walk, rock in a chair, soak in a tub, or sit on a birthing ball, depending on the hospital. (If you decide to take pain medication, you'll be kept in bed after it's administered. See "How Do I Decide on Pain Interventions?," page 187.) These

## FORWARD INVERSIONS

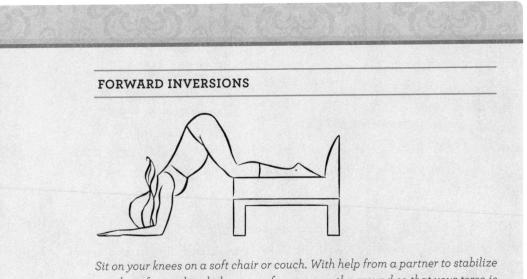

*Sit on your knees on a soft chair or couch. With help from a partner to stabilize you, lean forward and place your forearms on the ground so that your torso is upside down and your back looks like a slide. Tuck your chin, rather than looking up, to ease tension in your neck. Consult your doctor before trying an inversion if you have high blood pressure. Hold for up to 30 seconds, or repeat it several times for shorter intervals. Return to your seated position slowly so you don't become light-headed.*

options are intended to increase your comfort and help you feel at home. If you have any soothing or special music you'd like to play, now is the time to set it up in your room.

## WILL I BE INDUCED?

About one in five births is induced in the United States, according to the Centers for Disease Control, for a number of reasons, including:

- Abnormal fetal heart rate
- The baby is not growing at the normal rate
- High blood pressure or preeclampsia
- Insulin-dependent diabetes
- Uterine infection
- The due date is 1 to 2 weeks past
- Water (amniotic fluid in the membrane around your baby) breaks, but labor doesn't start
- Nonmedical reasons (elective induction)

If you and your doctor decide that birth should be induced, the doctor will check your cervix to see if it has softened and will assess the baby's position. There are several methods for inducing labor and starting your contractions:

* Dilating your cervix with medication (prostaglandins), taken by mouth or inserted vaginally
* Ripening the cervix by inserting a catheter that fills a balloon with water to open the cervix
* Using a small hook to make a hole in your amniotic sac in order to break your water (if your cervix is already partially dilated)
* Starting contractions with medication (Pitocin), administered in an IV drip with a small dose that the doctor can increase to stimulate contractions strong enough to deliver the baby

After you're induced, it can take anywhere from a few hours to a few days for labor to start.

## WHAT IS "ACTIVE" LABOR?

During active labor, your cervix should dilate 1 centimeter (cm) per hour if this is your first vaginal delivery, or 1.5 cm per hour if you've had a vaginal delivery before. This is an estimate, however, and every woman's rate of progression will be different. While the whole birth process is the human body's most awesome workout, you'll be in a phase known as latent labor until you become 4 cm dilated, which often takes hours (and sometimes days). This is the time when you'll be best served by distraction techniques (e.g., mantras), breathing patterns, and visualizations. When you're between 4 and 10 cm dilated, you are in active labor.

If you stop dilating over time, it may be that your baby is too big for your pelvis, which is called cephalopelvic disproportion, or that your uterus isn't contracting sufficiently. To determine whether your uterus is contracting properly, your doctor might place an intrauterine pressure catheter (IUPC) inside your uterus. The catheter, which sits between the baby and your uterine muscle, will measure the strength of your contractions (using mm of mercury). If your contractions aren't strong enough, you might receive Pitocin to increase the strength of contractions. Pitocin may be started before the IUPC is placed, as the catheter is sometimes inserted only if no change in the cervix is occurring with Pitocin.

## WHAT IS BACK LABOR?

Most women experience some lower-back discomfort during contractions, though it usually dissipates between them. A specific pain known as "back labor" afflicts some women, who feel intense cramping in the lower back during contractions and some degree of pain between contractions. Often the baby's position is responsible for causing back labor, such as when it faces your pubic bone (occiput posterior) and the hard part of the back of the head pushes against your spine.

To relieve this pain, it's best to avoid lying on your back. You can walk, sway, or sit and rock on the birthing ball, or ask your significant other to massage your lower back just above the sacrum. It can also help to get on your hands and knees (see the Pelvic Tilt exercise on page 178), especially if you're trying to assist the baby in finding a more optimal position. Being on all fours will take the pressure off your cervix, too, decreasing the intensity of contractions. If you try the hands-and-knees position, pelvic tilts while you're on all fours can also reposition the baby and take the pressure off your spine.

If you want to sit, use the ball to sit and lean forward onto the bed, or sit backward in a chair so there is no pressure on your back, placing a hot or cold compress on your spine while you lean forward. You can also perform pelvic tilts while sitting on the ball. A shower or warm bath, if permitted by the doctor, is also an option.

Although the baby's position does matter for the ease and duration of delivery, back labor in and of itself is not a risk for the mother or baby. Regularly repositioning your body and trying gentle movement that takes pressure off your spine is the best way to reduce the pain in your lower back.

## WHEN DO I PUSH?

Once you're 10 cm dilated, it's time to use those ab muscles you've been strengthening with your core work to push that baby out. It can take three hours to push out a first baby, though this isn't the rule. Women who are active athletes or who have had a vaginal delivery before can take less than an hour to push. This is one of the biggest benefits to staying active and fit throughout pregnancy!

Pushing is hard work, and you'll need every muscle fiber you've strengthened during your pregnancy. Engaging your athlete's mental strength will be key, too. There are many positions you can use to push out your baby, from hands and knees to squatting. Sometimes rotating from side to side will help the baby move down through the pelvis on its final path to the outside world. You'll need the help of everyone in the room to push, as nurses and your birth partner can help hold your legs back so you can bear down to push during contractions. The nature of pushing is akin to having a bowel movement, and some doctors will invite you to look at the baby's emergence with a mirror between contractions.

Crowning occurs when a baby's head appears in the vaginal opening. If you aren't using pain medication, this feeling is marked by a burning or stinging sensation followed by a period of numbness. The numbness occurs because the baby has stretched the vaginal tissue so thin that the nerves are blocked. When the baby crowns, you'll need to stop pushing in order to decrease the amount of tearing.

Usually the doctor will massage your perineum with mineral oil while the baby is crowning to protect it from tearing. That said, a baby's head is bigger than the vaginal opening, so it is common for some tearing to occur, and you probably won't be able to sit without some discomfort for a week after the birth.

If you've been pushing for hours and are unable to push any longer, or the baby isn't tolerating this part of the labor and needs to be delivered expeditiously, the doctor may use a vacuum or forceps. While not a routine part of delivery, the use of these instruments is safe and effective and can decrease the

## WHAT IS AN EPISIOTOMY, AND WILL I NEED ONE?

There was a time when an episiotomy, or an incision in the perineum (the area between your vagina and your anus), was a routine aspect of childbirth to aid delivery. Now, because it makes tears in the anus and rectum more likely, it's performed only in certain cases. Many women will naturally tear during delivery, and a doctor will stitch a tear after the birth. An episiotomy is done with local anesthesia (if you don't have an epidural), and a doctor will often perform one only if extreme natural tearing seems likely due to the size of the infant's head, the baby is positioned abnormally, or a quick delivery is imperative for the baby's health.

chance that you'll need a C-section. The equipment will be used during a contraction to pull while you are pushing, and a baby who is delivered with this method will be immediately assessed in the room by a pediatrician.

A baby delivered with a routine vaginal birth will be "caught" by the doctor, who will likely place your infant on your bare stomach so the support person of your choosing can have the option to cut the umbilical cord. It's important for the baby to cry loud and often, as well as to hear that the infant's respiration is clear of mucus. The baby will then be placed on your bare chest because research shows that immediate skin-to-skin contact with the mother is important for attachment and an auspicious start to breast-feeding.[2] Encouraging the baby to latch on for breast-feeding can usually occur right away.

Even though you've had your baby, you're not quite done and will need to deliver the placenta, which usually comes out on its own in the 30 minutes after delivery, typically after the baby has been weighed, measured, and checked for its Apgar Score (the numerical summary of the baby's health at birth). The placenta is very soft and easy to push out, compared with the baby you just birthed. After the placenta is delivered, a nurse or the doctor will massage your uterus, an important step to slow the bleeding. If your perineum tore when you were pushing, the doctor will sew it with sutures that dissolve on their own.

## WHEN IS A C-SECTION NEEDED?

There are several reasons why you might need a cesarean section. According to the American Pregnancy Association, the reasons for a C-section include:

- Placenta previa (complete or partial covering of the cervix by the placenta)
- Placental abruption (1 percent of women experience a separation of the placenta from the uterine lining, which interferes with oxygen reaching the baby)
- Prior C-section birth
- Breech position
- Uterine rupture (only 1 in 1,500 births results in tearing of the uterus, which leads to a hemorrhage)
- Fetal distress
- Cephalopelvic disproportion (the baby's head is too large for the cervix)
- Active herpes (to prevent the baby from infection during passage through the birth canal)
- Preeclampsia (severe)
- Multiple fetuses
- Failure to progress

### WHAT HAPPENS DURING A C-SECTION?

A labor is deemed a failure to progress if contractions slow or stop or if the cervix does not dilate completely. If your cervix does not dilate enough over the course of a few hours after you receive a Pitocin drip, it's possible that the baby is unable to be delivered out of your pelvis. A C-section is a life-saving surgery that is performed when labor doesn't progress because the baby can't fit through the pelvic opening; when the baby isn't tolerating labor; or when labor becomes life threatening to either you or your baby, such as in the case of severe preeclampsia. While a C-section is major surgery that requires a longer recovery than does a vaginal delivery, the good news is that athletes and fit women often experience a faster healing period than do sedentary women.

If you need a C-section, the anesthesiologist will increase the medication in your epidural so that the numbness reaches up to your chest. If you haven't had an epidural up to this point, the anesthesiologist can administer spinal anesthesia, which is similar to an IV drip and will last about two hours. In rare, emergency cases, general anesthesia is needed, such as when there is umbilical cord prolapse (i.e., the umbilical cord hangs outside the cervix and into the vagina) or there is fetal distress and no time to wait for a spinal to kick in.

A woman undergoing a C-section is usually wheeled in her bed to the operating room of the labor and delivery suite. There the doctors will ensure that your anesthesia is working, usually by pinching you hard. After they lift you onto an OR table, you'll be draped with a sterile covering and your abdomen will be prepped with betadine, a topical antiseptic.

During the surgery, an anesthesiologist will stay at your head to watch your vital signs. Your significant other can also stay by your shoulder while the baby is delivered, a process that takes about 30 minutes when uncomplicated. Just before the baby is delivered, you'll feel pushing on your abdomen by the surgeons, but it won't be painful. As soon as the baby is born, he or she will be handed off to the waiting pediatrician, who will dry and assess the baby in a spot you can see. Oftentimes your significant other will be invited to cut the cord after a C-section, too.

As soon as the doctors are sure the baby is doing well, he or she will be swaddled and given to your partner to hold next to you. You'll have to undergo about 15 more minutes of surgery to complete the process and will then be taken back to your room to recover and breast-feed your baby, if you choose.

*As an athlete, I saw natural childbirth as a challenge that I was looking forward to conquering. I trained for it throughout pregnancy, and when he finally emerged, I think I was as excited that I had accomplished my goal as I was about the arrival of my son . . . momentarily.*

CRISSY | RUNNER AND MOM OF LEXI AND ZACH

*At the time of my first child's birth, I was cavalier in my ability to manage pain, having run multiple ultramarathons and having run through all nine months of pregnancy. I wasn't antimedication and was keeping my options open. Good thing. At 1 cm dilation, I was nearly vomiting from pain and begged for the sweet relief of an epidural. With my second child, my only question was "Is it too soon to get an epidural?" At that point I was only 5 months pregnant!*

JENNIFER SUSAN | ULTRAMARATHONER AND MOM OF TWO

## HOW DO I DECIDE ON PAIN INTERVENTIONS?

There is absolutely no shame in opting for pain medications. Many women, hard-core athletes or not, opt for medical pain intervention during childbirth, for a range of reasons. Whatever your choice in the matter, pick the course that is best for *you* and don't choose one option or another because you feel you have something to prove to anyone. Remember, there's no trophy for best birther.

If you do want pain medication, there are usually two options. One is a narcotic that is administered intramuscularly as a shot. Often a type of morphine, narcotic pain relief is commonly described as a method that "takes the edge off" the pain of labor, letting you relax between contractions. This option is offered only if you aren't going to deliver in the next several hours, as narcotics cross the placenta and will depress the baby so that it doesn't cry or take nice, deep breaths at delivery. Narcotics will also not be an option if the fetal heart rate pattern isn't reassuring.

The other option for pain relief is an epidural, administered by an anesthesiologist. If you think you'll be unable to relax and cope with pain through breathing techniques or other distractions, an epidural might be the right option for you. You'll need to be hydrated intravenously before receiving an epidural because it may lower your blood pressure. An epidural is a drip of continuous medication into the fluid surrounding the nerves of your back and can cause you to lose feeling in your legs. While that can be a little unnerving (literally), the medication will relax your body and eliminate the pain of contractions. An epidural will not increase your risk of C-section.

Many women opt to first try the narcotic, waiting to go with the epidural if the pain is unbearable. Remember, you don't get a medal for unmedicated childbirth, and opting for narcotics or an epidural doesn't make you weak. Everyone feels the pain of labor differently, just as every woman's pregnancy exhibits different physical and mental symptoms. Most importantly, every birth experience that has the outcome of a healthy and happy mom and baby is the right kind.

## Gear: What Do I Pack for the Big Day?

Just as you don't want to throw together your race kit the morning of the event, you don't want to scramble to pack a hospital bag after you start labor. As mentioned in Chapter 4, it's a good idea to pack for the hospital or birth center about 4 weeks before your due date so that you're ready to go and don't find yourself searching for your aunt's swaddling blanket between contractions. When you pack, consider that you can expect to be in the hospital for two nights for a vaginal birth and three for a C-section, although that can vary based on your health insurance. Here is a list of ideas to get you started:

* Favorite pillow
* Bathrobe
* Nightgown (two) or pajamas designed for nursing
* Slippers
* Comfortable shoes
* Socks
* Comfortable changes of clothes (two to three)

* Photo ID and insurance card
* Toiletries
* iPod with soothing music and small portable speakers
* Camera
* Video camera
* Batteries/chargers for the cameras
* Reading material (especially important if you'll be induced)
* Snacks you like (don't count on a hospital cafeteria)
* Cash for parking
* Cell phone and charger
* List of the people whom you want to call with updates
* Nursing bras (or comfortable regular bras)
* Maternity underwear
* Book on infant care
* Clothes for your newborn
* Clothes for you to wear home
* Infant car seat (installed)
* Receiving blanket (two)

Remember to leave other valuables at home. Your most precious asset will be asleep in your arms, and you don't need the hassle of worrying about where you put your favorite earrings. You also don't need to bring diapers or formula, as the hospital will have plenty of both. The hospital will also have a breast pump available if you need one.

## Chapter Summary

Congratulations! You started this chapter in a body built for two and finished it with a baby in your arms. With mental strength and physical fitness, you completed one of the human race's most challenging and awe-inspiring events. The bibs don't have numbers, and the only safety pins at the finish line are used on diapers. In the process of putting your body to the test, you qualified as an elite athlete, enduring a tough and exhausting event to place first in the eyes of your biggest fan.

In Part II, you'll read about adjustment in the "fourth trimester," or the first months with your baby, the second event in this biathlon of pre- and postpregnancy. You changed your life by choosing to bear and raise a child and are a strong example of the 21st-century woman. Being a mother is the world's most difficult extreme sport, but with your fitness focus, you'll excel with this new baby and find your way onto the podium of motherhood.

## TO REVIEW ... THE DOCTOR'S NOTES

- ✳ Write a list of things to pack for the hospital as well as gear to have at home when you get back (see Chapter 6).

- ✳ Keep at least five days' worth of dinners in your freezer to have ready when you come home from the hospital so you don't have to cook.

- ✳ If you plan to opt out of pain medication during labor, take a course on pain management with the technique that appeals most to you. You might be a tough athlete, and your experience with hard races and high efforts will help, but you need a class to learn how to manage the pain of this highly unique endurance event.

- ✳ Meet other women who can be a support system after birth by taking a prenatal exercise, Lamaze, or birthing class.

- ✳ Bring comforts as well as necessities to the hospital, such as the pillow you like, music that soothes you, and soft slippers.

- ✳ Your labor experience depends on your mind as well as your body. Practice breathing techniques and visualization prior to the first contraction and think of a mantra that you can recite in your head to relax during labor.

THE

# Fourth Trimester

# 6

## From Bib Numbers to Bibs
*Your First 3 Weeks with Your Baby*

CONGRATULATIONS! You completed the best endurance event of your life and came home with a medal no one else can match. In less than a year, you achieved a goal that's more significant than any race or event you've done. It has put you on the podium as first overall female in the life of your baby—a title you won't ever have to give up. The "fourth trimester" is a time full of joy and firsts that are exciting—while also possibly making you feel like a deer in the headlights. Life in the first 3 months after birth bookends a pregnancy with an emotional cyclone that is similar to the first trimester's hormonal vortex. It's a major change for your family and for you as a woman. The trick to successfully keeping your cool with this new juggling act is to continue to apply an athlete's mind-set: Keep your wits and use your determination to define your possibilities and priorities.

This chapter covers the details of the first few weeks after the birth of your little cooing machine, focusing on the healing and recovery process and readiness for mild exercise, which will leave you prepared to resume a training program. Here you'll read information about:

* What's happening to my body?
* What can I expect from breast-feeding?

During the first few weeks after delivery, your body returns from an internal riot to postpartum calm, at which point exercise is safe. Every woman follows a different trajectory and timeline between these points. While some women will recover quickly, stop bleeding, and be ready for workouts in a few weeks, others might take months, especially if a C-section was needed.

## What's Happening to My Body?

You're full of bliss while holding your heart in your arms, but your body is feeling the effects of the tough road that got you there. Even "easy," routine births cause some physical damage that needs to heal. If you had a vaginal delivery, you can expect it to be about two weeks before the swelling in your lower extremities abates and you feel like you can sit on a hard surface comfortably. Cycling will probably be on the back burner for at least four to six weeks. Over the first six weeks postpartum, many of the changes your body went through will reverse, and most of that healing takes place within two weeks.[1] However, it took 40 weeks for your body to get to this point, so don't anticipate an immediate return to your prepregnancy body. It will take roughly six weeks for muscles to recover fully from any strains, and nerves can require four to six months to heal. Your vaginal muscles, weakened from pushing, or prolapse, will take about six months to return to their prior strength.

If you had a C-section, you may need six months to return to normal, with no pain. The incision of a C-section is the same as for a hysterectomy, and that takes time to heal. The skin over the incision will be the last part of your body to heal because the nerves have been cut by the incision. Because of that, you may be playing an easy round of tennis, jogging, or gently swimming a couple months after the birth and feel a quick tug in the pelvis, which is normal and safe.

Even when labor and delivery go smoothly, you'll probably feel flat-out tired with little chance to think about workouts very much. Your body might even look

## COMMON SIDE EFFECTS OF BIRTH

Your body's hormones go wild to help you deliver your baby and can lead to some side effects in the first few weeks that you might not have expected. Don't worry; they'll go away after your body recovers from the birth process. Here are a few of the initial changes to look out for:

- Enlarged uterus for the first two to three weeks
- Difficulty sensing when you need to urinate
- Stretched or sore vaginal muscles
- Increased thirst
- Retaining fluid and swelling
- Constipation
- Dry skin
- Chloasma (dark patches of skin on your face)
- Hot flashes
- Mood swings

and feel more foreign than when you were pregnant. Where it was once either muscular or distended, in the first several weeks the postpartum body can be described as one that doesn't quite fit itself. Your flesh is soft and might feel as if it's folded like a sweater. Don't lose faith; with the activity you maintained during pregnancy and a safe return to exercise after the birth, you'll be back to form in a few months.

## WHAT HAPPENED TO MY UTERUS?

Many women, especially athletes or women used to being fit, are surprised that the uterus doesn't spring back to its prepregnancy shape right after birth. Although it does shrink in size, you'll have a bulge, and your abdomen might appear as it did in the early weeks of the second trimester. Your watermelon belly is now more like a grapefruit. Within about six weeks, your uterus will shrink back from 2 pounds to about 12 ounces and will shift downward from your abs to your pelvis. As mentioned in Chapter 5, your provider will massage it until it's firm or administer Pitocin right after delivery in order to reduce vaginal bleeding. The nurses will later teach you to massage it, and you can do that at home if you have heavy bleeding. Don't stress about the postpartum baby bump; it will continue to shrink. Try not to fixate on your body during this recovery period, as everything about you is settling back to its prior state. Instead, try to be patient and direct your attention to your baby's healthy weight gain and your own opportunities for rest.

## WHY AM I BLEEDING?

It is normal to continue bleeding in the days after delivery. The discharge, known as lochia, is a combination of uterine lining and blood and should stop after a few weeks of changing color from red to pink to white or clear. Expect vaginal blood to stop and start during this phase of your recovery. If the bleeding soaks a pad within 15 minutes, immediately call your provider, who might limit your activity. In addition, if you find you're changing pads every 30 minutes for several hours, regardless of activity, notify your provider. He or she will want to make sure you don't have a uterine blood clot or any ripped stitches, which dissolve naturally. This level of bleeding means you should severely limit activity, discontinue exercise, and wait for at least three days past the decrease in bleeding before you increase activity again.

**TRAINING TIP** Staying hydrated is important. Carry a large, insulated water container with a straw everywhere you go. The straw makes it easier to drink when you're holding a baby because you don't have to fuss with a cap, and the ice will melt slowly over time, keeping your water cool and decreasing the number of times you have to get up to refill it.

**Use pads rather than tampons** for four to six weeks after birth. While many women find pads annoying, you don't want the tampon to rub against any lacerations in the vagina, and as a foreign body, tampons carry bacteria that can cause infection. They also may fall out because vaginal muscle strength is lower after giving birth.

Attempting to jump back into exercise in your first two weeks after the birth will likely increase your bleeding during and after the activity, and as a result, workouts so soon after delivery are usually not advised. Try not to lift anything heavier than your baby in the first two weeks after birth, and consult your doctor if you would like to try any exercise more intense than a stroll. You will see your doctor in person for a checkup after the first month postpartum, at which point he or she will likely okay both exercise and sex. However, because every woman has a unique pregnancy, birth, and postpartum experience, you should talk to your doctor about your own recovery and the kind of activity you want to do. If you'd like to exercise before the fourth week, call your provider to discuss your recovery, specifically your bleeding and the type of exercise you'd like to pursue.

If you opt to feed by bottle, you may find that your period returns soon after the lochia stops, as early as the fourth week, and your first period could be particularly heavy. Do not be concerned if there are clots or if your periods are irregular for a few months. If you breast-feed, your period might not restart until after you're done nursing, and at this point, you'll be clear to use tampons again. If you do menstruate while you're breast-feeding, note that your period can decrease your milk production temporarily. If you drink water consistently to keep yourself hydrated, your lactation should be fine. This is especially important for active women, who need to drink plenty of fluids to replenish their systems after sweating.

## HOW DO I TREAT PERINEAL SORENESS AND LACERATIONS?

The perineum is the outer edge of the vagina and can be very sore and inflamed after the birth, particularly if you had an episiotomy or tearing with delivery. It will take at least four weeks for perineal or vaginal lacerations to heal. The swelling should decrease within the first week, and any stitches will dissolve on their own. You can help the healing process along with a few steps:

* Use a peribottle to clean the perineum several times a day, following the instructions on the package.
* After a bowel movement, always wipe from front to back to avoid infecting the area with bacteria.
* Sit on an ice pack three to four times per day for 8 to 10 minutes to ease the inflammation in your perineum.
* Use a sitz bath to alternate heat and cold with the ice pack and reduce pain (see "Doctor's Note" above).
* When sitting on a hard chair, squeeze your buttocks together before sitting, and hold the position to buffer your perineum from the hard surface.
* Take a mild pain reliever if necessary, but consult your doctor about dosage and the right medication for you.

## HOW DO I ELIMINATE?

Urination or defecation in the days after the birth can feel scarier than actually delivering your baby. To make matters trickier, it's common for women to feel either uncertain of when their bodies need to go or an overall increased need to urinate, in part because they are so thirsty from breast-feeding that they'll likely be drinking more water than usual. It might be uncomfortable to urinate or have a bowel movement in the week after the birth, but severe pain could indicate a different problem, such as a bladder infection or hemorrhoids. If you experience more than discomfort and feel any pain or burning, contact your provider. Use the peribottle or sitz bath to keep your perineum clean and free of infection.

While you might feel the urge to urinate more often, it's not uncommon for women to go a few days without a bowel movement after giving birth. You probably haven't eaten much since you started the labor process, and your body might not feel the urge due to lacerations or hemorrhoid symptoms. To prevent constipation, walk as much as feels comfortable and does not increase bleeding. In addition, stay hydrated and try to eat a lot of fiber from fresh fruits and vegetables and whole grains. You can also use an over-the-counter stool softener.

## WHEN DO I SLEEP?

If you heard only one piece of advice before your baby was born, it was probably "Stock up on sleep." Although you expected to feel tired, the level of fatigue that new moms experience can be crushing. During the early weeks, it's crucial that you devote as much commitment to rest as you ever did to fitness. A lot of factors conspire to exhaust you, including the physical trauma of labor, a demanding feeding schedule, a revolving door of visitors, and your baby's inability to sleep for long stretches overnight. Your new life might not seem feasible when you're crippled by fatigue, but as with any race you weren't sure you could handle, you are tougher than your circumstances, and you will make it through this phase of sleep deprivation. Here are some tips to help you endure what can be an exasperating period of sleeplessness:

* As much as possible, sleep when your baby is sleeping. This can be a challenge, but napping or just lying down and closing your eyes can be your saving grace.

* Institute a bedtime routine for your infant on day one, even though it might seem silly in the first week. The rituals of bath, pajamas, rocking, feeding, and a lullaby at a specific time each day can settle a baby into a dependable pattern of stimulus and response to promote sleep.
* Get as much help as possible from family and your partner when it comes to household chores, food shopping, cooking, and infant care so you can sleep instead of doing the dishes at night.
* Pump milk (see "What Can I Expect from Breast-Feeding?," below) so that your partner can feed the baby and you can rest.
* Wear comfortable clothes all day, if possible, so you can grab sleep whenever it's available to you. Yoga pants and big, soft shirts are great for this phase so you can sleep without taking time to change.
* Eat foods high in protein and iron to sustain your energy as much as possible.
* Continue taking your prenatal vitamins, and ask your provider to extend your prescription for an additional 6 months.
* Resume an exercise routine by the sixth week after the birth to boost your energy.
* Consider using a bassinet next to your bed, at least for the first 6 to 8 weeks.
* Go outside to walk at least once a day, and keep your curtains open in daytime so you and your baby experience natural biorhythms for day and night.
* Don't feel as if you always have to answer your phone.
* Institute "visiting hours" so you can nap without guests showing up all day during the first week.
* If your baby sleeps for hours at night (lucky you!), don't wake him or her to feed. A baby will wake up when hungry and needing to eat.

## What Can I Expect from Breast-Feeding?

Just as your sport performance isn't all in your legs, not everything about having a baby takes place below the waist. You'll probably be giving more thought to your breasts than you have since puberty, and not just because they're the first thing you see when you look in the mirror during that initial week. In the first weeks, you'll need to feed your baby at least 10 times per day. Many women try breast-feeding to give their babies the superior (and free) nutrition that their bodies are making. According to the Centers for Disease Control, almost 80 percent of infants are breast-fed at some point, with about 50 percent nursed for the first six months. Regardless of your decision about how you'll nourish your baby (or for how long), your breasts will probably be swollen and ready to go to work on the first day.

Your milk supply will engorge your breasts in the first 24 to 72 hours after your baby is born, with the thick substance known as colostrum coming in right away. Colostrum is highly nutritious and loaded with calories because all babies are at risk of losing weight in the first week of life. A breast-fed baby will lose 7 to 10 percent of its body weight, and a bottle-fed infant will lose about 5 percent of its weight, according to the American Pregnancy Association, which also states that most babies will return to birth weight within the first 10 to 14 days of life. Colostrum helps the baby keep weight on while your milk descends.

When your milk descends, your breasts will feel heavy and tender and can become so swollen that it becomes difficult for a baby to latch on. Expressing milk into the sink or pumping and freezing your milk will make it easier for the baby to latch. While sucking is a human reflex, many babies have difficulty learning how to nurse. Don't be discouraged. Latching on can be something of an acquired skill that takes patience on your part. Try holding your baby at different angles, and invest in a nursing pillow to support the baby's weight so you can direct your nipple into his or her open mouth. There is a lot of information available on a "good" latch, but rest assured, as long as the baby is gaining weight and you aren't in pain when nursing, it's a good latch.

Once your baby has figured everything out, he or she will probably root to find your breast when in your arms, and nursing can be a wonderful way for the two of you to connect. Another benefit of breast-feeding is the ease with which

## BREAST-FEEDING BASICS

- Support your baby's head with one hand, and use your nipple to stimulate his or her bottom lip or chin so that the baby will lower his jaw to open the mouth wide. The baby's mouth should open wide enough to circle around the outer edge of your nipple.

- You can also open the baby's mouth by pressing your forefinger softly on his or her chin and gently pulling downward.

- Guide your baby's open mouth over your entire nipple by placing your hand at the back of his or her head to support the neck and direct the latch.

- To reposition the baby's mouth, insert your finger between your breast and his open mouth to release the suction.

- Let your baby empty one breast before changing to the other side, and start with the second breast for the next feeding.

- Use lanolin on dry nipples after each feeding to prevent cracking.

- Be patient. Your baby will learn how to nurse with practice. He or she might prefer a specific position, so switch up how you sit, and try lying down to help both of you get comfortable.

- Some insurance companies will cover a session with a lactation consultant, who can be invaluable if you're having trouble with nursing.

- A baby who spits up frequently is likely still receiving plenty of nutrition (think about the size of an infant's stomach), but if you note that he or she spits up after every feeding or the vomit is projectile (across the room), consult your pediatrician.

you'll drop the weight you gained during pregnancy. "Nursing off the pounds" is great, as long as you're vigilant about drinking plenty of water and eating enough protein, iron, calcium, and healthy carbs to nourish both of you. It takes a lot of energy to be Wonder Woman.

Some babies are sensitive to certain foods and can become cranky due to gassiness that comes from what you're eating. Because infants react differently, it might take some trial and error to figure out what foods your baby can't stomach. If you suspect your baby is reacting negatively to something you ate, remember that it takes 4 to 6 hours for anything you eat to find its way into your milk supply. Don't blame the pizza you ate 10 minutes before nursing if your baby starts to fuss right after you fed him or her.

Foods high in acid, such as tomatoes, sometimes trigger infant gas, as can broccoli; beans; and cow's milk, which is meant to feed calves, not humans. A baby's difficulty with the cow's milk you drink doesn't necessarily point to lactose intolerance, however—just a tiny, growing, sensitive tummy. Keep in mind that most babies don't have food sensitivities or allergies, even though we tend to want to find a food source for any inconsolable crying. Chances are, your baby's fussiness isn't linked to breast-feeding.

An infant will usually nurse every 90 minutes to 2 hours, though there are some hungry babies who look for your breast every hour. When you and your body are ready to resume exercise, it can be as much of a challenge to time nursing with your workout as it is to strap down your newly voluptuous breasts. Your baby's feeding schedule and your need to recover from the birth will likely keep you from overexertion in the first few weeks, but you can also pump milk before a longer exercise session when that time comes.

On average, women who breast-feed produce about 25 ounces of milk per day, and that can make for swollen breasts.[2] Find a nursing sports bra with adjustable straps that can handle potential engorgement while you work out. Your nipples are working overtime, so slather on some petroleum jelly to keep chafing to a minimum and just wash your nipples before feeding.[3] If you swim in either a pool or the ocean, you should also wash your nipples prior to nursing because of the chlorine and salt.

**DOCTOR'S NOTE**

While you are **breast-feeding**, you need to eat 200 to 500 calories in addition to your regular diet. Women burning calories through exercise will need to eat even more. To stay hydrated, drink when thirsty and check your urine for clarity. Women who overhydrate (more than 12 glasses per day) can actually see a decrease in milk supply, so don't go crazy.

It's important to stay mindful of preventing infected breast ducts. Mastitis, an infection of the mammary glands, is both painful and debilitating, as it causes fever; aches; and exhaustion, which is, of course, the last thing you need. Most common in the first three months after birth, mastitis often occurs when engorged breasts do not get the relief of expressing milk or when a baby dribbles milk and bacteria back into the glands. The afflicted breast usually feels very sore, lumpy, and swollen and looks red and irritated. Call your doctor if you experience any of these symptoms. You'll probably be instructed to take a mild pain reliever, such as ibuprofen or Tylenol, which are safe while nursing; your provider will prescribe a course of antibiotics if the infection is more serious. For additional pain relief, use a warm compress on your breast, but don't apply ice before nursing because it can slow lactation. You'll want to continue breast-feeding, even though it will probably be painful, because expressing milk can clear the ducts. Nursing with mastitis is safe for the baby because the germs that resulted in the infection likely originated in your baby's mouth.

## HOW DO I CHOOSE NURSING BRAS?

Nursing moms will want to invest in a sports bra that is geared to breast-feeding. When buying your bras, be sure to go up in size from your usual, prepregnancy bras because nursing has increased your bust, as you've no doubt noticed. Many women find that sports bras are far more comfortable and supportive than other nursing bras and choose to wear them exclusively.

Sometimes a regular sports bra has features that make it more comfortable and perfectly fine for breast-feeding. In any bra, look for adjustable straps, particularly the kind that use Velcro to change their length. You can quickly open a

## TIPS FOR PREVENTING MASTITIS

- Prevent your breasts from becoming engorged by pumping or expressing milk between feedings if you feel any swelling, pressure, or lumps.

- Massage any lumps.

- Avoid bras that are too tight in order to keep from smashing down the nipples.

- If you return to work while breast-feeding, pump regularly throughout the day.

- Empty your breasts entirely during feedings and when pumping to prevent engorgement.

- Nurse equally from each breast by alternating sides.

- Stay well hydrated.

- Clean your breasts thoroughly with warm water and mild soap a few times throughout the day to prevent milk from drying in the glands.

## FEATURES TO LOOK FOR IN A NURSING SPORTS BRA

Here are some features of comfortable, reliable sports bras that breast-feeding moms like:

- Mesh panels that promote moisture wicking, cooling, and breathable comfort

- Drop cups that allow for unfastening and closure with one hand

- Wide straps that adjust in length

- Cups that can hold nursing pads in place

- Wide underband for support and comfort

- Multiple back fasteners for stability

- Soft fabric that doesn't chafe

Velcro attachment to drop the fabric and nurse, then easily reattach it, all with one hand. This format tends to be more user-friendly than a cup that attaches to the strap with a hook-and-eye closure. Regardless of which bras you end up with, don't buy any with underwire, as this can affect your milk production.

Because so many athletes want to train while nursing, many sportswear companies now make nursing bras, giving you a few options to choose from. Moving Comfort, CW-X, Medela, Bella Materna, and La Leche League all now make sports bras for nursing moms. Some women wear two bras at once, and most will suggest that you feed the baby (or pump) right before exercising to reduce the swelling and discomfort, not to mention the awkwardness of two wet circles on the front of your shirt. Wicking fabric can only do so much.

Always take off your sports bra right after you finish exercising because it will be laced with bacteria from sweat that can clog and infect your ducts. But before you throw off that bra, check to make sure that no milk has dried and glued the fabric to your breasts. If the bra has dried onto your skin, just use a little water on the cup to moisten and release the skin. As much as you might love working out, it's not a good idea to be that attached to it.

## DO I NEED A BREAST PUMP?

A breast pump is pretty much your ticket to freedom if you plan to return to work and working out. A pump is also great for relief from engorged breasts, especially in the first couple of weeks after birth, when your milk descends like Niagara and your body hasn't yet figured out its supply-and-demand ratio. The trick is to not get carried away with a pumping frenzy because that will convince your body that you gave birth to quadruplets, and it will simply produce more to meet that demand.

There are many different options for breast pumps, but the fundamental choice comes down to manual versus electric. Buying an electric pump is well worth the money; the cost doesn't even come close to what you'll save by not buying formula. The Internet is full of reviews of breast pumps, and you can also seek out other moms you know for advice on the pros and cons of theirs. When comparing models, bear in mind that a pump with exceptionally powerful suction doesn't necessarily collect more milk. Your body decides what it will produce, and the most effective pumping mimics the suction of your baby.

You can pump anytime, but a good approach is to pump any remaining milk from your breast after your baby finishes a feeding. After the initial phase of engorgement, you won't be able to pump very much after a feeding because your body will be producing the right amount of milk for your baby. Your milk supply will increase by pumping, but the idea is to do it gradually. Simply put, you're going for locavore milk, not mass-produced milk from a factory farm. This is why it's a good idea to start pumping and freezing milk well before you return to work (and/or workouts) so that you've amassed a good supply next to the pints of ice cream that are equally essential to your survival. It's also wise to pump on a schedule, ideally once per day at the same time, to simulate a feeding so your body will learn to lactate in order to meet the demand. After you return to work, you can pump once for every missed feeding.

It takes practice to figure out a comfortable pumping position and to find ease with attaching a machine to your breast, which takes on an eye-widening appearance when the suction is operating. Try to find a relaxing space to sit while you pump, and do your best to be patient with the process. It can make you twiddle the thumb that isn't holding the machine, but ultimately a breast pump will set you free.

TRAINING TIP Pumping milk gives your breasts a workout. To coach your breasts through the process, try compressions on them. Massage your breast from the armpit toward the flange of the pump with one hand, gradually increasing the pressure you're applying. When you're done, firmly squeeze your breast a few times, as you do when expressing milk.

## How Do I Fuel My Recovery?

Fuel is energy, and energy is probably what you're lacking, so eating well and staying hydrated will help you endure this period of exhaustion. In particular, if you're nursing, your baby is still nourished by your body, and you need a healthy balance to support the two of you. Postpartum nutrition should follow the same guidelines you used during pregnancy: balancing nutrients, taking in adequate calories, and focusing on whole grains for carbohydrates.

You need 2 to 3 quarts of fluids every day to stay hydrated, especially if you're breast-feeding, and most of it should be water. Keep water in arm's reach while you're nursing and on every walk you take with the baby, as both will make you thirsty. You'll probably find it hard to shuffle to the kitchen with a baby latched on. As much as it might seem like a mechanism for survival, coffee might make you jittery, especially if you've gone several months without it. However, the USDA reports that it's safe for nursing moms to drink two to three cups of caffeinated coffee per day. Just remember that anything you drink, including coffee, alcohol, and sugary drinks, gets passed through your breast milk to the baby. If you're not keen on water, look for flavored waters as a substitute.

Nutritionally, women who are nursing require more calories than those who are bottle-feeding because, obviously, the baby consumes a large bulk of the nutrition you take in. The amount of your increase in calories will depend on how much milk you need to produce. On average, you need 330 extra calories per day in the first six months of breast-feeding and an average of 400 additional calories per day in the second six months. As you can see from Table 6.1, a woman who is 5'4" and 140 pounds and choosing to breast-feed exclusively needs 2,600 calories every day at 6 weeks postpartum. As Tables 6.2 and 6.3 show, a woman of the same height and weight who is using at least some formula will require 2,200 calories/day.

When it comes to vitamins and nutrients, continue to focus on calcium, iron, folic acid, protein, omega-3, and vitamin B12, which some women lack post-pregnancy (see Table 6.4). As when you were expecting, it's much better to eat your vitamins than to pop a supplement. Vitamin B12 is critical to infant health, and deficiencies can cause developmental delays, lethargy, and a failure to thrive. Full-term babies of well-nourished moms will be born with enough vitamin B12 for the first eight months of life, though infants of vegetarians or women with a nutritional imbalance may have inadequate stores.

If you're a nursing mom, your omega-3 stores will decrease by breast-feeding, and because these essential fatty acids are key to a baby's neural development, it's important to keep them replenished with the foods you eat. Insufficient omega-3s may also be tied to women's depression, so this is a critical area of your balanced diet. It isn't hard to get enough omega-3s in your diet if you eat salmon, or you can supplement with fish oil or flaxseed oil if you don't eat seafood. Because mercury content transfers in breast milk, some fish and shellfish can harm a breast-fed infant's nervous system, just as when your baby was in utero. Limit your fish consumption to 12 ounces per week. As noted earlier, shrimp, catfish, and salmon are fine to eat in this quantity, but avoid shark, swordfish, and king mackerel altogether (their mercury content is too high). Albacore (white) tuna also has more mercury than canned light tuna, so limit that to 6 ounces per week.

Calcium is essential to prevention of training injuries, such as stress fractures and muscle tears, not to mention your own overall strength. The babies of women who nurse leach calcium from their moms' milk supply, and your bone health depends on replenishing those losses. As you probably know, dairy

## IS ALCOHOL OKAY WHEN I'M BREAST-FEEDING?

You can drink limited alcohol if you're breast-feeding by taking a few precautions. Don't drink alcohol before you've established a set feeding pattern for your baby and can predict when you'll need to nurse him or her, at about three months. Either wait at least four hours after one drink before nursing or pump a bottle of milk before you have any alcohol so you can feed the baby with it later.

**TABLE 6.1** Nutritional Guidelines for New Mothers
(Breast-Feeding, No Formula)

*These USDA recommendations are for a 28-year-old woman who is 6 weeks postpartum. She has a moderate exercise plan of 30 to 60 minutes per day. These guidelines are based on postpartum weight and are meant to be general guidelines. You can use the Choose My Plate feature on the USDA web site (www.choosemyplate.gov) to customize your plan to your weight and height. Please consult your provider for nutritional guidelines that are specific to your exercise volume, dietary needs, and target for weight.*

| CURRENT WEIGHT | 5'4", 115 LBS. | 5'4", 140 LBS. | 5'9", 135 LBS. | 5'9", 170 LBS. |
|---|---|---|---|---|
| CALORIES/DAY | 2,400 | 2,600 | 2,600 | 2,600 |
| Vegetables | 3 cups | 3 cups | 3 cups | 3 cups |
| Fruits | 2 cups | 2 cups | 2 cups | 2 cups |
| Grains | 8 oz. | 9 oz. | 9 oz. | 9 oz. |
| Dairy | 3 cups | 3 cups | 3 cups | 3 cups |
| Protein | 6½ oz. | 6½ oz. | 6½ oz. | 6½ oz. |
| Oils | 7 tsp. | 8 tsp. | 8 tsp. | 8 tsp. |

Source: USDA Daily Food Plan for breast-feeding mothers, 2012.

products are great sources of calcium, and meat is the primary source of the vitamin B12 that is so important to postpartum nutrition. Calcium intake is easy to accomplish if you're not vegetarian, vegan, or lactose intolerant but can be difficult for anyone who doesn't eat dairy products.

Remember that calcium prevents the absorption of iron, so if you're maintaining your bone health, your iron levels could be compromised by calcium-rich foods. Try to wait about two hours after taking calcium before eating foods with iron. Many women need to increase iron after having a baby because during childbirth, your body produces too few red blood cells to give you enough oxygen. Anemia can make you feel very low in energy, which is the last thing you need during your baby's first weeks and months. Some women find out they're anemic after having undiagnosed anemia during pregnancy, and others develop the deficiency from blood loss during birth. Many believe that delivering multiple babies can also lead to anemia.

Typically, you can treat anemia by eating foods that are high in iron, although severe blood loss during delivery may have led your doctor to order a

**TABLE 6.2** Nutritional Guidelines for New Mothers
(Mostly Breast-Feeding, Some Formula)

*These USDA recommendations are for a 28-year-old woman who is 6 weeks postpartum. She maintains a moderate exercise plan of 30 to 60 minutes per day. These guidelines are based on postpartum weight and are meant to be general guidelines. You can use the Choose My Plate feature on the USDA web site (www.choosemyplate.gov) to customize your plan to your weight and height. Please consult your provider for nutritional guidelines that are specific to your exercise volume, dietary needs, and target for weight.*

| CURRENT WEIGHT | 5'4", 115 LBS. | 5'4", 140 LBS. | 5'9", 135 LBS. | 5'9", 170 LBS. |
|---|---|---|---|---|
| CALORIES/DAY | 2,400 | 2,200 | 2,400 | 2,400 |
| Vegetables | 3 cups | 3 cups | 3 cups | 3 cups |
| Fruits | 2 cups | 2 cups | 2 cups | 2 cups |
| Grains | 7 oz. | 7 oz. | 8 oz. | 8 oz. |
| Dairy | 3 cups | 3 cups | 3 cups | 3 cups |
| Protein | 6 oz. | 6 oz. | 6½ oz. | 6½ oz. |
| Oils | 6 tsp. | 6 tsp. | 7 tsp. | 7 tsp. |

Source: USDA Daily Food Plan for mothers who are breast-feeding and using formula, 2012.

blood transfusion. This only happens in about 6 of every 1,000 pregnancies, though. When you take iron supplements, remember that taking vitamin C at the same time will help your body absorb the iron. Broccoli, citrus fruit, and potatoes are great sources of vitamin C, and iron can also be found in spinach and meats. And don't forget to fill your fruit bowl. Oranges are great sources of C, they're beautiful on your kitchen table, and babies love to see them roll across the counter. Everybody wins!

More generally, simply focus on balancing your food groups and eating vegetables in many different colors. It is possible to achieve healthy balance in your nutrition even when you're giving most of your attention to your new baby. For instance, when it comes to breakfast, raw fruits and vegetables are easier to prepare and yield a higher vitamin content because the value hasn't been removed by heat. Yogurt, cottage cheese, steel-cut oats, and low-fat granola also provide various high-quality nutritional must-haves: calcium, healthy fats, and protein among them. When combined with raw fruit, you get a fast and furious source of long-lasting energy.

**TABLE 6.3** Nutritional Guidelines for New Mothers (Mostly Formula)

*These USDA recommendations are for a 28-year-old woman who is 6 weeks postpartum. She maintains a moderate exercise plan of 30 to 60 minutes per day. These guidelines are based on postpartum weight and are meant to be general guidelines. You can use the Choose My Plate feature on the USDA web site (www.choosemyplate.gov) to customize your plan to your weight and height. Please consult your provider for nutritional guidelines that are specific to your exercise volume, dietary needs, and target for weight.*

| CURRENT WEIGHT | 5'4", 115 LBS. | 5'4", 140 LBS. | 5'9", 135 LBS. | 5'9", 170 LBS. |
|---|---|---|---|---|
| CALORIES/DAY | 2,000 | 2,200 | 2,200 | 2,400 |
| Vegetables | 2 cups | 3 cups | 3 cups | 3 cups |
| Fruits | 2½ cups | 2 cups | 2 cups | 2 cups |
| Grains | 6 oz. | 7 oz. | 7 oz. | 8 oz. |
| Dairy | 3 cups | 3 cups | 3 cups | 3 cups |
| Protein | 5½ oz. | 6 oz. | 6 oz. | 6½ oz. |
| Oils | 6 tsp. | 6 tsp. | 7 tsp. | 7 tsp. |

Source: USDA Daily Food Plan for moms using mostly formula, 2012.

---

{ **TIMESAVER TIP** }

For lunch and dinner, use a slow cooker to prepare a meal well in advance of your baby's witching hour. A slow cooker also provides leftovers, which make cooking the next day a whole lot simpler. Add some whole-grain bread and a quick salad, and you're good to go.

---

It's easy to get distracted by a baby who needs cuddling, cooing, or nursing during dinner, but don't forget to eat. Learning to eat while nursing is a skill that comes in handy during those first six months of infancy. You can also wear a sling to hold the baby while you make meals and eat, but of course not in front of a hot stove. There are many healthy and high-calorie foods that are convenient to eat but don't contain empty calories or a lot of sugar, such as avocados, nuts, nut and seed butters, bean dips, hummus, trail mix, and soy products.

While you might not be incorporating training back into your life during the first month after having your baby, any amount of physical fitness means you need to refuel your body more than if you're sedentary. On the flip side, if you're

**TABLE 6.4** Core Vitamin Needs for Postpartum Women

| VITAMIN | DAILY RECOMMENDED INTAKE | SOURCES |
|---------|--------------------------|---------|
| B12 | *2.8 mcg (breast-feeding)*<br>*2.4 mcg (formula)* | *Meat, yeast, supplements* |
| Iron | *10 mg* | *Squash, chard, shellfish, tuna, meat and poultry, sweet potatoes, tofu* |
| Calcium | *1,000–1,300 mg* | *Yogurt, milk, cheese, spinach, broccoli, fortified cereal* |
| Folic acid | *500 mcg* | *Leafy vegetables, citrus fruit, beans, whole grains* |
| Protein | *71 g* | *Meat and poultry, fish, nut butter* |
| Omega-3 fatty acids | *300 mg* | *Salmon, fish oil, flaxseed oil, eggs* |

Source: www.perinatology.com/ Reference/RDAlactation.htm

used to being in training and going for long workouts and find yourself needing extra time to rest after delivery, you might not need the calorie intake that you had during peak fitness periods before you were pregnant. Eat when you're hungry, not just tired, bored, or antsy. Don't deny yourself food, but pay attention to what your body needs when your mind craves a block of cheese because you haven't had adult conversation in eight hours.

## How Do I Keep a Fit Mind?

Becoming a mother is a wonderful and exciting aspect of your life, but it often causes women to feel alienated from the identities they had before. The Fit Self you cultivated and knew as yourself can get a little lost in your softer body and the attention you devote to caring for an infant. Pretty much overnight, a woman must compromise an independent, free sense of self in order to care for a baby 24/7, and it's common to feel elated one moment and panicked the next. Take a deep breath and remind yourself that your Fit Self isn't AWOL. She isn't even on sabbatical.

## NUTRITION FOR BREAST-FEEDING VEGETARIANS

It's fine to keep a vegetarian diet while you're breast-feeding. Like omnivores, you will need to attend to a healthy balance between grains, proteins, vegetables, fruit, and fats, deriving nondairy calcium from figs, calcium-enriched tofu, soy milk, calcium-enriched juices, canned salmon with bones, white beans, kale, and collard greens. To achieve a healthy vegetarian balance of nutrition while nursing, the American Dietetic Association recommends the following distribution.

| FOOD GROUP | SERVINGS PER DAY |
|---|---|
| Vegetables | 3 cups |
| Fruits | 2 cups |
| Grains | 6–8 oz. |
| Calcium | 1,000 mg |
| Protein | 5–6½ oz. |
| Healthy fats | 6 tsp. |

It isn't hard to obtain the calcium you'd get from dairy products from other sources. For instance, 1 cup of bok choy will give you almost as much calcium as a cup of milk, and ½ cup of ground sesame seeds will yield the same amount of calcium as 2 cups of milk. Vegetarian moms who are nursing sometimes show low levels of vitamin D, too, when they don't drink milk, but the best way to boost your vitamin D is from natural sunlight, as opposed to supplements.

Because you don't eat animal proteins, you will probably need to increase your intake of vitamin B12, which can be found in supplements or by adding yeast to your diet.[4] You can also find B12 in fortified cereals and some soy milks.

She's in a recovery cycle. It's more than possible to achieve great goals in life, sport, and fitness after you have children. Just look at Dara Torres, who medaled in the Beijing Olympics at 42 years old after the birth of her baby. It's easy to absorb the negativity that Torres describes below and make it your own perspective, and it's easy to operate from your own apprehension about what's possible. But in truth, that apprehension and fear are the only limits to your potential.

## TENDING TO YOUR FIT SELF: BABY BLUES AND POSTPARTUM DEPRESSION

At some point, many new moms will pull up to a stoplight with Elmo singing through the speakers and a baby crying in the backseat and wonder, "Who *am* I?" For many women, the initiative and pursuit of sport and fitness help to counteract conflicted, confusing, and even sad feelings about a major change in who you are.

Postpartum depression (PPD) affects about 15 percent of women after the birth of a child, but its milder relative, known as the "baby blues," is experienced by 80 percent of new mothers.[6] Marked by emotional lows, exhaustion, anxiety, and decreased energy and motivation, PPD is known to lead women to feelings of shame for wanting to run away from it all, and breast-feeding can exacerbate these feelings, as it can be stressful and exhausting for a lot of women. These feelings usually begin in the first few days after the birth and disperse after 10 days, though you should seek help if you're still depressed, anxious, and weepy after two weeks.

Molly found running ameliorated the shake-up she felt after becoming a mom. When Molly's son was born, her sense of herself was fractured by new motherhood. She tried to get back to running a few days after his birth but didn't really resume it for a couple more weeks. Running was the familiar, core part of herself that she could use to bridge the gap between her former and new lives.

As Molly started exercising again, she found parts of herself that she recognized. Once she'd recovered from the birth, Molly focused on her fitness as much as she was able to during her baby's first year, finding a way to meld her new identity as a mom with the athlete she'd always been. Molly credits running for saving her from postpartum depression because it helped her stay connected with friends and with a part of her life that made her feel strong.

The postpartum blues, which can give way to depression, are maybe best described as a stress fracture of a new mom's self, and it's a feeling that's completely normal. Don't be embarrassed by it, and don't feel guilty. If you feel this way, know that sadness and crying are common after you have a baby, and you can get help to feel better.

## HOW DO I DEAL WITH POSTPARTUM LOWS?

Studies show that women who exercise in the third trimester have lower rates of postpartum depression.[7] This may occur because pregnant women with lower levels of endorphins at 36 weeks show more symptoms of the blues and depression after birth.[8] What's more, the opiates your brain generates from exercise during pregnancy can help you cope with the emotional whirlwind of those early months spent adjusting to motherhood. Not only is it important for you to stay consistently active throughout your pregnancy for the sake of your physical health, but your postpartum mental health will benefit, too.

Given that aerobic exercise triggers the release of endorphins, resuming regular exercise activity is an important tool for helping you to fight the mental lows that can accompany new motherhood. When your body has recovered from childbirth, exercise is known to be one of the best therapies for overcoming depression.

While many women experience the most severe lows in the days and weeks before they can resume cardio exercise, you can address anxiety and depression with even mild activity, particularly in fresh air. After your weeks of recovery, it can still be a challenge to *work in* a workout during your baby's first year. Remind yourself that exercise will restore you in a way that definitely outweighs your fatigue. After finishing a workout, most moms say they feel more energetic and less frazzled than when they left. For a lot of postpartum women, exercise links a familiar no-nonsense, independent self to a new-mom-self.

At the same time that you need to honor your body's recovery from childbirth with rest, find time to go for an easy daily walk after your first few days at home (following a vaginal delivery) so that you can return to a routine of activity. A daily session of gentle stretching after the first few days home (see "Postpartum Stretching and Flexibility," page 221) is also a good way to introduce a ritual of mind-saving, stress-busting activity. Before, during, and after, it can make you feel more present, active, and self-possessed. "I appreciate my body more after having my son and I am more awed by what I have been able to accomplish, running-wise, since his birth than I was of any of my prebaby accomplishments," says one mom.

## How Do I Safely Get Back to Training?

Between the baby, placenta, blood volume, and other fluids, a woman can expect to lose 15 pounds of "baby weight" on the day of delivery. It is an endurance event, after all. While you might be chomping at the bit to return to exercise and lose the weight quickly, remember that you've just completed a 40-week phase of weight gain and stress on your body, and don't ignore the bleeding that typically continues for a few weeks after delivery. Exercise can worsen bleeding, so if your activity causes the flow to return or increase, take a few more days before resuming it. If you're breast-feeding, also keep in mind that a woman who is lactating usually stores about 3 pounds of additional breast tissue. You need to hold on to enough calories to feed your baby, so no fit mother should exercise to drop pounds in the first 6 weeks because her body needs to produce milk. In simple

**DOCTOR'S NOTE**

**Prepregnancy exercise routines** can be resumed gradually postpartum based on an individual woman's physical capability. The competitive athlete with an uncomplicated pregnancy may resume training soon after delivery.

RAUL ARTAL, M.D.[9]

terms, exercise in the first 4 to 6 weeks after birth should center on achieving feelings of wellness, not weight loss.

Even if you're bottle-feeding, give yourself a couple of months to recover and adjust to your new routine and lifestyle before thinking about weight loss. Relax the pressure on yourself to shed weight too fast, for your sake and your baby's. With an active lifestyle and some goal-setting, you'll get back to prepregnancy weight in about 4 to 6 months. A study of endurance athletes after pregnancy found that most women who start running 5 weeks after delivery get back

## PREVENTING POSTPARTUM SADNESS AND STRESS

In addition to a daily walk, here are 20 suggestions to help prevent and treat postpartum sadness and stress. Find what works for you, and take solace in knowing thousands of women have been through a period of darkness after childbirth.

1. Ask others for help with babysitting to give you some needed time and space to yourself.

2. Rely on your spouse for help with practical details such as cooking, cleaning, running errands, and feeding the baby.

3. Resting is an essential part of your recovery. Lie down whenever you can in the first two weeks.

4. Use the mindfulness meditations in Chapter 2 to manage your stress, even if it's only in 5-minute increments a few times per day.

5. Use a daily shower to take 20 uninterrupted deep breaths and refresh your mind.

6. Take photos of anything interesting or beautiful on a daily walk to keep you connected with the world around you.

7. Go outside every day.

8. Search for a guided daily meditation on iTunes or YouTube.

9. Find a support group of new mothers through your doctor or midwife.

10. Try art therapy with paint or clay to express your range of emotion.

to prepregnancy weight within 5 months.[10] In the first few 2 to 3 months, exercise should focus on fitness that allows you to feel good, with sweat.

When it comes to exercise for wellness, realize that working out in the weeks after delivery can compromise your health, your recovery, and your ability to actually exercise at all if you end up exhausted or hurt. Maintaining a consistent level of fitness and activity during pregnancy will help your labor and delivery to progress more smoothly and expedite your return to working out after the birth, but the effects of delivery on your body still demand rest. It might feel like

11. Do 8 sun salutations each day, in class at a yoga studio or using a DVD, book, or web site at home.

12. Write a paragraph about the blessings in your life.

13. Find a daily ritual that you look forward to, such as your morning cup of tea or your regular walk with the stroller.

14. Connect online with someone who is also experiencing postpartum lows through www.ppdsupportpage.com.

15. Grab the calendar and mark five events in which you want to participate over the next five months, such as a race, dinner with friends, a continuing-ed class, or a charity event.

16. Listen to music or talk radio during the day when you're alone with the baby.

17. Find a quotation that gives you strength, and stencil it on your wall or write it on paper to frame.

18. If possible, hire a babysitter for a few hours every day so you can nap, exercise, or meet friends.

19. If you experience a panic attack when alone with the baby, get help immediately by calling a friend, your partner, or 911.

20. Find a therapist through your doctor, pediatrician, family member, or trusted friend.

a slow road back to form, but it's more than possible with some faith and patience. The key elements to a safe and speedy return to training are:

* Exercise as consistently as possible throughout pregnancy.
* Rest as much as possible in the weeks after delivery, resisting the temptation to do too much too soon.
* Start slowly and conservatively, with strolling walks every day after the first several days at home.

Your movement for the first 7 to 10 days can be painful and slow. Balance might be difficult, and you may feel dizzy if you stand for too long. Be careful in the shower, and give yourself extra time so you don't have to rush and risk slipping. With your mind in a bit of a fog, too, everything can seem surreal, and you might feel the furthest from an athlete you've ever felt. In the first few days after birth, sit or recline as much as possible; it will help you return to a familiar level of activity sooner.

Typically, a woman who had a vaginal birth will stay two nights in the hospital after she delivers and leave on her third day. (A woman who delivered by C-section can expect to stay three nights.) After you return home, don't draft a training plan to start right away. Don't even grab the vacuum or start unpacking in the first few days. Resting can be hard for women who are used to being active and getting things done themselves. Keep in mind that the postpartum experience isn't altogether different from taking on a tough race: It's rough on your body, which takes some time to recover fully. In short, it's unwise to try to get to your previous level of activity or exertion before your body is ready. Your life-changing event was a major shake-up for your body—inside and out—and

**DOCTOR'S NOTE**

Do not exercise until **bleeding** has stopped. If you do too much activity before the fourth week, you may experience very heavy flow or even hemorrhaging. You can safely return to moderate exercise (see Chapter 2 for the definition of "moderate") at 4 to 6 weeks, as long as you're no longer bleeding. See guidelines in Chapter 7.

although birth is the most common human process, it's also a major physical event. As Chapter 7 covers in more detail, your body will be ready to exercise more than your daily stroll and stretch (see "Postpartum Stretching and Flexibility" for stretches) when your bleeding stops. Until then, rest as much as possible, taking the time to establish a feeding and sleeping routine with your new baby. Increasing your exertion while you're still bleeding can lead to infection of the lacerations and hemorrhage.

If you had a routine vaginal birth, it's okay to **go outside for a slow 20- to 30-minute walk** every day in the first 4 weeks, as long as the walk doesn't increase bleeding or exhaust you.

Consult your doctor if you have high blood pressure, preeclampsia, or other circumstances that make you unsure of activity in the first week postpartum. Women with C-section births will need to take much longer (at least 6 weeks) to recover before pursuing even gentle activity (see Chapter 7).

## Postpartum Stretching and Flexibility

This series of stretches will relax you and help your body with some gentle lengthening while you rest through your recovery. One set of 30 to 45 seconds per stretch done a couple times a day is a great release for tired new moms. If you experience pain or your bleeding increases, call your doctor before doing these stretches again. Women who had C-sections should wait a few weeks before trying this sequence.

**OUTER HIP STRETCH**

1–3 sets of 40–45 sec.

*Repeat on both sides, trying to keep the shoulder of your extended arm as flat on the ground as possible.*

## HAMSTRING AND LUMBAR STRETCH

1–3 sets of 30–45 sec.

*This can be done with a resistance band to help you if you can't reach your ankles. Don't force the stretch, and keep it gentle.*

## QUAD AND HIP FLEXOR STRETCH

1–3 sets of 30–45 sec.

*If the ground hurts your knees, try placing a pillow underneath you for cushioning. Repeat this stretch on both sides, and again, don't force the stretch. Your upper knee shouldn't extend past your toes.*

## GLUTE AND HAMSTRING STRETCH

1–3 sets of 30–45 sec.

*Don't pull your leg into your chest; the stretch you get from wrapping your arms around your leg is plenty. Repeat on both sides.*

## Gear: Bringing Home Baby

When you bring your baby home, you want to be sure you have what you need in arm's reach. The last thing you want to do is stop by Target for diapers with your infant on the way home from the hospital. It's also a good idea to stock your freezer with meals you prepared before the trip to the hospital so you won't have to cook for about a week. Here is a list of essentials for your first week. A more detailed explanation of some items is found in Chapter 7.

* Nursing pads (disposable or washable)
* Nursing bras (4 to 6)
* Baby monitor
* Bathtub for infants
* Breast pump
* Bottles with newborn nipples (10, if feeding exclusively with formula)
* Brush for washing bottles
* Nursing pillow
* Bibs (4)
* Bulb syringe for sucking mucus from an infant's nose
* Burp cloths (6 to 8)
* Layette (clothes for baby)
* Socks for baby
* Infant skull caps
* Footed baby pajamas
* Diapers (12 per day for the first few weeks)
* Diaper cream
* Diaper pail
* Diaper bag
* Hairbrush with very soft bristles for babies with hair
* Hemorrhoid cream
* Ice packs to sit on
* Wipes for baby
* Maxi-pads and liners for your bleeding
* Nail clippers for an infant

* Nipple cream
* Freezable breast pads to soothe and cool engorged breasts
* Formula, if using (talk to your new pediatrician about formula choices)
* Nightlight
* Pacifiers (4 to 6)
* Shampoo for babies
* Sitz bath
* Sling or front pack that can support an infant head
* Stroller that can recline flat for a newborn (see Chapter 7 for details on baby joggers)
* Swaddling blankets (6 to 8)
* Mechanical swing or bouncing seat for an infant
* Towel for bathing an infant (hooded towels are great for warmth)

## Postpartum Clothes

It's fun and exciting to prepare a layette for your baby, but a new mom needs some new threads, too. For the first few weeks, you can wear stretchy maternity clothes, but there will soon be a time when you'll want to burn them and dress like a hot mama. You can easily find yourself living in your husband's button-down shirts for six weeks because you can't find the time or energy to shop for your own clothes, so buying a few new items in the third trimester might help postpartum morale and the desire to be seen in public when you're feeling too tired to leave the house. Here are some flattering basics to have ready before the baby comes because it can be hard to shop (even online) with a newborn.

* Yoga pants with a lower rise and a wide waistband
* Empire-waist tops
* Nursing tops
* Large scarves that you can use for modesty when nursing, if desired
* A-line or empire-waist dresses in a wrinkle-free fabric

* Button-down shirts in soft cotton with female tailoring
* Cardigans
* Pajamas designed to make nursing easy

## Chapter Summary

You just completed one impressive endurance event, which launched you into another test of stamina more or less overnight. Like transitions in a triathlon, the recovery from birth can be disorienting because you're simultaneously finishing one challenging phase (labor and delivery), looking for your groove as a new mother, and perhaps wondering when you'll get back into the groove of your former lifestyle, as a woman and an athlete. The key is to listen to the needs of your own mind and body and to rest both as much as possible while you adjust to this big change in your family and your identity.

It's normal and okay to feel anxious, sad, and weepy. Talking to other women will help with your transition. If you feel depressed, don't feel guilty or ashamed to seek help from a therapist. The laundry can wait, and the house really does look fine. While your body and mind are in this recovery and adjustment period, your primary need is to recharge both. When you're ready, you'll set new goals; achieve new personal records; and, of course, conquer the world.

✱ A sitz bath can help your perineum heal from the birth by keeping lacerations clean and soothed.

✱ When your body is ready to resume exercise, it will have stopped bleeding during your daily walks, which can take 2 to 4 weeks after a vaginal delivery and 6 to 8 weeks after a C-section.

✱ Stay well hydrated; carry water with you everywhere, particularly if you're nursing.

✱ Focus on getting enough nutrition to support a growing baby and your own energy needs. On average, you need 330 extra calories per day in the first 6 months if you're breast-feeding.

✱ Avoid mastitis by pumping or expressing milk between feedings if you feel any swelling or lumps, as well as washing your nipples with warm water and mild soap.

✱ If you feel anxious, depressed, or isolated in the weeks after childbirth, don't think you have to face these feelings alone. Contact your doctor or pediatrician or talk to your friends, any of whom might be able to help you find a therapist.

# 7

## Mamas on the Move
### *Getting Back on Your Feet*

A RETURN TO TRAINING can be as daunting as it is exciting, even after your body has fully recovered from having given birth and you've adjusted to your new daily routine. A baby swells your heart as much as your ankles at 40 weeks, and "love" can't begin to describe the awe you feel for this person you've brought into the world. But there comes a day when you might want to run—or bike or swim—away from home to rediscover the feeling of being a woman with a mind and body of her own. Chapter 6 helped you transition from pregnancy to the fourth trimester of life with an infant. This chapter will help you move forward in your life as a fit athlete mom.

In this chapter, you'll learn:

* What's happening to my body?
* What can I expect from postpartum fitness?
* How to manage breast-feeding and training
* Sport-specific workouts that give you flexibility
* How to plan a return to racing
* How to choose the right gear: a treadmill, jogging stroller, or bike trainer

Knowing what your body needs and setting expectations that your postpartum body can put into action will help you succeed as you build training intensity. Pregnancy and childbirth are normal, wonderful parts of life, but they're also traumas to your body, and as any athlete knows, you don't overcome injury by taxing your body. This chapter helps you get back to training with that in mind. It covers the physical aspects of rebuilding stamina and strength, and it gives you concrete advice for digging into goal-focused training.

## What's Happening to My Body?

Your body slowly returns to its prepregnancy equilibrium during the first 4 to 6 weeks after adding a new baby to your family, but a few lingering changes are common. Many women feel a loss of strength in their pelvic floor, resulting in incontinence or difficulty with sex, but there are simple treatments for these issues. While the differences in your body can be unsettling, remember that this is a period of transition, and many of the changes will revert when your hormones rebalance.

### INCONTINENCE AND YOUR PELVIC FLOOR

Many women find "leaking" during workouts to be an unwelcome by-product of having had a baby. The cause of urinary incontinence (UI) after vaginal birth is primarily the weakened muscles in the wall of the bladder. Babies in utero rest their weight on the bladder and pelvic floor, which can weaken those muscles during pregnancy and labor. The process of vaginal birth further weakens the nerves that control the bladder. While bladder control should return after you

**DOCTOR'S NOTE**

To reduce the **incidence of UI**, lower your consumption of diuretics, such as alcohol, tea, coffee, and carbonated drinks—with or without caffeine. If diet and bladder training don't work for you, talk to your doctor about medication, nerve stimulation, or surgical options.

## EXERCISES FOR THE PELVIC FLOOR

There are surgical treatments and prescribed medication that can help with severe cases of UI, but you can also strengthen your pelvic floor with Kegel exercises, found in Chapter 4 and reviewed here. After you have your baby, you have more options for strengthening the pelvic floor to alleviate vaginal pain and to treat incontinence and prolapse. You can do any of these exercises once the postpartum bleeding has stopped. In addition to these exercises, it is possible to "retrain" your bladder by going to the bathroom on a schedule every day, before you have the urge, and slowly increasing the time between bathroom visits. If you have not returned to your prepregnancy weight by the end of your baby's first year and experience UI, you may find that healthy weight loss can restore your bladder control.

### FOR INCONTINENCE

*1 set 3x/day*

*Kegels: Pull your vaginal and rectal muscles up and in at the same time to contract so that you're squeezing and lifting simultaneously. These are performed as you exhale (not when you breathe in). Resist tightening your ab, glute, or leg muscles as much as possible. One set is 8 reps lasting 5 seconds each.*

### FOR VAGINAL PAIN OR PAIN FROM SITTING

*8–10 reps*

*Lie on your back with your knees bent and feet flat on the floor. Imagine a compass on your abdomen: Your belly button is north, your pubic bone is south, and your hip bones are east and west. Pull your belly button toward your spine so that your pubic bone tips up, then tip your pelvis west, rotating around so that you then tip east. Return to the original position, then reverse directions.*

### FOR UTERINE PROLAPSE

*2 sets of 10–12 reps*

*Sit on the floor with your knees bent and a ball between your thighs. Squeeze your thighs together, contracting the vaginal muscles as if you're trying to stop the flow of urine. Hold each contraction for 10 seconds.*

heal from birth, many women continue to experience difficulty and more frequent trips to the bathroom. Workouts, particularly running or other high-impact exercise, can also prompt UI, which is frustrating for the many women waiting in long bathroom lines at races.

## SEXUAL HEALTH

After having a baby, you should wait to have sex until your body stops bleeding and heals from any lacerations, which will usually be 4 to 6 weeks after delivery. Regardless of this time frame, you need to listen to your body and let your own needs dictate your timeline for sexual activity. It's very common to feel too tired and depleted for sex, so honor your body and mind when it comes to your desire. Your vagina may also feel dry or tender as a result of hormonal changes, and sometimes your sensations of pleasure can be compromised because childbirth stretched you and reduced the muscle strength of your pelvic floor. This situation is usually temporary, and performing the pelvic-floor exercises described earlier in this chapter can make a positive difference.

A common myth holds that women can't get pregnant while breast-feeding, but this isn't true. You need a dependable method of birth control whether you're nursing or not. If you resume sexual activity 6 weeks after delivery, you're fine to take birth-control pills with estrogen and progestin (known as "combined birth control" pills), though this combination does increase your risk of blood clots if taken in the first month or so after birth. If you're sexually active before this time, you're advised to take progestin-only birth control or to use an intrauterine device, condom, or spermicide.

If your body and mind aren't interested in sex during your baby's first months, take heart in knowing that you aren't the first or only woman to feel this way. It can be hard to feel sexy when your days are soaked in spit-up and you don't have time to brush your hair. Be reasonable with your expectations for yourself; respect your need to rest; and engage in some physical fitness every day, which will boost your self-confidence and sense of well-being. Don't worry that your partner might be turned off by your softer body; speak up with any concerns, and no doubt you'll be reassured that you're desired. Here are some other tips for resuming a rewarding sex life after your body has healed.

* Try different positions to determine what feels most pleasurable to you.
* Use lubrication if your body doesn't feel moist or you experience discomfort as a result of dry friction.
* Start slowly with massage to reduce the pressure to have sex.
* Do your Kegel exercises every day to increase pelvic-floor strength, which will improve your sense of pleasure.
* Tell your partner what hurts and what feels great so the experience is enjoyable.

## HAIR AND SKIN

Changes in your hair and skin are common after childbirth. Many women lose clumps of hair, which occurs because pregnancy hormones prevented shedding while you were expecting. Once those hormones decrease, you start to lose the lush hair you had when you were pregnant. This will usually occur within a few months after childbirth, and it doesn't last beyond the first year. Women who nurse may lose their hair at a slower rate than those who bottle-feed, but either way, you won't lose enough hair to be noticeable to anyone else. You won't go bald; your body is just resetting the estrogen balance from the thick hair you cultivated and didn't shed during pregnancy.

To keep your hair as strong and healthy as possible, try the following:

* Don't shampoo every day, and use a leave-in conditioner.
* Continue taking prenatal vitamins during your baby's first year.
* Allow your hair to air dry, if possible, as blow dryers and straighteners can dry it out.
* When you work out, pull your hair back with a soft band or tie that has no metal on it to prevent breakage.
* Wear a hat during outdoor activities to shield your hair and skin from the sun.
* Swimmers should wear a cap to protect hair from chlorine damage.

Women also often experience dry or particularly sensitive skin after childbirth, again as a result of hormonal changes. The glow you had while pregnant often gives way to splotchy skin from a surplus of melanin as well as unexpected acne from the shift in hormones. Don't worry, though. Dry or splotchy skin and postpartum acne won't last, and taking care of your skin with sunblock, washing your face regularly, drinking plenty of water, and exercising will improve the quality of your skin. Some women who take a birth-control pill with estrogen (e.g., the combined pill, the ring, or the patch) may experience more splotchiness in their skin. If this is the case for you, ask your doctor about birth control without estrogen (e.g., the minipill, which contains only progestin).

Stretch marks affect at least 50 percent of women who give birth, so if you have them, you aren't alone. While there is limited hard evidence that lotions and potions will expedite the disappearance of stretch marks, you can reduce their appearance with cardio and strength building exercise that tones and tightens your legs and core. The plank poses presented on page 91 are excellent for

**DOCTOR'S NOTE**

**That stripe you may have developed down your abdomen** during pregnancy, known as the *linea nigra*, isn't permanent and disappears within a few months after childbirth.

core strength that tones your oblique (side) and rectus abdominus (center) core muscles. Combine basic and side planks with leg lifts for a series of ab and leg strength building exercises. Perform 10 to 15 leg lifts per side while holding a straight-spine plank, repeating for 1 to 3 sets. While you may not be able to get rid of all of your stretch marks or cellulite, building strength and cardio fitness builds confidence and will help you care less about superficial skin variations.

## BACK AND AB PAIN

There are many reasons why new moms continue to feel back and abdominal pain after the baby is born and the rest of the body has healed. For one thing, when pregnancy relaxed your ligaments, it affected the ligaments in your back, too, causing them to loosen. Your core muscles also put stress on your back when your posture adjusted to accommodate shifting abs and a baby as well as when they worked overtime to push out an infant. Simply put, after birth, your back may experience lingering pain as a result of strain and the need to regain its strength. Your abdominal muscles may feel sore, too, from the strain they underwent during pregnancy and delivery.

## NIGHT SWEATS

Unusually heavy sweating frequently affects women in the postpartum period, even when they aren't working out. Night sweats are particularly common, so you may want to wear loose, light cotton fabrics when you go to bed, keeping a fan nearby. As with many of your other postpartum symptoms, the cause of post-pregnancy sweating is hormonal. Your pregnancy hormones are instructing your body to rid itself of the extra fluids it retained to nourish a baby in utero, which occurs through sweating. The perspiration will abate in the first month, when your body has regained its equilibrium in fluids, although it can last longer

### DOCTOR'S NOTE

If your **sweating** is accompanied by a fever of 100° or more, call your doctor. You may have an infection or a virus instead of just the normal postpregnancy perspiration.

When strengthening your back with targeted exercises, start slowly, and emphasize quality over quantity. That means one set of just a few slow reps is more valuable to your back than several sets of many quick repeats. You can begin to do these exercises 2 weeks after a vaginal delivery or 6 weeks after a C-section.

To restore your back to a strong state, try to keep habits that protect your muscles and ligaments from further strains. You don't want to stress your back further by overdoing a strength building routine when you get back to working out or by the repeated motion of picking up your baby. While many baby slings are designed to protect your back, if you wear one much of the day, a sling can be exacerbate back pain by pulling down hard on your shoulders and straining your back. Choose a sling carefully and consider keeping a few different options for carrying your baby so you can distribute the weight differently every day. Always bend from the knees to pick up your infant or the heavy car seat, and try to avoid hunching your back when nursing or holding your baby.

You can treat back pain by applying a cold compress to the area for 10 to 15 minutes, followed by a warm compress for another 10 to 15 minutes. The cold will reduce the inflammation (and the pain), and the warmth will relax tight, sore muscles. In addition, don't be shy about asking your partner for a massage at the end of the day or investing in a massage therapist. All action comes from your core, so as a busy new mom balancing the components of an active lifestyle, you need your back to be strong and pain-free.

## HEEL SCOOP

8–10 reps per side

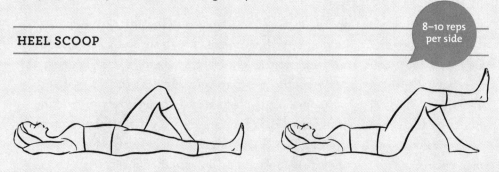

*Lie on your back with your legs bent and feet planted on the floor. Slowly straighten your right leg by pressing your heel along the ground until your leg is lying flat on the floor. Then slowly lift your right leg while bending it so that you're pulling it back toward your pelvis into its original position. Perform this entire scooping motion to a count of 6, being careful to keep your lower back on the floor while you straighten and then lift and pull your leg back to the starting position. Repeat on the left side.*

## COBRA LIFTS

10 reps

*Lie on your stomach with your legs straight behind you and your hands planted palms down next to your shoulders. Slowly lift your torso off the ground to a count of 4, using your lower back to lift rather than your hands to push you up. Hold for 2 to 3 seconds, then lower to the original prone position, taking another count of 4 to get there.*

## REAR LEG LIFTS

10–20 reps
per side

*From the same starting position as Cobra, slowly lift your right leg to a count of 3, then lower to the floor and lift the left leg in the same fashion. Your upper body and palms should stay flat on the floor, with the only motion occurring in your legs.*

## ARM/LEG EXTENSIONS

10–15 reps
per side

*Position yourself on all fours, with a flat spine and your gaze at the ground (but not tucking your chin). Extend your right arm and left leg simultaneously so that both are straight and parallel to the ground. Hold for 3 to 4 seconds, then return to the starting position. Repeat on the other side, extending the left arm and right leg at the same time. Keep the extension and retraction movements slow, about 3 to 4 seconds.*

in breast-feeding moms. Remember to drink plenty of water during this time, as the loss of fluids can result in dehydration. As long as it's not the heat of summer, get plenty of fresh air, too, which is good for keeping your body cool and your mind clear.

## What Can I Expect from Postpartum Fitness?

Many women with sleepless nights and a demanding nursing schedule don't know how they could possibly exercise in the first month. On the flip side, some are so eager to get back to working out that they want to hit the gym before the cord is even cut. Nurse-midwife and Ironman triathlete Marisa Rowlson works with countless athletes who become moms. She says some are ready to resume training—mentally—before they leave the birth room. Others take more time, whether they had a complicated delivery, experience exhaustion to the point of hallucinations, or simply have a body and brain in need of recovery. Marisa's advice to women trying to restart training as a new mother? "Don't compare yourself to anyone else. Listen to your body, and use perceived exertion as a guide." If you were active during pregnancy, you'll probably be able to resume training more quickly, but your timeline will depend on the pain and duration of your labor. If only the stork myth were real, we'd be back to training the same day. In the fourth trimester, when you're making the adjustment to motherhood, your fitness should focus on wellness, not weight loss or race wins.

This phase should be about "finding your feet" again—quite literally, as you may not have seen them in a while. Jumping back into high volume and intense workouts before your body has recovered and you're ready for that level of effort puts you at risk for training injuries and additional mental pressure you don't need. If you aren't bleeding and it feels good, go for it, but if workouts cause bleeding, deplete you, and leave you in a rut, rest three to four more days before trying another workout.

### WHEN CAN I EXERCISE AFTER A VAGINAL DELIVERY?

You may want to hustle out for a workout soon after you leave the hospital, but remember what your body went through to bring you that beautiful little person. You have a placenta-sized wound that needs to heal, and bleeding after birth requires recovery time. Also, remember that every woman's body will be ready at a different point in time. It's perfectly okay to take weeks to rest and recover. The details of the delivery will influence how easily you return to activity. Even after a routine vaginal delivery, your uterus and ab muscles need to heal, with soreness in the 10 to 14 days it takes for your uterus to clamp back down. Muscles and tendons can take up to 9 months to fully recover.[1] In addition, your blood will continue to be diluted because iron levels drop in the third trimester, when your baby consumes much of your iron. Because of this, avoid any activities that increase bleeding.

If you try an activity and find that your bleeding increases, then that activity is too demanding. **Take three to four days before trying again** to exercise at that level of intensity.

A reliable guideline for resuming exercise holds that when you can take your daily walk with no bleeding, you can begin to increase the intensity of your activity, as long as you've conferred with your doctor by phone or in your follow-up appointment. As you build your base with effort-based walking, remember that your training will benefit from being respectful of your body's healing process. It can be frustrating to resume gradually and cautiously, but if your body isn't ready, it will tell you with exhaustion, bleeding, and/or injuries that bench you from your sport and potentially impede your mobility with the baby.

### WHEN CAN I EXERCISE AFTER A C-SECTION?

A C-section is major surgery. You'll be on strong narcotics for three to four days after the birth, weaning off them after one week. Any activity on narcotics is ill-advised, and most women who have a C-section aren't anxious to train immediately anyway. Women with C-section births take much longer to return to a fitness routine, as just getting out of bed is difficult for a while, and the incision takes 6 weeks to fully heal. A C-section mother can attempt a return to gentle exercise anywhere from 6 to 8 weeks after the birth. However, easy walking and gentle abdominal exercises can help you heal. Consult your doctor about your specific healing process to determine when it will be okay to return to walking for exercise and ab exercises such as those below.

## EXERCISES FOR ABDOMINAL STRENGTH AFTER A C-SECTION

### LOWER ABDOMINAL

8–10 sec.
3x/day

*Pull your belly button in and up at the same time and hold the contraction. This can be performed while sitting or lying down.*

### PELVIC TILT

10 reps
3x/day

*Lie on your back with your knees bent. Slowly tilt your pelvis up so that your lower back pushes against the floor. Hold for 8 to 10 seconds, then lower your pelvis.*

### SIMPLE SIT-UPS

12–15 reps
3x/day

*At 6 to 8 weeks postbirth, when your incision has healed, you can start some slow and gentle sit-ups. Lie on your back with bent knees and tighten your pelvic floor and abs while lifting your head and shoulders about 3 inches off the floor. If you find this movement difficult or painful, you aren't quite ready for sit-ups and should wait a few more days before trying them.*

When you return to exercise, use pain as your determining factor. As with exercise after a vaginal birth: If the exercise hurts, stop. Take your time when you get up from lying down. Roll to your side first, then use your arms to push yourself up so you don't put any pressure on your back and abs, which are still weak and healing.

## RESUMING WORKOUTS SAFELY

Research on competitive athletes and postpartum exercise indicates that highly competitive athletes with a normal pregnancy and straightforward delivery often resume training safely within a few weeks after childbirth.[2] Medical guidelines indicate that recreational athletes who don't train at an elite level will take

6 weeks to recover and return to prepregnancy readiness for training.[3] Your resting heart rate will return to its prepregnancy levels within that time, and your working heart rate will be much lower than when you were active during pregnancy, most likely because you will have lost at least 15 to 20 pounds.[4]

Women who are more active during pregnancy tend to have lower working heart rates in postpartum workout tests than those who exercised less when pregnant.[5] That means that if you exercised when you were pregnant, your postpartum heart rate and rate of perceived exertion will be able to handle a higher level of effort when you resume exercise. But there is a lot of variation between women when it comes to how active they can be during and after pregnancy, so don't compare yourself to the Ironwoman next door. Many very fit women take a long time to be ready, and it's up to you to pay attention to what you need. Instead of tackling a strict training plan right away, orient your return to training toward exercise that feels good for the first 6 to 8 weeks after you begin to rebuild your base. For those workouts, strive for 3 to 5 days per week of 45 to 60 minutes of cardio that feels good to avoid overtraining and overuse injuries.

For the sake of your health and healing, you may have to scale back your desire to push your lactate threshold. But if your body recovers quickly and the bleeding has stopped, there's no need to watch the calendar for your fourth week if you feel ready to exercise. Generally speaking, follow the guideline *If it doesn't feel good, don't do it*. If your bleeding has stopped before your follow-up appointment, call your doctor to clear an increase in the effort of your workouts.

When you and your doctor agree that it's go time, keep in mind three key elements:

* Be patient, and increase your volume and intensity as part of a mental and physical base-building phase.
* Focus on effort, using Borg's RPE scale, in the first 6 to 8 weeks back to regular training.
* Don't stress about weight loss for the first 4 months of your baby's life. It will probably happen as a natural result of birth, nursing, and increased activity, and if it doesn't, you will take it on when your workout routine is established and you're getting more dependable sleep.

## REBUILDING VOLUME AND INTENSITY

First, build your base by gradually increasing the time of your workouts. Three to 4 days per week is a good place to start for anyone returning to activity after pregnancy. As noted in Chapter 6, begin with strolling in the first 2 weeks after birth. Generally speaking, a 20- to 30-minute brisk walk is a reasonable expectation by 4 to 6 weeks, as long as you aren't bleeding. If your bleeding does not increase, you can increase the volume and intensity of the exercise by starting to run easy or use the elliptical machine at the gym. For the first 8 weeks of these workouts, continue to follow Borg's scale by sticking to a 13–16 RPE, and add 3 to 5 minutes every third workout to gradually increase the volume of your base. Don't focus on miles or meters in the pool, and be flexible with your expectations, as you were during pregnancy.

Increasing the intensity will come later. If you start by building your base volume without striving to increase intensity at the same time, your body will respond with strength and cardio power instead of breaking down from fatigue and stress on muscles, joints, and bones that are experiencing the lingering effects of pregnancy and labor. Postpartum changes in your body composition can alter your form and gait, which can trigger small aches and pains that, when ignored, become injuries.[6]

Similarly, fluctuations in estrogen and relaxin during pregnancy loosened your hip joints to prepare your pelvis for birth, and the increased flexibility lingers after delivery. The ligaments can be hypermobile, making stability harder

---

**FITNESS** $R_X$

A woman's knees, hips, and back are the main areas at risk when it comes to postpartum injury from endurance-oriented workouts and daily tasks, such as picking up an older child or lifting a car seat. Squat when lifting anything heavy, rather than bending from the waist. Look for softer ground to ease the impact of running on your body, such as soccer fields or well-groomed trails, or run in the grass or dirt beside a sidewalk or road. Combining workouts by cycling to an athletic field or trail will vary the muscle groups you're using so you can achieve a beneficial workout without repetitive stress on the same areas.

to maintain for postpartum women.[7] Overtaxing your muscles, joints, and ligaments with long, hard workouts can pose a risk for strains and sprains, so begin a training cycle with some willingness to build the duration of each session gradually. In order to prevent overuse, follow the 10 Percent Rule described on page 247 for increases in the time and mileage of your weekly training and longest workout, regardless of what type of exercise you're doing.

Some studies suggest that stress fractures are also a risk for postpartum athletes because of decreases in bone density as a result of breast-feeding.[8] Nursing leaches calcium from your body to your baby, and loosened joints can't absorb the impact of a run as well as before pregnancy. While mostly anecdotal, examples of marathoners such as Paula Radcliffe and other women who developed postpartum stress fractures suggest that you should be cautious about ramping up your workouts too quickly. It's perfectly safe to resume training and to train with increased intensity, but your body needs to rebuild its strength, so don't get overly aggressive and be sure to get your DRI of calcium as well as a mix of carbs and protein (e.g., chocolate milk) to aid recovery after a workout.

### BREAST-FEEDING AND TRAINING

During the 2007 Hardrock 100 Endurance Run, Emily Baer turned some heads when she stopped at every aid station to nurse her son. The milk breaks didn't seem to hold her up much—she finished eighth overall. Studies show that on average, athletes of all levels can breast-feed and train at an intense level with no negative consequences for their babies, their milk production, or their own bone density.[9] Even better, new research indicates that exercise will actually help you reduce the risk of bone-density loss that is a common result of the loss of calcium to your baby. Nursing women who do cardio and strength training at least 3 days per week show, on average, a lower bone-density loss than do women who breast-feed and don't exercise.[10]

Anecdotes from your mother-in-law or the ladies at the gym might tell you that strenuous exercise can inhibit milk production, but the medical consensus is that it is dehydration, not exercise in and of itself, that will limit lactation.[11] If you drink enough water, you will produce enough milk, and your baby will continue to gain weight and grow. Carry water with you everywhere so you stay hydrated (which an athlete should do anyway), and drink when thirsty. Remember to use the color of your urine to indicate hydration, looking for clear liquid.

Breast-feeding does not prohibit training or competing. For example, elite Ironman competitors Jessica Jacobs and Gina Crawford finished the 140.6-mile

## WORKOUT HINTS FOR NURSING MOMS

- Express or pump milk (or nurse your baby) to prevent discomfort that comes from blocked ducts, engorgement, and leaks while you work out.

- For longer workouts, pump a bottle prior to leaving so your baby won't miss a feeding.

- Find a supportive nursing sports bra (without underwire) so that you can feed just before you leave the house; buy several so you aren't doing laundry constantly.

- The more fasteners on a sports bra, the better; they structure the bra for more support and "containment."

- Before you leave for a workout, insert fresh nursing pads into your bra to avoid leaks and prevent infection.

- Change out of sweaty clothes immediately after you finish the workout to avoid infection of the milk ducts.

- If possible, work out at a gym that has a nursery so you can pause to feed, if necessary.

event in New Zealand when they were still nursing their young babies, showing that moms who breast-feed don't have to hand over the keys to their fitness drive. As long as you prepare for feedings during your absences and organize yourself, you'll be able to breast-feed and train regularly. Because an infant will last between 90 minutes and 2 hours between feedings, it's a good idea to nurse just before your workout. A benefit of preworkout nursing is that lactic acid buildup can sometimes temporarily change the flavor of breast milk after high-intensity workouts, such as speed work.[12]

## CREATING A SUPPORT TEAM AT HOME

Once it becomes a source of empowerment in our lives, sport often becomes an integral, restorative part of who we are. After giving birth, we're in a recovery phase that restricts activity, which can feel disorienting. Athlete moms frequently say that having a spouse or partner who understands how deeply meaningful their fitness is keeps them connected to that identity and able to pursue activity after a new baby. In the fourth trimester, in particular, a partner who will make space and time for you to take 30 to 60 minutes alone every day will be a huge help in your adjustment to life with your new baby.

Taking time alone to recharge with endorphins benefits the entire family because it keeps you centered and energized. Having a partner who encourages that and makes space and time for your activity can mean the difference between some exercise and nothing at all.

To get a spouse on board with the importance of your training program, try any of the following:

* When talking to your spouse about how important it is that you get support for workouts, pick a time that isn't stressful for the chat. Avoid the moment just before you want to head out to run.
* Use an online shared calendar, such as Google Calendar, to schedule your workout "appointments" so that your family schedule accommodates them.
* If necessary, barter your solo fitness time for his solo time.
* Suggest that both of you train for a family event, such as a 5K, so that you each must schedule time for workouts.
* Remind your partner that setting aside time for you to be active benefits your partner's relationship with the new baby, giving them time to bond without you there to get all the baby's attention.

## Sport Specifics: Guidelines for Run, Bike, and Swim Training

### FOURTH-TRIMESTER RUNNING

It is important to start with walking, slowly, in the first 4 weeks unless you consult with your physician and get the green light. Once your bleeding stops, you can pick it up to a brisk walking pace. If your bleeding doesn't return, you can build some jogging back into your program. Remember to start with short runs and go at a very easy, conversational pace when you return to running so that you don't tempt an injury from doing too much too soon. The exact distance or time and pace of your first run after delivery will depend on how much you were able to stay active while you were expecting and your training volume prior to pregnancy. If you're returning to running with a walk-to-run program, you can follow the interval program guidelines described in Chapter 4. For no-impact running, you can also use intervals on the elliptical or arc trainer by alternating

*I remember it was only for 30 minutes and maybe three or four times a week, but it was pure adrenaline . . . so refreshing to look forward to it every day.*

JESSICA | ULTRARUNNER AND MOM TO MAX AND MASON

The prerun warm-up is key to postpartum running. We're often short on time, so a lot of us skip the warm-up phase of a run, but a walk or very slow jog is solid injury prevention and wakes up our muscles. A few trips up and down the stairs in the house (jogging up and down) are a decent warm-up, and if you add a basket of laundry, you might actually raise your heart rate before the run starts. In a pinch, you can also warm up stiff muscles by using a foam roller. Whatever creative choice you make to warm up before heading off to run, the activity should not be too taxing on cold muscles. For efficiency's sake, a warm-up for an easy run does not need to exceed 5 minutes, but more intense pace work requires warmer muscles and a 10-minute jog to begin.

60 seconds at a higher resistance with 60 seconds of very easy striding, working your way up to 3- to 5-minute intervals.

Pay attention to any soreness in your muscles after the first few runs. Remember that postpartum women with relaxed muscle fibers and hypermobile spines may be more susceptible to training injuries, or strains from carrying their infants in a sling. This is the main reason that it's critical to resume your training program conservatively. If you're heading out for a run still full of aches and pains from the last workout, you're doing too much. Shin splints are a good indication that you might be overdoing a return to running, as are tight quads and hamstrings that prevent you from lowering yourself to the floor to play with the baby. It's a good idea to ice your shins after a run, and try to stretch your major muscle groups following a workout but not beforehand, when your muscles are cold and tight. The quality stretch that you will get from gentle yoga is a beneficial and portable form of exercise that you can do with a baby in your arms or lying next to you. Target your back, quads, calves, hip flexors, hamstrings, and iliotibial bands to cover all the areas that can develop strains or tears from doing too much too soon. Hold each stretch for 30 to 45 seconds per side, and repeat twice per day. You can use the series of stretches found on page 222–223 to target your major muscle groups as well as the stretches to prevent calf cramping, page 96.

In the fourth trimester, low energy and schedule limitations can prevent you from achieving a 30- to 60-minute run. Running doubles is a way to creatively increase your cardio time. If you have a few short openings in your day, for example, because of your job or other kids' schedules, try a run in the early morning for 20 minutes and follow up with another 20 minutes at lunch or after you put your baby to bed. Breaking up your workout by doing a double is also great if you are nursing but not pumping milk because it allows you to be away from your baby in shorter increments while still getting your run in. Running doubles is also an ideal way to conservatively increase your exercise base when you're getting back to a training schedule. Whereas you might have difficulty jumping in with a 6-mile run, you'll benefit from two 3-mile runs with a lower risk of overtraining.

## Strides

After gradually increasing your running time, it will be safe for you to begin working on your pace. Once you've built a base of running 25 to 30 minutes at a conversational RPE at least 3 days per week, you can start to incorporate speed work. A blessing of speed work is that, by definition, you get it done faster. If you can't get to a track, you can perform speed intervals when you run on the road. Strides are a great way to improve speed in a safe and gradual format when you've been away from intensive training for a while. At the end of a run, stride out a series of 6 to 10 60- to 100-meter pickups, performed on a flat stretch of road, a path, a football field, or a track. With a longer warm-up (2 to 3 miles), they

TRAINING TIP Strides are a great option for incorporating speed work into your return to running, but be careful not to stride out too far with each step, and don't sprint. The level of effort should feel invigorating, not debilitating, about a 16–17 on Borg's RPE scale. Because your joints are still loose from the hypermobility caused by pregnancy hormones, start with 4 20-second strides on your first attempt, adding another 2 strides the next week. Max out at 10–12 60-second strides in a run, jogging 60 seconds between each one.

can give you a decent workout on their own, boosting your speed by triggering your fast-twitch muscles. If you're a new runner and crunched for time, strides are a great option for inserting some high-value cardio in a short amount of time. If you're an experienced runner who wants to increase the intensity, do some strides on a hill.

To do a stride, build up your speed over the distance that you're running (60 to 100 meters). Start from a jog and increase the pace to approximately 80 to 85 percent of your top sprinting speed by the first third of the stride. Hold that pace for another third, concluding with a gradual deceleration over the final third. Strive for quick, short turnover of your feet, landing on the midfoot. Insert a slow jog and shake out your arms and legs for 60 to 90 seconds between strides.

If you've been running steadily for 4 to 6 weeks, you can progress from strides to perform shorter intervals (400 to 800 meters) at the same intense level of effort. You can find sample interval workouts at the end of this chapter. Speed work at this level of effort is versatile because it benefits your power for running longer at more conservative paces, and you can get a cardio-pumping session from a short track workout.

If you're a distance runner, get creative to achieve long runs with a baby. One new mom started a long run on the treadmill, getting in 7 miles while her baby slept, and when he woke up, she bundled him into the stroller and ran another 5 miles outside. Long runs with a new baby can be hard to plan due to feeding schedules, but pumping milk and planning ahead will get you much of the way.

### The 10 Percent Rule

After you've increased the time of your runs from 20 minutes per run 3 days per week to 30 minutes total (adding 3 to 5 minutes every third run), it's fine to reorient your running to mileage as opposed to time. Whether you're on the road or on the treadmill, rebuild your running routine by following the 10 Percent Rule: Add to your mileage by increasing the total weekly distance by only 10 percent over that of the previous week. You should also add only 10 percent to the distance of your longest run each week. While scheduling can be tough with a new baby, don't go from 3 days of 4 miles one week to 1 run of 13 miles the next week because you followed the 10 Percent Rule. If you're running 3 days per week and have been back at it for 4 to 6 weeks, you can vary the type of run to improve speed and cardio fitness. Make one of your runs an easy run (perhaps with a few strides at the end), one a speed session of 400- to 800-meter (¼- to ½-mile) intervals (see "Running" on page 255 for a suggested workout), and then do one longer run to increase stamina and endurance. Try to space your runs out during the week instead of cramming them into 3 consecutive days and taking 4 days off because your body needs the recovery day between each run to rebuild muscle fibers. As you add any more days of running to this three-run base, don't run speed work and a long run on consecutive days. Insert a slow and easy recovery-run day between any runs that require a harder effort, such as going long or fast.

## FOURTH-TRIMESTER SWIMMING

Swimming is fine to do in the first few weeks after giving birth, although you will want to wait for any tearing to heal before getting into the water, as chlorine can irritate a laceration and inhibit the healing process. Once you've healed, swimming is a great way to resume exercise, just as it's the perfect pregnancy activity, because movement in the water is gentle on a body in recovery from physical stress. It also provides a total-body workout in a relatively short session of 20 to 30 minutes, ideal for nursing moms, and the water can be therapeutic for many women.

Some women are deterred from swimming because tampons can fall out before the uterus clamps down again, and doctors will advise that you not use tampons for 4 to 6 weeks after delivery. Ask your provider for advice on your particular risk for a uterine infection from using tampons after delivery, and don't wait for your 6-week appointment to ask about swimming or any other form of exercise you'd like to pursue. As soon as you feel ready in body and mind, call your doctor to discuss your options. You'll likely hear that, as with a return to running or any other form of exercise, you should start short and slow, taking breaks as needed.

## FOURTH-TRIMESTER BIKING

A month after having her third baby, professional cyclist Kristin Armstrong was back on her bike and training for the 2012 Olympics. Having retired from cycling because she wanted a baby, Armstrong found that having a baby and having her sport weren't mutually exclusive. And like other competitive athlete moms, Armstrong believes her toddler improves her performance, even though being a mom can make training complicated.

While cycling, like swimming, is technically safe, it might be painful to sit in the saddle in the first 6 weeks after delivery, and you'll want to wait until you're comfortable. If you have stitches, it could take longer to get back on your bike, and your mind might be ready to roll before your body gives you the go-ahead. As one mom said, "Mentally and emotionally, I needed to ride my bike for the freedom. You can go faster and farther."

To figure out when you can get back in the saddle, keep in mind that stitches as a result of tearing or an episiotomy take 2 weeks to dissolve, and the muscle soreness lingers for a good while (up to 6 weeks) because the prolapse from pushing takes a long time to heal. In addition, midwife Marisa Rowlson reminds her athletes that the nerves that were damaged during labor take a whopping 4 to 6 months to recover. Even though endurance training prepares us to push through pain and probably helped you get through labor, let your maternal instincts take care of your health as much as your baby's.

When you're ready to get back on the bike, you can have it fitted to a geometry that—to put it bluntly—favors your crotch. Have a bike specialist configure the seat so you sit further back on your sitz bones rather than forward and higher on the spot from which your baby entered the world. To start back on the bike, begin with a road bike (not a tri bike) because the angles will keep you from leaning too far forward and will be more physically comfortable. A bike fitted for nontriathlon cycling will allow you to sit back.

*The biggest challenges are not going to be about my training or nutrition, the things that a lot of people struggle with to be at the top. It's going to be about the challenges of raising a child.*

KRISTIN ARMSTRONG | PROFESSIONAL CYCLIST AND MOM OF LUCAS

Some women don't ride after having babies because they're afraid of the dangers of riding in traffic. Minimize your risks by riding on less busy roads, during daylight, and at times of day with fewer cars on the road. You can also get used to cycling again by starting on a spin bike or a bike trainer.

A solid cycling workout does not have to take several hours to reap a fitness benefit. An hour of high-quality spinning will do plenty for your fitness. As with running, as soon as you're healed up from the birth, there are options that can help a mom train hard on the bike, such as using a bike trainer or attending a spin class at a gym. A spin class is an efficient way to squeeze a high-quality workout into a short amount of time—with adult music and grown-ups to keep you company. You'll adjust the bike's resistance to simulate various elevations, and the class can allow you to blend power-based training for speed with hill repeats that build aerobic strength. Even though a spinning class likely won't match the specifications of a workout that's prescribed on a training plan, it can give you child-care-enabled crosstraining—and a shower. It might be worth it just to have a shower in peace.

For a cardio workout on a bike trainer or spin bike, warm up for 10 minutes at an easy effort. Then try a few sets of intervals that have you at a 14–16 RPE with equal-length recoveries between your hard efforts. For example, do 3 sets of 3 intervals of 2 minutes at 14–16 RPE with 2 minutes of easy spin between the exertions and 5 minutes of easy spin between the sets. That's a solid interval workout in under an hour.

If you want a speed session to focus on power for sprinting or as a substitute for lifting weights, do more intervals of shorter duration, such as 3 sets of 3 × 20 seconds, 4 × 15 seconds, and 5 × 10 seconds. Insert recovery periods of 2 minutes between each burst of sprinting, standing up on the pedals during the bursts. If you don't have a power meter, you can use perceived exertion to guide your input; a heart rate monitor is unreliable when the repeats are so short. The bursts should put you at a 16–18 RPE.

## ELLIPTICAL

If you're not running or want an alternative to the treadmill, you can get a run-like workout by using an elliptical (or a Cybex Arc Trainer) at the gym. The motion of your legs on the elliptical is as close to a running stride as you can get, without the impact of running so you can accumulate some miles without the pounding. Set the incline to at least 50 percent, and choose a steady-state effort (same level of resistance for the entire session) or interval training (see "Elliptical Workouts," page 258, for workout options). Don't hold on to the hand grips; pump your arms in a running motion instead. This keeps you from leaning on the machine so that you work under your own power. To get the best simulation of a run, aim for at least 130 steps per minute on the elliptical (155 on the Arc Trainer), which you will probably be able to read on the machine's display. You might not hit that endorphin-rich flow state you score from a run, but the elliptical can get you some serious sweat, a higher heart rate, and aerobic training. Hopefully your gym has a good TV setup, too.

## Returning to Racing

After the birth of her first baby, Ryan made the bold move of registering for a marathon several months away. When a running-store clerk saw her jogging stroller, sized her up, and suggested she train for a 4-mile race instead, she was even more determined. Completing the marathon was a huge source of power for her, and unlike the small daily tasks of motherhood, the race was a feat that would not be "undone," as she put it.

One of the best motivators for helping you return to a regular training schedule is to pick an event that's at least 4 months from your first workout without bleeding. Consider it a celebration race, your chance to strut your athlete-mom self. If you're nursing, you're probably not drinking much alcohol, so this is a healthy alternative for toasting yourself and your new family.

When it comes to a postpartum event in the first several months, you'll probably need to tweak your plan compared with how you approached it prior to having a baby. Many women report that they performed well above their expectations because their training was so focused and they didn't waste any time during workouts. Others set their goal at "just finish" because of the challenges of balancing workouts with family life. Regardless, it's not just about finding someone to hold the baby while you're racing, or making sure the tires on the jogger are inflated for you to push in the event. Write a master checklist of your race essentials, and use that to pack your bag for each race. You don't need to pack a month in advance, as you did for the birth, but try not to leave it until the morning of the race, when you also have to give attention to a baby. Remember to wear nursing pads if you're still breast-feeding and to leave enough time before the race to nurse or pump a bottle. You'll also want to build in enough time for at least one trip to the bathroom.

As with training, your race pace should be oriented toward effort—how you feel—and not toward hitting specific splits, at least for the first half of the race. You can set multiple goals for yourself so that you're satisfied with the outcome even if you don't set a personal best (see Chapter 8 for more on that). Your first goal should be to finish the major achievement of a postpartum race, not to set a personal record or win a medal, as getting out to a race at all in the first year is a big achievement.

It's fine to pick an event that exceeds any distance you've covered before, such as your first marathon or century ride, providing you're able to do the train-

> As mothers, so much of what we do is undone in an instant—the laundry gets washed and folded, only to be dirty again; it takes all afternoon to make dinner, but it's eaten in a flash, leaving only a sinkful of dirty dishes. For me, running a marathon was a way to achieve something that couldn't be undone. I am, and forever will be, a marathoner.
>
> RYAN | MARATHONER AND MOM OF SAMI AND MAX

ing without risking injury by overreaching the 10 Percent Rule to increase your volume. Discuss your intentions with your doctor, and consult a coach about your training and goal. A skilled coach in your sport will ask about your health, fitness history, schedule, and lifestyle and determine whether your individual circumstances can safely lead to meeting your race goal.

Childbirth teaches women that they can accomplish physical feats they never thought possible, and many then want to strive for ambitious fitness goals in the first year postpartum. As long as you've let your body fully recover from the birth, there's no stopping you. Listen to what your body tells you, get input from a coach about a timeline for reaching your specific goals, and enjoy the process of training to meet them.

## Does Childbirth Actually Boost Fitness?

Giving birth to a baby is taxing work, obviously, and even with the benefit of anesthesia, the physical and emotional workout of labor and delivery will probably leave you wiped out and sore. But take heart: Some researchers think that giving birth can actually boost women's athletic potential. For example, a woman's blood volume rises by as much as 60 percent when she's pregnant, and her resting heart rate can increase by as much as 15 beats. Nadya Swedan, M.D., author of *The Active Woman's Health and Fitness Handbook*, believes that pregnancy can amount to "hypertraining" and that a return to running within weeks of the birth may allow women to capitalize on their oxygenation levels.[13] Some theorists even wonder if women's high oxygenation during pregnancy amounts to natural blood doping, the illicit practice of increasing an athlete's mass of red blood cells to aid performance. During pregnancy, the body generates more erythropoietin (EPO), which increases the production of red blood cells to supply both mother and child. According to *Sports Illustrated*'s David Epstein, who covered the topic in a 2008 article, "Once the baby is born, the additional red

*I really thought that once I got pregnant and had Sophie, my days of PRs were over. I've only just now realized that this is endless, and I can still keep improving. I thought this was as good as I can do and as fast as I can run. And I was wrong about those things.*     HEATHER | RUNNER AND MOM OF SOPHIE

blood cells that remain in the mother's system carry extra oxygen to the muscles, an effect akin to doping with EPO."[14]

Athlete moms often swear that having babies makes them faster and fitter than when they were childless. As Chapter 8 explains, this may be as much due to their determination and focus as it is to red blood cells. Anxiety about balancing our multiple roles with training seems to make many of us "more fervent" about training, as one mom put it. And the need to balance can be a protective factor against injury and burnout, improving both your race experience and your race performance.

If you're feeling discouraged by a slower road back to fitness than you'd wanted, remember that the discipline of the passionate athlete isn't squelched by motherhood. Your passion and commitment just need a body to recover in order to fulfill your training goals. Just because your motivation and the oxygenation of your blood may point to new fitness or training potential, there are other parts of your body that need a solid recovery period from the physical trauma of giving birth.

## Workouts to Build Cardio and Muscle Strength

Many athlete moms will tell you that they saw major improvements in their athletic performance in their babies' first year of life. By the time a baby is 9 months old, a schedule is pretty much set, and you have the base for sustaining an active life. Make that 1-hour appointment with yourself. Here are a series of great workouts that build stamina, release tension, and increase aerobic and muscle strength—specifically designed to be efficient so you can strike the athlete-mom balance and train with some intensity.

*Was it pregnancy and birth that contributed to some decent race results? I say yes. Not because of changes my body went through . . . but because of what changes my life is going through. Now quality workouts outweigh quantity workouts. . . . I have learned to balance. This contributes to less burnout and more enjoyment when I actually get to train or race.*

BREE WEE | PROFESSIONAL TRIATHLETE AND MOM OF KAINOA

# RUNNING

## EFFORT-BASED LADDER

*This is an ideal workout for shaking off the dust and returning to training. The variation gives you a chance to run at five different paces, with generous recovery periods between. If you're on a treadmill, set the incline to 1 percent to mimic the effort of running with some wind resistance outdoors and jog the recoveries at a 0 percent incline.*

2 × (5:00, 4:00, 3:00, 2:00); 3-minute easy jog between sets

   5 minutes at 13 RPE (2:30 recovery jog)

   4 minutes at 14 RPE (2-minute recovery jog)

   3 minutes at 15 RPE (1:30 recovery jog)

   2 minutes at 16 RPE (1-minute recovery jog)

## THE STRESS BUSTER

*Try this series for an efficient, muscle-stimulating speed session that varies your effort level within each interval. If you're on a treadmill, set the incline to 1 percent to mimic the effort of running with some wind resistance outdoors and jog the recoveries at a 0 percent incline.*

8–10 × 800-meter variation intervals; 90-second easy jog or walk between intervals

   400 meters or ¼ mile at 14–15 RPE

   200 meters or ⅛ mile easy jog

   200 meters or ⅛ mile at 16–17 RPE

## 2-MINUTE MOM TAG

*Hit the track with another mom to tag-team the child care. Bring some balls or other distractions for the kids. One person takes her recovery break and watches the kids while the other person runs her interval. Use the recovery to stretch or push a stroller while walking so that you keep moving to prevent your heart rate from dropping too much.*

16–18 × 2 minutes
>
> 2 minutes at 16–17 RPE
>
> 2-minute recovery on the infield

## TREADMILL HILL GRIND

*Not everyone loves the treadmill, but this is a fun one. The intervals keep changing to stimulate your brain, helping you avoid boredom when an outdoor run is not an option. It's a great way to get a challenging workout when you need to run during naptime, for example. The workout can be run at any pace, so it's suited for all levels.*

8–10 × 4-minute incline shifts
>
> After a 5- to 10-minute warm-up jog, set your pace to a comfortable run at a 1 percent incline. Change the incline *for every minute* of each 4-minute interval. Take a 2-minute recovery jog or walk between each numbered interval.

| INTERVAL | INCLINE |
| --- | --- |
| 1 | 2, 3, 4, 1 |
| 2 | 0, 2, 4, 0 |
| 3 | 2, 3, 4, 1 |
| 4 | 0, 2, 4, 0 |
| 5 | 2, 3, 4, 1 |
| 6 | 0, 2, 4, 0 |
| 7 | 2, 3, 4, 1 |
| 8 | 0, 2, 4, 0 |
| 9 | 2, 3, 4, 1 |
| 10 | 0, 2, 4, 0 |

## CYCLING

Here are two great interval workouts that build your aerobic base and muscle strength in an hour.

### BIG-GEAR INTERVALS

*After a 15-minute warm-up ride, head to a shallow hill (about 3.5 to 4 percent incline), and get ready to grind without maxing your heart rate. Set your bike to a big (hard) gear, and push the hill for strength building, standing up on the pedals if you like. You can also use a bike trainer and change the gears to increase the level of resistance or difficulty. This workout is about a challenging hill climb, not speed.*

Options (in order of difficulty)

> 5 × 1 minute with 60-second recoveries back down
>
> 4 × 2 minutes with 2-minute recoveries back down
>
> 3 × 3 minutes with 3–4-minute recoveries back down

### SIT 'N' SPIN THRESHOLD SERIES

*Great for boosting your aerobic threshold, these workouts alternate sitting and standing while cranking as fast as you can up a hill. Standing on the pedals generates more power, but it demands so much energy that you can't sustain it for more than 30 seconds. Varying the workout between the two positions works different muscles and gives you a high-quality session. Find a long and gradual incline for this workout.*

Options (in order of difficulty)

> 8 × 1 minute: intervals 1–4 sitting and intervals 5–8 standing, with 60-second recoveries
>
> 6 × 90 seconds: odd intervals standing and even intervals sitting, with 90-second recoveries
>
> 4–6 × 3 minutes: first 1:30 of each repeat sitting and second 1:30 of each repeat standing, with 2-minute recoveries

## ELLIPTICAL

You can get a solid, muscle-burning aerobic effort in 45 to 60 minutes on the elliptical, using a motion that approximates running without any impact.

---

### ELLIPTICAL WORKOUTS

---

*Set the incline to 50 to 80 percent, and warm up for 5 to 10 minutes at a low, easy level of resistance.*

Options

  44 minutes short speed: 8-minute warm-up, 18 × 1 minute at 16–18 RPE, 1-minute recoveries

  65 minutes tempo speed: 5-minute warm-up, 10 × 4 minutes at 14–15 RPE, 2-minute recoveries at a low resistance, 2-minute very easy cooldown effort

  60 minutes progression: 10-minute warm-up, 10 minutes at 13 RPE, 10 minutes at 14 RPE, 10 minutes at 15 RPE, 5 minutes at 16 RPE, 4 minutes at 17 RPE, 1 minute at 18 RPE, 10 minutes very easy cooldown

## STRENGTH TRAINING

Lifting your baby or toddler will no doubt build your biceps. The workouts below employ his or her weight for strength training.

---

### BABY-LADEN LUNGES

**1–3 sets of 8–15 reps**

*Set your feet wide to assist with balance. Your forward knee should not reach beyond your toes as you bend your knees. The forward thigh dips no further than parallel to the ground. Repeat on other side.*

## BABY-LADEN SQUATS

1–3 sets of 8–15 reps

*Feet are hip width apart and slightly turned out. Keep your back upright as you bend your knees, resisting the urge to tip forward.*

# STRETCHING

As you may have noticed, babies and toddlers are extremely flexible. Contorting themselves like pretzels helps them figure out space and how their bodies move, and their love for twisting into seemingly impossible positions can give you a few minutes to lengthen the muscles and open the joints you've been training. It only takes about 30 seconds per stretch to release some tightness.

## DOWN DOG

4–10 sets of 5 deep breaths

*Down Dog stretches the hamstrings and calves while lengthening the Achilles tendons. Babies and toddlers love to crawl or walk through your open legs for upside-down kisses.*

## HAPPY BABY

1–3 sets of 30–45 secs

*Happy Baby releases the piriformis and opens the groin and hip joints. As you might guess, your baby could teach you how to do it.*

## Gear: Buying a Trainer, Jogger, or Treadmill

It's as important to "pack a bag" for the fourth trimester as it was to pack one for the hospital or any endurance event. Having good tools on hand becomes even more valuable to moms who want to resume a regular exercise or training program.

### BIKE TRAINER

When the weather spells misery or you have a napping baby with no babysitter, set your bike up on a basic indoor trainer to create nearly any kind of workout you want. Cheaper than a treadmill, it's convenient for moms with infants, and you can get a hard effort in very little time. If your baby will tolerate the mechanical swing for 15-minute spans, you can bike a 45-minute triple on a mechanical trainer over three sessions throughout the day. You get a great sweat and a way to burn off the stress of cabin fever in just your nursing bra and a pair of shorts without anyone else around. For those who are self-conscious about how they look exercising postpartum, it's ideal.

There are a lot of choices when choosing a trainer. You might want a simple setup that uses a fan to simulate the feel of wind on the road, though this doesn't give you any resistance beyond your pedaling action. While more expensive, a fluid trainer is capable of increasing difficulty because the fluid allows for hydraulic resistance. Because the heat you generate increases the viscosity of the fluid as you work, resistance builds as you ride, allowing for a superb workout. You can further change the difficulty by using a block under the front wheel to elevate it. This type of trainer is more versatile than a wind trainer. A magnetic trainer is pretty quiet, and you can adjust the resistance manually or electronically, depending on the brand you pick.

Not only does a bike trainer give you versatility and flexibility to work out with a baby at home but you can actually get a strong workout on an indoor trainer relative to the road, where it's easy to go lax by coasting. Likewise, there are no stop signs or slow merges—moms on trainers yield to no one! You can sit or stand in the clips and push your watts hard against the resistance of the trainer without needing to slow for traffic or other hazards. You'll be able to get an indoor workout that is equivalent to an outdoor one in less time because you can keep your heart rate elevated throughout. As a bonus, you can listen to music or catch up on shows that you're missing now that you crash in bed at 7:30 every night.

Just remember to ease back into cycling on a trainer, as your ligaments are still loose, and you likely haven't been on a bike for quite a while after pregnancy. Begin with 20 minutes of pedaling on an easy gear, and don't add hard stand-up pedaling back into a spin workout for a few weeks after you resume cycling, or when your cardio fitness can handle 6 to 8 30-second bursts of effort during a 30-minute session on the trainer.

## BABY JOGGER

A jogging stroller becomes such an object of attachment for mothers that some shed a tear when they finally pass one along to another new mom. Pregnant runners look forward to buying a jogging stroller perhaps more than any other gear. For some moms, a jogging stroller may be the only way to manage to run or power walk at all; it exponentially increases your ability to get outside for a run.

In addition, pushing a stroller up hills is great for building back strength. A stroller run can also be quite soothing to a baby, much like a car ride, and little ones enjoy the opportunity to get out of the house and see the world as much as we do. You can also use a stroller run to get to the playground, day care, a play date, or preschool. And if you run it to the supermarket, you can add challenge to your workout with the weight of groceries on the way home! The stroller helps you multitask various daily obligations and gets your run in when you start to feel as if the baby on your hip might just be glued there with epoxy.

Running behind a jogger can also be excellent race preparation. If you train for a race behind a baby jogger, the race usually feels vastly easier once you ditch the effort of pushing the weight of a stroller and a baby. Unless the temperature outside is unsafe for adults, you can bundle up a child safely for a cold run or use a sunshade to protect a baby from heat and the summer sun. When the walls of the house seem to be closing in on you—as they often do for mothers at home—a run with the stroller can recharge you and take both of you out into the world.

Used jogging strollers are fairly easy to come by, and as long as you test certain features, they are dependable. A newborn needs to have neck support until he or she can hold the head up without help. Some strollers now have neck supports for younger babies, but remember that an infant will need to recline for months. Talk to your pediatrician about your baby's readiness to ride in a jogging stroller while you're running.

You will want your jogger to have a sun shade that can be adjusted for all directions of sunlight, because chances are, you will make several turns on a run. You will also want a jogger that can be folded. If you are running on brick or cobblestone sidewalks or city sidewalks that are cracked, you might want a jogger with shocks, though these can add to the weight of the stroller.

In order to test a jogging stroller, you should jog behind it with some weight in the seat for 50 to 100 yards. The handlebar height should feel natural, and you shouldn't feel as if you're kicking the rear wheels. Test the hand brake to ensure that the stroller stops quickly and completely. The front tire on any good jogging stroller should be fixed in place or able to lock; turning a jogger is a fun and humbling lesson in coordination, but in order to retain control, it is important that you don't run with a stroller that has a front wheel that rotates. Wheel height is another factor to consider if you are a taller person.

Additional desirable features include a rain cover and a basket underneath for supplies and snacks. Some joggers now come with adjustable handlebars and speakers so you can play music from your digital player to entertain both yourself and the little one.

## TREADMILL

For new mothers, access to a treadmill can provide flexibility that is a saving grace as you adjust to life caring for an infant. While for many, being outdoors is fundamental to the salvation that running offers mothers, there are times when a treadmill is the only option. Once you own one, a treadmill in your home can feel like owning a microwave for the first time: How on earth did you ever get by without it? It is an expensive piece of equipment—and a heavy one—so the treadmill you buy and move in will need careful thought and planning. Buying a used treadmill will save you some money, but you must be careful of expired warranties and the mileage already on the machine. Be wary of equipment that was once housed in a health club, as these tend to be high-mileage (albeit sophisticated) machines.

When buying a treadmill, issues to consider include noise, power, size, and extra features. Start by planning where it will go, what that will mean for its use, and how much you can spend to be able to use it when you need to. Strategizing the location is key. Consider that the treadmill's noise likely means you can't have it in the same room where your kids will be watching TV, unless they wear headphones. Nor do you want it next to the home office if your partner can't work to the sound of feet slapping on the belt. Likewise, treadmills can get quite large and take up an entire room, so measure the space beforehand and be aware that the machine will look smaller in the store than in your home. A folding treadmill may seem appealing, but the decks and belts of folding treadmills can be flimsy.

You should test any treadmill before buying it. If you opt to buy one on eBay or Craigslist, be sure to try the same model in a store beforehand. You want to know how smoothly the belt moves, how loud the motor runs, and how you feel on it. Asking your running friends with children is another way to determine whether the model will collect dust in your basement because it is too loud or underperforming.

If you plan to use the treadmill while children are sleeping, prioritize the noise factor, especially because runners often need a more powerful motor.

Treadmills with aluminum frames generate more reverberation than do steel-framed treadmills, and DC motors tend to be quieter than AC motors. Be sure to test the treadmill when the store is not busy so you can hear the noise it generates, and when researching reviews of quiet treadmills, be sure to take note of how fast the reviewer was running on it. Place a rubber mat underneath when you set it up to minimize noise (and to increase the longevity of the machine by preventing dirt and dust from being sucked up into it).

Most treadmill motors range from 1.5 to 3.0 horsepower (HP), but a durable, quieter home treadmill will have a DC motor of at least 2.0 HP. If you will be doing some speed training or running faster paces, you will want a more powerful motor, and a less taxed motor is a quieter motor, so it should be a minimum of 2.5 HP for a runner.

Finally, after you buy the treadmill and set it up, consider the safety of your kids around it. Placing it in a room with a safety lock on the door is wise in a home with a small child. The treadmill should be unplugged when not in use, which also saves money and electricity. Many treadmills have a cord with a safety clip at one end for your own safety when you're running, but there are cases of children dying from strangulation when they find these cords, so detach it and store it up high when not in use.

## Chapter Summary

Being a new mom adds dimension to your athlete life, but it by no means prevents you from striving for your best performance and then meeting those goals. If anything, your baby makes you a stronger, fitter athlete. Nothing prepares you for the stamina demands of endurance sports like getting a baby safely and happily through the day. Knowing *your* body—not what Kara Goucher could do after she had her baby—is the first step in resuming your training base. Figure out your fueling needs and your breast-feeding schedule—not to mention the sleep intervals you can depend on—and then dig in to planning your workout type and intensity. The workout-family balance is less overwhelming when you can predict your body's needs to balance your daily mom life. In the next chapter, you'll read more on that balance and how your love of fitness benefits you and your family.

## TO REVIEW . . . THE DOCTOR'S NOTES

* Before resuming swimming, make sure your cervix has clamped back down to the point where a tampon will stay in. Any lacerations should heal before you swim in chlorine.

* Once you can walk for 20 minutes without bleeding, it's okay to resume a cardio and strength training program. Start with an easy jog or walk/run of 20 minutes.

* While cycling is safe, it might take some time before it is comfortable. If it hurts to sit on a bike, wait until the pain goes away before spinning.

* Nurse or pump milk prior to workouts to make the session more comfortable for you and to buy more time before you must return to feed the baby.

* Focus on effort level and duration instead of pace and distance for the first 4 to 6 weeks of workouts.

* Increase your workout duration or mileage by adding only 10 percent of the total weekly time or distance each week.

* Don't cram workouts into several consecutive days with several days off in between. This makes it harder for your muscles to recover and strengthen.

# At Home with Your Fit Self
*Striking the Workout-Family Balance*

WHEN BOBBI GIBB SECRETLY RAN the Boston Marathon incognito in 1966 as the first woman to complete the race, the *Boston Globe* lauded her as a housewife who broke barriers for women in endurance sports. A decade after her famous race, Bobbi had a baby and a law degree and was determined to keep running. At that time, she was a rarity. You'd see moms on the sidelines, rooting for their kids, but athlete moms were uncommon. Bobbi put her baby in an old-fashioned pram and ran it down the streets of her Massachusetts neighborhood—into a field outside her town. "I'd park the creaky pram and run in circles around it," she remembers. "People thought I was amazing but a little eccentric." While her baby slept in the carriage, Bobbi ran figure eights. "I even used to run in place if I had to." Bobbi's strength sums up our determination as 21st-century athlete moms. Raising her baby was the happiest time of her life, and sport was her passion. It didn't cross her mind to give it up; nor should you feel that you need to sacrifice your love of fitness or sport. Bobbi created conditions to run, showing that our fitness barriers can be dismantled and rebuilt like Legos: The wall becomes the road. Being an athlete mom can sometimes be a challenge, but it's absolutely worth it.

Fortunately, 21st-century athlete moms are well equipped to strike the workout-family balance. Bobbi had a pram, not a technical baby jogger, and without a gym nursery or a treadmill, she ran loops in a field. Today's moms have fun options, varied networks, and a culture that supports our passion for sport. Sure, there are times when guilt creeps up, but we can still craft a rewarding and successful life as athletes. What's more, we can answer that guilt with the knowledge that fitness is not an impediment to motherhood but rather a successful, fulfilling part of it.

This chapter gives you the practical guidance to maintain your fit motherhood and support your training success. You'll read how other athlete moms keep sport in their busy lives and how you can motivate your Fit Self to get going and keep going. In this chapter, you'll find:

   &#10051;   What's happening to my body?
   &#10051;   How to fuel your active family
   &#10051;   How to nurture a family life of fitness and health
   &#10051;   Ways to empower your Fit Self and inspire your kids
   &#10051;   Strategies for striking the workout-family balance

## What's Happening to My Body?

Now that you've recovered from the birth and are well established as your baby's mama, you might be facing the task of balancing dual roles as loving mom and independent athlete. Your parenting is in full swing, likely with a more predictable routine, and you are starting to get reacquainted with yourself and your training. There are a few key health issues that come into play as you adjust to training with your postpartum body. Specifically, staying mindful of your menstrual, bone, and breast health will give you a sound body and peace of mind.

### MENSTRUAL HEALTH

After a woman has a baby, it's common for her menstrual cycle to change, either becoming heavier or much lighter in flow, especially if she is very active or exercising so much that her body burns more fat than it needs to support her reproductive system. If your cycle becomes unpredictable, you can regulate your periods with the birth-control pill, which will also supplement low estrogen if your period is very light or missing.

If you're planning to have another baby, you can go off the pill and expect to get pregnant within a couple months of trying, though this span of time varies from woman to woman. Because you can become pregnant as soon as you start ovulating again, some women will conceive in a matter of weeks, whereas others may take more time. It isn't unusual for several months to go by after stopping the pill before you conceive, so consult your provider if you haven't become pregnant after 6 months of trying. It's a good idea to start taking folic acid as soon as you decide you'd like to have another baby because 2 months of additional folic acid in your system greatly reduces the risk of birth defects, such as spina bifida and autism. Take 400 mcg (0.4 mg) of folic acid daily prior to conception, then increase the dose to 600 to 800 mcg (0.6 to .08 mg) once you're pregnant.

## BONE HEALTH

Busy moms need to be sure to protect their bone strength, in particular, to prevent osteopenia and its corresponding disease, osteoporosis. Women achieve peak bone mass when they're 30, and breast-feeding babies combined with the aging process decreases your bone density. You can take care of your bones with both diet and exercise and take estrogen replacement through the birth-

**DOCTOR'S NOTE**

On top of a calcium-rich diet and weight-bearing exercise, you can **lower your risk for bone loss** by cutting back on caffeine (no more than 16 to 24 ounces of coffee per day), doing 10 minutes of daily yoga to improve balance and strength, and asking your doctor about a regular bone-density test.

control pill. After menopause, medications such as Fosamax will supplement your estrogen. Look to low-fat dairy sources, leafy greens, fortified juices, and cereals for the 1,000 mg of calcium you need every day to maintain bone strength. Vitamin D will also protect your bone strength; daily sources of vitamin D include a cup of fortified milk, egg yolk, 3 ounces of canned salmon and tuna, and 15 minutes of sun exposure (with sunscreen). Weight-bearing exercise complements a diet rich in calcium and vitamin D, so your active lifestyle of mixing cardio workouts with resistance training (e.g., light weights) will help to protect you from bone loss.

Research shows that athletes have higher bone density than do nonathletes, even when they engage in only 30 minutes of daily exercise. At the same time, athletes who train extensively can be hard on their bodies and often have low body fat, which can put women at risk for osteoporosis. If your doctor deems them necessary, bone-density tests will help you monitor any losses over the long term. If you show signs of osteopenia, or loss of bone density, you can build your bones with muscle strength using any of the resistance training exercises that appear earlier in this book.

## BREAST HEALTH

Even though you may have given your breasts more attention than ever before while breast-feeding, it's common to forget about breast exams after you wean your baby. In addition to the exam your doctor performs at your annual visit, conduct breast self-exams on a monthly basis. The shower is a great opportunity for uninterrupted time to conduct a breast exam to find lumps or new irregularities, such as a nipple that is inverted. If you find anything that seems new or different, consult your doctor. Many lumps are benign fatty deposits, but a visit with a doctor is the only way to determine whether further tests are needed. Don't ignore any changes you notice.

## Fueling: Nutrition for Active Moms and Families

As an active woman, you need to continue to focus on adequate hydration and your nutritional needs just as you did when your baby was in utero. It's imperative that you get high-quality foods that will provide you with a long-term energy source, as you must stay on your toes in your busy life. Although you may be concerned about losing pregnancy weight, do not neglect carbohydrates in favor of fad diets that center on one food group, such as high-protein/no-carb approaches. A diet that is heavily weighted away from carbohydrates won't sustain your energy for training, work, and family life. As a woman with an active lifestyle, seek balance in nutrition, particularly sufficient carbs, which provide glucose for energy. Inadequate energy from carbs can compromise your performance in training and races, as you need to replenish the glycogen stores your body burns during endurance efforts. In long workouts that exceed an hour, you'll want to replace 100 calories for every hour you exercise, through carb gels, chews, or any other easy-to-eat source of carbs, such as a granola bar.

Any weight-loss efforts should focus on balanced nutrition and energy for the demands of parenting and training. Don't rush into a restricted diet when your baby is under 6 months old and you're resuming workouts, especially if you're breast-feeding. A severely restricted diet or skipping meals will result in exhaustion and, ultimately, the inability to meet training goals. You need energy for your busy life, and a crash diet tends to be counterproductive, starting a cycle of yo-yo weight loss and gain. Be sensible and think in terms of a healthy, balanced lifestyle that is neither depleted of nor saturated with comfort food.

In general, your daily calorie intake should be 50 to 65 percent carbohydrates (4 calories per gram), 15 to 20 percent protein (4 calories per gram), and less than 25 percent from fat (9 calories per gram). For example, if you have a daily intake of 2,500 calories, you might strive for 1,375 from carbs (55 percent), 500 from protein (20 percent), and 625 from fat (25 percent). Alternatively, the USDA recommendations for a 2,400-calorie-per-day plan with 2.5 hours of exercise per week suggest the following daily distribution of grains, fruits and vegetables, dairy, and protein.

**8 1-ounce equivalents of grains, with half of these servings as whole grains. Examples of 1-ounce servings include:**
>1 slice whole-grain bread
>½ cup rice or pasta
>1 ounce cereal

**3 servings of vegetables, as many different colors as possible, with 1 serving equaling:**
>1 cup raw or cooked vegetables
>1 cup 100 percent vegetable juice
>2 cups leafy greens

**2 servings of fruit, with 1 serving equaling:**
>1 cup raw or cooked fruit
>½ cup dried fruit
>1 cup 100 percent fruit juice

**3 servings dairy, with 1 serving equaling:**
>1½ ounces natural cheese
>1 cup cow's milk or soy milk
>1 cup yogurt

**6½ ounces protein, with one serving equaling:**
>1 ounce lean meat
>1 egg
>1 tablespoon peanut butter
>¼ cup cooked beans

A sample menu for a day in the life of an athlete mom might look like this:

{ BREAKFAST }

 1 slice toast
 1 cup cereal with ½ to 1 cup milk
 1 banana
 1 hard-boiled egg

{ MIDMORNING SNACK }

 1 cup juice
 2 tablespoons peanut butter on 2 slices whole-wheat bread

{ LUNCH }

 Leafy salad with 2 cups greens, ¼ cup chickpeas or other beans,
    1½ ounces cheese, and 1 cup mixed raw vegetables in many
    different colors, plus 1 ounce (fist size) grilled chicken if desired
 Toasted whole-wheat pita bread with 1 tablespoon olive oil for dipping

{ AFTERNOON SNACK }

 1 cup yogurt
 1 small/minibagel with 3 to 4 tablespoons hummus

{ DINNER }

 2 ounces grilled salmon
 ½ to 1 cup cooked brown rice
 8 ounces (1 cup) grilled asparagus spears drizzled with olive oil
 1 cup strawberries dipped in dark or bittersweet chocolate

## FAMILY FITNESS IN THE KITCHEN

Your time in the kitchen is a great opportunity to begin to teach your growing family about nutrition, healthy balance, and food as fuel. While a baby or toddler won't comprehend the relationship between burning and replacing fuel, it's never too early to model that food isn't only something we put in our mouths because we're bored. If you talk openly about how your body needs food for energy, your young child will develop a healthy relationship with food and learn that eating isn't taboo. Then, when your toddler is older and sees you eating a bowl of cereal at 4:00 p.m., it will be more clear that you aren't "ruining your dinner" with a snack. With older children, you can give the simple explanation that bodies burn food the way a car uses gas; food fuels our activity, and we need to replace the calories we burn with exercise throughout the day. No matter what, don't talk about dieting around your kids or discuss your weight when they're present; kids benefit from learning about various foods as energy sources, but fat talk doesn't do anyone any good.

About 6 months after his or her birth, you'll be helping your baby adjust to solid foods by introducing easily digestible options. Try whole-grain oatmeal or iron-fortified rice cereal, as these meals are easy to digest and known to lower the risk of food allergies when introduced at this age. And because cereals are so simple, you'll be able to cook for yourself without adding a lot of time prepping something separate for your baby.

Also at the 6-month point, you can introduce other foods, such as whole-grain breads (mashed), pureed meats, fruits, and vegetables, starting with sweeter options (breast milk is quite sweet) such as bananas, yams, and sweet potatoes. If you've been breast-feeding, your milk's zinc and iron content will drop at about this point, and so incorporating varied sources of nutrition into

**TRAINING TIP** A quick way to refuel after vigorous exercise is by drinking a glass of chocolate milk; you can achieve the same benefits with soy, almond, or cow's milk. The milk contains protein, and the chocolate will replace your carbs (as will the milk). It's an easy and convenient treat to replenish yourself after a workout, when your attention turns back to your baby.

your baby's diet, including meats, will replace those lost nutrients. Wait until your baby is 9 to 12 months old, however, before serving citrus fruits, wheat, and corn. Dairy products are best saved for a baby who is 1 year old.

As a busy athlete and mom, you can save time by preparing the same foods for everyone. With a food processor, you'll be able to mash your vegetables to a consistency that your baby can eat, too. This enables you to save money, provide foods without preservatives, and control the ingredients in your baby's meals. You'll be able to offer a wider variety of foods to your baby than is available in jars—good luck finding pre-made jars of mashed guava. And by including your baby in the family diet, he or she will adjust more quickly to eating the same meals as everyone else in your family. In your baby's first year, he or she is more likely to accept the foods you like—before the pickiness sets in—so this is a chance to reduce the workload in the kitchen. If you crave that guava at lunch after a workout, your baby can enjoy it, too.

Preparing a different dinner for each person in the house is expensive and exhausting, and you don't need to be a short-order cook to satisfy yourself, your partner, and your baby. If you make a pot of stew or a casserole, you can puree each of the components for the baby: vegetable, dairy, protein, and starch.

If you want to stock up on different options for your baby, particularly if you're using a nanny or babysitter, you can cut down on the time it takes to make your own baby food by steaming and mashing a selection of foods and using ice-cube trays to premeasure and prepare in bulk. Puree the foods with a bit of liquid to keep them palatable, and freeze or refrigerate anything you make.

When it's time to feed the baby, warm anything you've stored in the fridge and allow it to cool before serving.

## ORGANIZING YOUR FIT KITCHEN

The key to a fit kitchen is organization. Try writing a menu for the week that takes activities and schedules into account and will help prevent five trips to the store by Friday. In addition, keep one cumulative grocery list going throughout the week to take with you on shopping day. A master grocery list will expedite your grocery trip and, like your menu, it reduces the number of times you need to go to the store. You can also order your groceries online to be delivered, or simply order the standard supplies you always need (diapers, wipes, milk, eggs) if you like to pick out your own meat and produce. In warmer

{ **TIMESAVER TIP** }

Tools and gadgets can make meal preparation faster or easier when you live a busy and active lifestyle:

- **Pressure cooker:** cooks meat quickly without your involvement while keeping the meat tender
- **Slow cooker:** allows you to "set it and forget it" during your busy day
- **Electric grill:** cooks meat quickly with a nonstick surface that drains the fat
- **Juicer:** encourages a diet of fresh, raw fruits and vegetables that you can eat on the go
- **Handheld electric blender:** makes soups and smoothies quickly with little cleanup
- **Baby food processor:** steams and purees baby food for convenient one-step preparation
- **Mandolin for chopping raw vegetables:** cuts large quantities of vegetables in fun shapes

months, consider joining a produce co-op so you'll have a steady supply of vegetables each week. These programs sometimes even deliver your weekly cartons of produce.

To the extent that you can, include your growing baby in your time spent in the kitchen, even if it's just bouncing in a swing while you cook. When you talk to your baby during kitchen time, talk about what you're doing and why. You may be explaining food groups and vitamins in the simplest terms with a cooing voice, but your baby will develop an understanding of food as fuel over time. A baby who learns the language of healthy, balanced meals will develop a lexicon of nutrition that lasts.

## Empowering Your Fit Self

As a mom, you have many competing demands on your energy and time. Fortunately, athlete moms quickly learn that confident multitasking is key to feeling capable and covering our bases.

It's important to feel empowered as an athlete mom, whether in training or on race day. Although a new body and a different shape can feel discouraging, you can create a strong mind-body perspective that not only will carry you through workouts and races but also will fuel your sense of calm determination when you face multiple life demands at once.

Here are some strategies that will help empower you to achieve fitness and training success as you multitask your way through fit motherhood:

* Scale your goals
* Focus on the positive
* Model self-empowerment

### SCALE YOUR GOALS

Although busy athlete moms face unpredictable challenges and training disruptions, they can still achieve positive fitness outcomes or a successful race. Even if your child contracts a head cold and passes it on to you, or work takes away your hour to lift at the gym, you can find success by creating a list of scaled goals, being patient with yourself, and staying flexible. Setting goals for yourself is a great motivator for your postpartum return to workouts and training, and even lofty goals, such as a marathon or a yoga-teacher certification by your baby's first birthday, are fine. Ambitious goals are a way for you to grasp your own independence and create an identity that's separate from motherhood. So don't shy away from imagining and then planning a concrete, explicit, and reasonable path to get there, either on your own or with the help of a coach or trainer.

When approaching goals of any size, remember to be flexible and patient with yourself as you strive to meet them. With children and other responsibilities, you will often be tired, and unforeseen limitations can challenge your best intentions for training. Set a list of goals, but leave the timeline open for meeting them and be patient with yourself throughout training. It's crucial to recognize how your life and priorities will change as your family grows and to release pressure on yourself to workout if you're facing stress. Take care of yourself, whether it's through training for new records and goals or accepting yourself where you are.

To empower yourself in mind and body, remember to pick goals that promote strength and action, not how you look or what size you wear. While it can certainly feel good to lose weight or fit into prepregnancy jeans, the feeling of strength from accomplishing a race or event is a long-lasting boost to your sense of personal power. Not to mention, those types of *appearance* goals are often met on the way to meeting an *accomplishment* goal. It's important to accept your body for the things it can do—having a baby, among them—while you also seek to accomplish new personal records and goals. Your body's form should be a badge of motherhood, not a source of discouragement.

At the same time, you can pick a few goals of different types, such as a race combined with training your way to a 3-minute plank pose. That approach will help you prevent injuries with a multifaceted training plan, tone and strengthen

TRAINING TIP Choose goals that focus on accomplishments rather than appearance, and stick to two or three ambitions that won't overwhelm you, such as a weekly yoga class, volunteering at a race or other event, or trying a new race distance.

## GOAL-SETTING: BUILDING YOUR SCAFFOLD TO SUCCESS

Establish a hierarchy of goals to scale your accomplishments and ensure a rewarding experience. For instance, if you are fairly new to running, pick a big goal to motivate your running, and then formulate a few subgoals to foster success:

- Goal A: Run the entire 5K
- Goal B: Run/walk the race
- Goal C: Complete the race, walking or running

If you're an experienced athlete, scale your goals more competitively. For example, maybe you want to achieve a half-Ironman to celebrate weaning your baby. You might scale your goals like this:

- Goal A: Place in age group, overall
- Goal B: Finish under 5.25 hours
- Goal C: Place in age group in bike
- Goal D: Set a personal best in bike
- Goal E: Finish 70.3 miles!

To create a scaffold for your success as an athlete mom, choose a few goals for yourself. Make some of the goals ambitious and others easily doable. Consider consulting a trainer or coach to assist you with creating your list of goals for the next 6 months or 1 year, with either a training plan or an ongoing partnership.

your core, and give you a public event where you can achieve a celebratory medal. Don't be overzealous with creating a list of multiple goals; two or three will give you variety without overwhelming you or your schedule. If you can find goals that require a formal registration, such as classes, workshops, and races, you'll be more likely to see them through.

*[Before having a baby,] if I had a bad workout, it would eat at me. I don't obsess over the little things anymore. I come home and I don't think about it at all. I only think about Colt. It's been really good for me. It's mellowed me out.*[1]

KARA GOUCHER | U.S. OLYMPIC MARATHON RUNNER AND MOM OF COLT

## FOCUS ON THE POSITIVE

For most of us, being a successful athlete mom involves setting goals, crafting plans, and training to the best of our ability. When you feel frustrated by the changes in your lifestyle, it's important to stay positive toward yourself as an athlete and a mother. Remind yourself often why you love the experience of sport and fitness, and try to see each workout and race as a chance to connect with that passion. Remember to be kind to yourself—as forgiving and encouraging as you would be to a friend or your children. We're usually much harder on ourselves than on others, so when you're feeling low or disappointed, ask yourself, "What would I say to a friend?" Then say it to your Fit Self.

Training yourself to focus on the positive is like finding the perfect sports bra: It's about how you support yourself, often through trial and error. It's common to feel overwhelmed as a busy mom, but don't let stress demolish your self-confidence, training, or sense of efficacy. Use different tricks for maintaining a centered positive outlook, such as:

* Find a guided yoga session on iTunes or YouTube or through an app on your phone.
* Visualize inspirational images (such as your family cheering at the finish line).
* Plan to cross the line with your baby in your arms.
* Take a day off to recover and rest after a tough workout or race.
* Be patient, understanding, and flexible with your training.
* Use any frustration as fuel for your workouts.
* Jot down why you love sport, training, or races to reset your frame of mind.

If your thoughts turn negative, picture the unconditional love you get from your children and family and the empowerment you feel from fitness. Bad self-talk interferes in your training and your fitness and is basically a waste of energy that would be better used for kicking butt in workouts. Alter your negative thinking so that you see it as an opportunity to meet a challenge and a chance to consider the value you have to your family and in multiple other aspects of your life.

## MODEL SELF-EMPOWERMENT

Training and fitness permeate a family for the betterment of everyone. What sport gives to women passes to the kids in spades. Children learn from their moms how to strive for goals and how health and fitness enrich life. While medals and cute clothes are nice perks of an athletic lifestyle, the most valuable medal comes from the ways that an active motherhood models self-empowerment for your family. They see you as a successful athlete because your striving, perseverance, and performance teach them about being a strong individual.

Research shows that moms who exercise in pregnancy and early infancy tend to have more active children,[2] and parents who value exercise and fitness in their own lives tend to have older kids who are more active, too.[3] Kids pick up on our behaviors and emulate what they see us doing and saying, so much so that children who think their parents are inactive tend to demonstrate lower cardio fitness themselves,[4] which means that kids benefit from involvement in their moms' fitness.

Modeling the mind-body benefits of sport to your kids—beginning in the womb—creates the best kind of domino effect. Training will create a win-win

*❝ I want to make [my children] proud. I want to do it as a mom.... As an athlete specifically, I feel like they've made me tougher. I am determined to be the best I can be so I can be a great example for them.[5]*

KERRI WALSH JENNINGS | THREE-TIME OLYMPIC GOLD
MEDALIST IN BEACH VOLLEYBALL AND MOM OF JOEY, SUNDANCE, AND SCOUT

dynamic for everyone in the house because you feel good, and children learn the connection between fitness and happiness. Your kids will inherit your fitness practice even if they don't take up the same sport. Your son might show little interest in running for running's sake, but maybe he loves to bike for miles while you run next to him. Health habits are part of his lexicon, and mind-body fitness is a popular topic.

Many moms want their daughters, especially, to benefit from their own love of sports. We tend to see boys as naturally predisposed to active lifestyles, but daughters need encouragement to pursue sport, too. As athlete moms, we know that it's not about being skinny, it's about feeling good about what your body can do. When daughters see their mothers doggedly pursuing goals for themselves, they learn what it means to feel strong and to work out for health more than for a dress size.

Even if you prefer to separate your training and racing from family life, the strength you embody and the value for activity you exhibit will trickle down. Heather, an attorney and new mom, was determined to return to running as much as possible and to bring Sophie along. As much as running filled her own needs as an individual, it was important to her that Sophie see her taking care of herself. "It will hopefully help Sophie to have a better self-image because she sees Mom can be proud of her body and take care of her body and do this."

**TRAINING TIP** Involve your kids in your passion for sport by going for a run while they ride their bikes, and model a love of sport by bringing them to watch your races.

To model and empower your fit family, try these simple options for your play time:

- Involve your kids in some of your races. Push the baby in the jogger (when permitted by the event), or sign up older kids for a tot trot or the fun run associated with your longer race.

- Create a "science experiment" to test simple exercise science, such as the time it takes to run up versus down a hill or how long it takes to run a lap around the perimeter of your house.

- Do yoga with your kids, who will love the animal names and contortions involved.

- Create a scavenger hunt that requires kids to run between challenges or a treasure hunt as part of a hike in the woods, challenging them to find objects of different colors, shapes, and sizes.

- Exercise with your children. For example, go to a track and chase each other or practice fun activities such as the standing long jump or triple jump.

- Use a bike chariot to visit friends so you get a workout before and after a play date.

- Roll a tennis or other ball across your yard and "race" your kids in sprints to get the ball.

- Learn a sport together that you've never tried, such as tennis or ice skating.

## Mastering the Workout-Family Balance

When it comes to striking the workout-family balance, good shoes and good friends certainly cushion the impact of life as a mom and an athlete, helping us to keep perspective and enjoy the ride. How can we strike the balance? Focus on:

- \* Understanding the many reasons you stay fit
- \* Staying motivated
- \* Creating structure
- \* Adapting when necessary
- \* Building support networks

## PRIORITIZING STAYING FIT

A stay-at-home mom of two boys, Renae says that one of her prime motivations for training is that she doesn't want her brain to turn to oatmeal. Before running, she went through the day "one foot after the other," feeling lethargic and low. She says she felt a little trapped in the day-in, day-out responsibilities of caring for home and family. Having always admired runners, Renae decided to join a local boot camp to get in shape. When she found herself struggling just to run a quarter mile, she started running between sessions. She wanted to complete a 5K; that was all. A year later, Renae had done two half-marathons. Six months after that, she ran her first marathon, and within a couple of years, she qualified for the Boston Marathon.

To see Renae now, an athlete mom who strikes the workout-family balance every day, it's hard to imagine her without joy on her face. Her race photos show a strong athlete with obvious pure bliss, even at mile 17 of a marathon or waist-deep in swamp water during an adventure race. Once an introvert who was hesitant to try unfamiliar activities, Renae explains that she has gained new confidence and energy from running. When she feels guilty for taking the time for workouts, she reminds herself what sport does for her as a mom, and also for her family.

Even elite athletes who get paid to compete and train feel some guilt over it.[6] But there is a mental edge that being an athlete gives to moms, as Renae illustrates, which we can tap to get the initiative to train when the workout-family balance is daunting. Remind yourself that you are a better mother *because* you take care of your own strength. If you perceive your physical fitness as a component of your strength as a mother, it's harder to push a workout aside.

Michelle Simmons is a 10-time Ironman finisher, endurance coach, sales rep, and mother of 3-year-old Moana. Within 2 weeks of having Moana, Michelle surprised many athletes she knew by showing up for a swim workout at the pool. "I needed to get back to it," she remembers. She'd missed the intensity of her workouts as well as the camaraderie. As Michelle sees it, her choice to get back to her training was a simple reflection of her priorities. She skips evening TV and goes to bed early, knowing she needs the rest to train and be a mom to Moana.

Michelle works creatively to schedule her training early in the morning or with babysitting help from friends, and her husband supports her priorities. She coaches other moms to elevate the status of fitness and training in their lives and to make those things a priority the same way they prioritize their children's or spouse's activities. That way, their own needs are much less likely to be sacrificed.

## STAYING MOTIVATED

We know why we feel good when we train and want it to be a priority, but sometimes we just can't translate that into action. You've found your time slot and your shoes, but where did you put your initiative? When your motivation has temporarily gone missing, you can train yourself to get moving anyway by attaching the behavior to an extrinsic goal when the intrinsic motivation isn't there.

Sometimes we need to add on layers of motivation. Make it about more than just the activity. Look for a meaningful payoff, such as achieving a big distance, giving to charity, or honoring a loved one. If you really want to challenge yourself when you pick your payoff, look for goals that will hold you accountable, such as a race that requires charity fund-raising or any performance that is public. Name a goal that is hard but not so daunting that you'll give up on it. Easy goals are convenient to slough off because you can afford to miss workouts, and impossible goals are easy to slough off because you're intimidated and give up. Find the right level of challenge in your goals by recruiting a friend to join you in the training and consulting a coach or trainer.

Remind yourself that you will feel better physically and mentally from the effort; that reminder can help get you up in the morning or energize you at night. As Michelle tells the athletes she coaches when they're prone to procrastinating, remind yourself that very few moms return from a workout feeling worse than before they left. Whether or not you hit a runner's high, you've

*Running makes me feel like I have a secret weapon. I am empowered.*
*I am not weak.*　　　　　　　　　　　　　TRACY | TRIATHLETE AND MOTHER OF FOUR

achieved the fitness equivalent of an oil change—draining the mental and physical junk and refilling with the opiates of training and muscle-building lactate. So when you're dragging your feet, prioritize the aftereffect over the "before" feeling.

## CREATING STRUCTURE

As new moms, we quickly find out that familiar schedules help build confidence and security in our kids. Knowing what to expect from everyday life is a pretty big deal. In the same way, we often depend on forecasts, training plans, and routes that don't throw surprises at us when we're training. When you review a course before you race it, you have a known entity. Being an athlete and a mom means sometimes leaning heavily on organization and structure so you don't feel like life is a free-for-all. Simply put, it's a good idea to structure yourself in training in the same way you would create a predictable routine for your child.

Once you nail down a goal, come up with a plan. Jumping into training with a vague idea of what you want to do can derail you or leave you without accountability. Because an athlete-mom life requires balance, it also requires creative organization. Start with a training plan—if possible, one that a coach customizes to your life. The challenge, the priority, and the accountability are your arsenal against inactivity.

A mother of four children under 12, Tracy describes the importance of keeping a disciplined schedule: "I think the one thing would be consistency—I try to maintain a schedule with running just as I help the kids understand about being

*My biggest tool is the kitchen calendar. We put everything on it for the day, so the kids kind of know who's doing what when and what they can expect.*

CATHERINE | TRIATHLETE AND MOM OF THREE

consistent—with homework, bedtime, helping around the house, [and] brushing their teeth."

Once you've got a plan, here are some ways to keep yourself on track:

* A great way to stay accountable is to tie your fitness calendar to a log (see Table 8.1). On one line of a spreadsheet calendar, write down your workout goal for each day of the week. On the lines below it, record what you actually did as well as any comments about the workout. Post the calendar on your wall at home or at work, or use an online forum that's visible to others. There's nothing like making your workouts public to motivate you.
* Put your workout times on the family calendar, in ink. Your training is an important task, and everyone should know it.
* Review your plan at the beginning of every week to confirm with yourself that you have childcare covered as well as any chores that might force you to bump a workout. Check the forecast and shift things around if, for example, a major storm falls on a day you'd planned to swim 2 miles.
* Find a training partner, and after a successfully completed cycle of 3 to 4 weeks, toast your fabulous life management skills over coffee or a glass of wine.
* Respect lists. They will keep your training and race gear organized and remind you to grab your timing chip when you're distracted by the details of being a mom.
* Set your workout clothes next to your bed before you go to sleep, and set the alarm on your mobile phone—across the bedroom. Don't let yourself hide from your training just because you're groggy or it's dark outside.

*" Running and motherhood have a lot of similarities. You have to get up early and often, you have to do it even when you don't want to, and most of all you don't get paid for this, but in the end it's worth it.*

MARCY | DISTANCE RUNNER AND MOM OF KEIRA AND CAMERON

Holding yourself accountable to your workout priority makes it a routine, not an indulgence in some me time. The structure reinforces and validates what you're doing. It's who you are: a hard-core athlete-mom. Make it matter by structuring your life to hold it and using a Sharpie to make it permanent.

## ADAPTING WHEN NECESSARY

When our kids get bored with an activity, we come up with something new for them to do. Workout schedules need variation, too; it makes athletes stronger and faster and prevents injury and stagnation. Even if you're satisfied with your regular route and routine, your training plan can be invigorated by adding some minor changes. Throw in a miniadventure to a new trail or part of town to stimulate your brain, taking you out of your comfort zone and regular stomping ground.

When a toddler decides one day that he absolutely will not sit in the grocery cart without screaming for a foster parent to rescue him, you'll probably let him out of the seat to cruise the frozen foods for a bit. A hug, a talk, and, when necessary, a cookie can mean the difference between a shopping trip in war or peace. The same goes for your workout. When you have a baby, you can't hold rigidly to your plan. Backup options and a motivating cookie are going to be your saving grace.

The key to making variation work when Plan A backfires is having a backup plan in place. Draft a quick list of options you can turn to when you can't get to your scheduled training session, such as a strength building DVD workout, 20 to 30 minutes of plyometric drills in your yard during the baby's nap, or a run over your lunch break at work. Think outside the box, and be willing to do alternative activities. You might hate doing squats and planks, but they're great total-body strengthening options when you're in a pinch. There are times when a treadmill or bike trainer can feel like our mail-order soulmates, but even without those

**TABLE 8.1** Logging Your Progress During a Training Week

| MON | TUES | WED | THURS | FRI | SAT | SUN | TOTAL |
|---|---|---|---|---|---|---|---|
| **12 WEEKS TO RACE** | | | | | | | |
| Off | Track: 1-mile warm-up ——— 5x 1mile at 10K pace ——— ½ mile recovery jogs ——— 1-mile cooldown | Spin 1 hour with heart rate monitor | Tempo run at lunch | 90-min. yoga class | Marathon pace | Easy trail run | — |
| **GOAL MILES** | | | | | | | |
| 0 | 9 | 20 | 5 | 0 | 10 | 6 | 50 |
| **ACTUAL MILES** | | | | | | | |
| 0 | 8 | 24 | 5 | 0 | 10 | 8 | 55 |
| **WORKOUT NOTES** | | | | | | | |
| — | No time for cooldown | Rode with friends before work; got lost and added 4 miles | Done as planned | Missed yoga but did 30-min. online yoga sequence after the kids went to bed. | Done as planned | Beautiful day— couldn't stop! | Nailed this week! |

> *Quite simply, I probably wouldn't still be running if it weren't for my friends who run.*
>
> CINDI | DISTANCE RUNNER AND MOM OF CHARLIE

*I'm pretty focused and organized with most things I do. I am the same with running and parenting. I think things through, plan them, and then go with the flow of what eventually happens, which is rarely the exact run I planned or exact activity the kids and I set out to do. Rolling with the punches is a life skill, and it shows up in running and at home.*

REBECCA | DISTANCE RUNNER AND MOM OF ADAM AND AUGGIE

options, you can think creatively and do whatever you can on the days when things are thrown out of whack, adapting your next high-quality workout to make up for the lost training.

## BUILDING SUPPORT NETWORKS

Like a roaming support group, a band of athlete-moms becomes a means of accountability, motivation, counsel, healthy competition, and even babysitting. When Michelle had Moana, she made a point of tracking down other running and biking moms—sometimes while they were working out—to set up a network of athletes who needed support and childcare to make their training possible. On top of the practical help that other moms can give, finding a like-minded group will validate your training priority and your desire to take the time to workout. Michelle set up a babysitting co-op to help each other get quality training without worrying about childcare. Each mom watches the kids one day while the others do what they need to do—bike, run, swim.

There are also online networks that help to organize running and training groups, such as Moms in Motion, which reports more than 5,800 members in 49 states and 5 countries. Andrea Vincent's social network, seeMOMMYrun.com,

TRAINING TIP  Don't feel wedded to one sport or type of event. By taking a cardio class at a gym, you get a rigorous whole-body workout in an hour that is fun, driven by music, and a quality activity for your whole body in the company of other people. Try a kick or groove class, Zumba, or even pole dancing.

## CONNECTING WITH OTHER ATHLETE MOMS

- *Third trimester:* Consult your physician, who can be an excellent resource for putting you in touch with other new moms. Ask him or her to share your contact information with other patients who may be interested.

- *Two weeks postpartum:* Visit online networks that focus on women athletes. These networks help you form or join a group; offer training plans; and provide a consistent, dependable source of motivation and information.

- *Six weeks postpartum:* Sign up for a race to benefit a charity. Team in Training and Race for a Cure are two of the largest organizations. Large programs often host events to connect you with others or organize group runs, where you can meet your teammates.

- *Eight weeks postpartum:* Join a local running, cycling, swimming, or triathlon club. Most such organizations are welcoming to new members of all levels and provide countless opportunities for training, socializing, and advice from fellow athletes.

now boasts more than 40,000 members and more than 4,000 groups. Members run together and use each other for accountability and motivation, not to mention a sounding board for struggles with a new baby.

Hooking up with other athlete-moms can be key to sticking to your training plan so you can meet your goals. And a training partner who is a mother will make a big difference, too. Of course there are wonderful workout friends who are men or nonparents, but a compatriot mom will get you in a different way. You don't have to do every session together, and it's entirely possible that you can provide support to each other without ever meeting in person, but another mom with a fitness interest can be a lifesaver. These women understand your athlete identity, your parenting struggles, and the importance of what you're doing. Other athlete moms can help you through some of the stress of juggling your sport and your baby while also providing care, encouragement, and practical advice on everything from strollers to a classy spot for an Ironman tattoo. And they know how important your training is to you.

Regardless of where you join a group—at the gym, online, or casually with play-group friends—don't feel intimidated about showing up. One of the most rewarding aspects of adult sport is that it is only as competitive as you want it to be. You will probably never be the fastest athlete in the world, but the odds are pretty good that you're not the slowest, either. No matter what, you're faster than the people sitting on the couch. Group sessions are rarely competitive events; in general, group workouts are times of camaraderie, not cutthroat competition.

## High-Quality Training with New Technology

Moms juggling fitness and parenting want training that's as efficient as possible because they don't have time for wasted training or junk miles that don't serve a direct goal. Thanks to new technology, there are now many ways to cultivate high-quality training time through apps you install on your phone or websites to log workouts with social components. These tools can be essential for keeping yourself on track with a plan and some personal encouragement from a team or trainer. They'll help you focus and organize your workouts to promote the best quality for every session.

Apps for your phone or tablet can help you save time, keep you from getting lost, and even remind you to work out when you're distracted, procrastinating, or glued to an office chair. For example, when you're running with a stroller, you don't want to find yourself lost with a baby who has a limited attention span for the outing. No mom wants her baby to finish a Zwieback cookie when she has no idea where they are! Not only do GPS and data-driven apps help you track your distance, speed, and elevation; they can also enable you to chart a course and follow a map for a workout on the road or trail that's a known entity before you head out. As an added benefit of compiling data with GPS, these apps can chart your progress over months or years and let you make comparisons with your friends' routes and data. Such logs also enable social motivation and incentive by posting your workout results to your Twitter and Facebook contacts, if you like, or by sending you encouraging texts from your friends while you're working out. You can use GPS apps for biking, running, hiking, and even skiing. Well-reviewed options in this category include Cyclemeter, Runtastic, and Edomondo.

The social motivators for training can't be underestimated for new moms, and many fitness apps center specifically on this element. Not only do they provide the user with both diet and workout programs, but each program includes a social component by using teams and discussion groups for motivation, accountability, and advice. If you're looking for friendly competition to go with your customized workout, you can get that, too, by comparing your progress to that of others at the same level of fitness. Runners, in particular, have sites that help them join other moms in online training plans and in-person local running groups. If you have a race in mind, you can connect with a local or national team of other moms in training for specific endurance events (running, walking, triathlon) and participate in motivational discussion groups for information on a variety of subjects that matter to athlete moms—from sports bras to smoothies. Apps and web sites for social athletes include SparkPeople, the Nike Women Training Club, seeMOMMYrun, and Moms in Motion.

If you want an app that will provide more instruction and coaching than social motivation, there are virtual personal training options that are great for 21st-century moms. Many of us are too busy with work and family obligations to meet with a trainer, especially if we have to train in the early hours of the morning. Virtual trainers meet the need for flexibility without sacrificing an individually tailored program that gives you exactly what you need and want in a training plan. You might not get a coach yelling in your ear to drop and give him 20, but your phone will still let your trainer keep tabs on your workouts and progress, checking in on you so you can't slack off. In the same vein, you can even download a virtual yoga teacher who uses your skill level and time available to generate a custom yoga workout, which is ideal for busy moms with only a few minutes to pose per day. Personal coaching apps and sites match you with a human trainer who will even tailor your workouts to a nutrition plan, adjusted whenever you both decide it's necessary. Examples of these programs include FitOrbit and Yogatailor.

Moms who are primarily concerned with managing diet and nutrition also have options that will track calories against their exercise. When you're busy and distracted by your baby's needs, it can be hard to keep tabs on what you're eating and drinking, so leaving that to your phone is one way to stay accountable without obsessing. Apps such as Daily Burn will track both exercise and diet in one program by logging your workouts against the calories you eat. You can even pay better attention to your fluid consumption with reminders from an app, such as Water Log. A friendly chime reminding you to drink water is perfect for when you're pregnant, nursing, or too busy to remember to drink your eight glasses every day.

Similarly, moms who are so busy that they have trouble logging one longer workout can find apps that remind them to get up and move for several minutes throughout the day, wherever they are. If your day gets away from you or you are balancing a job with family responsibilities, there are days when an hour in the gym feels impossible. Fortunately, there are apps that offer more than 1,000 exercises for various target areas, using objects you have around the house or office so that you don't need gym equipment. Some even include exercises specific to women's main postpartum target areas—core, thighs, and hips—reminding you to get up and move in several installments throughout the day and to accumulate as many minutes of activity per day as you wish. Fitness Buddy and Break Pal are just two examples of the apps in this category.

## Focus on Health and Wellness

As moms, we tend to orient ourselves to our children's health and safety; however, it's crucial that we attend to our health needs, too. Often we put our own health on the back burner, and as athletes, many of us are adept at ignoring symptoms and signs of pain. It's important to take care of ourselves—self-care makes us fitter as women and as moms.

### REST AND RECOVERY

As you rebuild your fit lifestyle, get as much rest as you can. Rest and recovery periods are essential ingredients in an effective training program because your body actually becomes stronger during its downtime. When you feel like you're going a mile a minute, take time for yourself by meditating (in the shower if you're tight on time) with deep, mindful breaths and doing your best to get enough sleep. When your kids nap, don't be shy about napping with them if possible. It's a chance to connect with your children and to rest at the same time.

When you look at your training schedule and strive for a certain number of days per week—3, 4, 6, or whatever your calendar permits—gear your fitness time to high-quality effort and a recovery cycle.

* Increase the quality by alternating intervals of higher exertion with recovery periods rather than slogging through your miles at the same pace.
* Not every workout should be hard-core. Alternate a high-intensity workout day with a day of an easier effort or a day off.
* Strive for negative splits on every workout to train your brain to increase exertion when you face fatigue. Start the workout at an easier effort than you finish it.

* Use a high-octane spin or aerobics class to accommodate baby needs with childcare at the gym rather than going for a more leisurely 2-hour session.
* Incorporate yoga or stretching into your time with your baby or toddler so you can devote more of your solo workout time to activity you can't perform with your baby around.

## RESPONDING TO INJURIES

As moms and athletes, we may dismiss how our bodies feel moment to moment, hoping that a twinge will take care of itself, or we may just get distracted by the millions of other things going on around us that demand our attention. When you get back from a workout, it's easy to blow off that pain in your left quad because the baby is crying for you, a client has left you six voicemail messages, or David Beckham is on the *Today Show*. To prevent this from happening, pay attention to the first whine your body makes, remember it, and adapt to the situation.

When you don't accommodate minor physical protests, your body often adapts anyway, overcompensating for damage and then developing a second problem in a different spot. As moms, we don't need long to learn that buying a toy when we're running errands with a bored and fussing child is a short-term response that has a lasting impact: The next time we're off to the post office, a new toy is expected, or we must pay the consequences. In other words, the response prolongs the problem.

Instead of compensating like this, pay immediate attention and respond in a proactive, rather than reactive, way. It is often hard to determine when we should push through the pain or cut a workout short because the appeal of sports—and the idea of stamina—can be conquering discomfort. Ask yourself a few questions to help you adapt to the problem:

* Has this pain happened before? What was your response? What was the outcome?
* When did it start?
* Has it gotten worse over time?

To adapt to the problem, you have some options, depending on what the issue is:

* If it's minor or goes away during a workout, research the area of trouble and incorporate a few daily stretches and strength exercises that target the problem spot.
* If it's moderate or getting worse with every workout (or over the course of a single workout), take at least 2 days off that activity before trying an easy or modified version (shorter in duration or distance).
* If the problem persists after a few rest days or while you're laying off the painful activity, experiment with crosstraining options that won't aggravate the problem, such as water jogging, the elliptical, or the arc trainer.

Reassess your goals in response to an injury—and be okay with doing that. When your body courts injury and seems unwilling to cooperate, it more or less throws a tantrum—familiar to those of us who have hauled a fighting toddler with spaghetti limbs from a playground. Respond to your body the way you'd respond to your little one: Adapt to the situation without panic or stubbornness. You'll get back on track after you recover from the setback by referring back to your priorities and motivations, your scheduling and organization, and with the support of the athletes in your circle.

## Chapter Summary

As much as athlete moms swear by sport to preserve their sanity, they'll be honest and tell you it isn't all medals and endorphins. Returning to goal-driven training after a baby can make you feel like a rookie, but it's all about perspective.

There will be a feeling of newness, and in some ways that's liberating. When you can't even go to the bathroom alone for a couple of minutes, the freedom to be *all by yourself* without interruption to work out can feel like someone has let you off your leash.

How you think about training matters as much as what you actually do to work out. We might get down on ourselves after frustrating days when we're not performing as we'd expected 9 months after labor. But the dividends of an athletic life for mothers far outweigh the disappointments. Just like the deep breaths we take to cope with a day when the baby acts like a little dictator, we need to dig deep and rely on some firm self-talk to prioritize, structure, and adapt to the unpredictability of life as an athlete mom. The workout-family balance might be overwhelming, but most athlete moms will tell you that the endurance challenges of pregnancy, motherhood, and training form the embodied whole of who they are.

## TO REVIEW . . . THE DOCTOR'S NOTES

- After the baby is born, ask your doctor when to schedule your annual gynecological exam so you won't forget to keep that routine appointment.

- Look for variety in your workouts to help you adapt to schedule changes and prevent injury with diverse training options.

- The menstrual cycle can change after having a baby, so don't worry if it's lighter or heavier. You can take the birth-control pill to regulate your period and replenish your estrogen if you aren't menstruating at all.

- If osteoporosis runs in your family or you're concerned about bone loss, ask your doctor about periodic bone-density tests that can track your bone loss over the long term.

- If you'd like to get pregnant again, you can go off the pill and conceive shortly thereafter, since birth-control pills have a short half-life.

- If you've had a C-section for your first baby, your odds of a vaginal delivery for your second baby are increased by planning the pregnancies at least 18 months apart.

- Increase your folic acid intake 2 months before conceiving your next baby, if possible. Take 0.4 mg of folic acid every day prior to conception, and increase to 0.6 to 0.8 mg when you're pregnant.

# Notes

## Introduction

1. Oliver Pickup, "London 2012 Olympics: Pregnant Malaysian Shooter Nur Suryani Mohamad Taibi Aiming for Historic Gold," *Daily Telegraph*, July 25, 2012, www.telegraph.co.uk/sport/olympics/shooting/9426433/London-2012-Olympics-pregnant-Malaysian-shooter-Nur-Suryani-Mohamad-Taibi-aiming-for-historic-gold.html.

2. S. B. Pomeroy, ed., *Women's History and Ancient History* (Chapel Hill: University of North Carolina Press, 1991).

## Chapter 1: Building the Base for Your Ultra-Event

1. L. M. Redman and A. B. Loucks, "Menstrual Disorders in Athletes," *Sports Medicine* 35(9) (2005): 747–755.

2. A. B. Loucks, M. Verdun, and E. M. Heath, "Low Energy Availability, Not Stress of Exercise, Alters LH Pulsatility in Exercising Women," *Journal of Applied Physiology* 84(1) (1997): 37–46.

3. J. W. Rich-Edwards, D. Spiegelman, M. Garland, E. Hertzmark, D. J. Hunter, G. A. Colditz, W. C. Willett, H. Wand, and J. E. Manson, "Physical Activity, Body Mass Index, and Ovulatory Disorder Infertility," *Epidemiology* 13(2) (2002): 184–190.

4. Ibid.

5. Redman and Loucks, "Menstrual Disorders in Athletes."

6. J. F. Clapp, *Exercising Through Your Pregnancy* (Omaha, NE: Addicus Books, 2002).

7. Ibid.

8. S. A. Kopp-Woodroffe, M. M. Manore, C. A. Dueck, J. S. Skinner, and K. S. Matt, "Energy and Nutrient Status of Amenorrheic Athletes Participating in a Diet and Exercise Training Intervention Program," *International Journal of Sport Nutrition* 9 (1999): 70–88.

9. M. Grundmann and F. von Versen-Höynck, "Vitamin D—Roles in Reproductive Health?" *Reproductive Biology and Endocrinology* 9 (2011), accessed October 24, 2012, at www.rbej.com/content/9/1/146.

10.  M. Manore, "Dietary Recommendations and Athletic Menstrual Dysfunction," *Sports Medicine* 32(14) (2002): 887–901.

11.  I. Lambrinoudaki and D. Papadimitriou, "Pathophysiology of Bone Loss in the Female Athlete," *Annals of the New York Academy of Sciences* 1205 (2010): 45–50.

12.  Manore, "Dietary Recommendations and Athletic Menstrual Dysfunction."

13.  S. N. Morris, S. A. Missmer, D. W. Cramer, D. Powers, P. M. McShane, and M. D. Hornstein, "Effects of Lifetime Exercise on the Outcome of in Vitro Fertilization," *Obstetrics and Gynecology* 108(4) (2006): 938–945.

14.  K. Melzer, Y. Schutz, M. Boulvain, and B. Kayser, "Physical Activity and Pregnancy: Cardiovascular Adaptations, Recommendations, and Pregnancy Outcomes," *Sports Medicine* 40(6) (2010): 493–507.

15.  J. F. Clapp, "Exercise During Pregnancy: A Clinical Update," *Clinical Sports Medicine* 19 (2000): 273–286.

16.  Clapp, *Exercising Through Your Pregnancy*.

17.  2008 Physical Activity Guidelines for Americans, U.S. Department of Health and Human Services, www.health.gov/paguidelines.

18.  M. R. Domingues, A. Matijasevich, and A. Barros, "Physical Activity and Preterm Birth: A Literature Review," *Sports Medicine* 39(11) (2009): 961–975.

19.  R. Artal, "Anatomical and Physiological Changes of Pregnancy and Exercise," *UpToDate* (2011), accessed September 17, 2011, at www.uptodate.com/contents/anatomical-and-physiological-changes-of-pregnancy-and-exercise.

20.  Melzer, Schutz, Boulvain, and Kayser, "Physical Activity and Pregnancy"; S. N. Morris and N. R. Johnson, "Exercise During Pregnancy: A Critical Appraisal of the Literature," *Journal of Reproductive Medicine* 50(3) (2005): 181–188; Domingues, Matijasevich, and Barros, "Physical Activity and Preterm Birth."

21.  R. Barakat, J. R. Stirling, and A. Lucia, "Does Exercise Training During Pregnancy Affect Gestational Age? A Randomized Controlled Trial," *British Journal of Sports Medicine* 42(8) (2008): 674–678.

22.  Domingues, Matijasevich, and Barros, "Physical Activity and Preterm Birth."

23.  Clapp, "Exercise During Pregnancy."

24.  B. Sternfeld, C. P. Quesenberry Jr., B. Eskenazi, and L. A. Newman, "Exercise During Pregnancy and Pregnancy Outcome," *Medical Science of Sports Exercise* 27(5) (1995): 634–640.

25.  J. F. Clapp and E. L. Capeless, "The $VO_2$ max of Recreational Athletes Before and After Pregnancy," *Medicine and Science in Sports and Exercise* 23 (1991): 1128–1133.

26.  L. A. Wolfe and T. L. Weissgerber, "Clinical Physiology of Exercise in Pregnancy: A Literature Review," *Journal of Obstetrics and Gynecology Canada* 25(6) (2003): 473–483.

27.  Artal, "Anatomical and Physiological Changes of Pregnancy and Exercise."

28.  2008 Physical Activity Guidelines for Americans.

29.  Ibid.

30. K. Å. Salvesen, E. Hem, and J. Sundgot-Borgen, "Fetal Wellbeing May Be Compromised During Strenuous Exercise Among Pregnant Elite Athletes," *British Journal of Sports Medicine* 46 (2012): 279–283.

31. R. Artal and M. O'Toole, "Guidelines of the American College of Obstetricians and Gynecologists for Exercise During Pregnancy and the Postpartum Period," *British Journal of Sports Medicine* 37 (2003): 6–12.

32. Clapp, *Exercising Through Your Pregnancy*.

33. Ibid.

34. Artal, "Anatomical and Physiological Changes of Pregnancy and Exercise"; Domingues, Matijasevich, and Barros, "Physical Activity and Preterm Birth."

35. Clapp, *Exercising Through Your Pregnancy*.

36. Helen Wrightson, "Guidelines for Exercising in Pregnancy," CEF Seminars, accessed March 19, 2013, at www.cef.co.nz/index.php?option=com_content&view=article&id=14:guidelines-for-exercising-in-pregnancy&catid=1:articles&Itemid=5.

37. Melzer, Schutz, Boulvain, and Kayser, "Physical Activity and Pregnancy."

38. Clapp, "Exercise During Pregnancy."

39. Wolfe and Weissgerber, "Clinical Physiology of Exercise in Pregnancy."

40. L. M. Szymanski and A. J. Satin, "Exercise During Pregnancy: Fetal Responses to Current Public Health Guidelines," *Obstetrics & Gynecology* 119(3) (2012): 603–610.

41. Institute of Medicine, *Weight Gain During Pregnancy: Reexamining the Guidelines* (Washington, DC: National Academies Press; Committee to Reexamine IOM Pregnancy Guidelines, 2009), accessed at www.nal.usda.gov/wicworks/Sharing_Center/NY/prenatalwt_charts.pdf.

## Chapter 2: Your First Trimester

1. S. S. Stutzman, C. A. Brown, S. M. Hains, M. Godwin, G. N. Smith, J. L. Parlow, and B. S. Kisilevsky, "The Effects of Exercise Conditioning in Normal and Overweight Pregnant Women on Blood Pressure and Heart Rate Variability," *Biological Research in Nursing* 12(2) (2010): 137–148.

2. J. F. Clapp, *Exercising Through Your Pregnancy* (Omaha, NE: Addicus Books, 2002).

3. Ibid.

4. K. North and J. Golding, "A Maternal Vegetarian Diet in Pregnancy Is Associated with Hypospadias," *The ALSPAC Study Team Avon Longitudinal Study of Pregnancy and Childhood, BJU International* 85(1) (2000): 107–113.

5. Clapp, *Exercising Through Your Pregnancy*.

6. R. Artal, "Anatomical and Physiological Changes of Pregnancy and Exercise," *UpToDate* (2011), accessed September 17 , 2011, at www.uptodate.com/contents/anatomical-and-physiological-changes-of-pregnancy-and-exercise.

7. K. R. Kardel, "Effects of Intense Training During and After Pregnancy in Top-Level Athletes," *Scandinavian Journal of Medicine and Science and Sports* 15(2) (2005): 79–86.

## Chapter 3: Wonder Woman, Activate Your Second Trimester

1. R. Artal, "Anatomical and Physiological Changes of Pregnancy and Exercise," *UpToDate* (2011), accessed September 17, 2011, at www.uptodate.com/contents/anatomical-and-physiological-changes-of-pregnancy-and-exercise.

2. R. W. Hale and L. Milne, "The Elite Athlete and Exercise During Pregnancy," *Seminars in Perinatology* 20(4) (1996): 277–284.

3. Artal, "Anatomical and Physiological Changes of Pregnancy and Exercise."

4. C. Zhang, S. Liu, C. G. Solomon, and F. B. Hu, "Dietary Fiber Intake, Dietary Glycemic Load, and the Risk for Gestational Diabetes Mellitus," *Diabetes Care* 29(10) (October 2006): 2223–2230.

5. J. F. Clapp and E. L. Capeless, "The $VO_2$max of Recreational Athletes Before and After Pregnancy," *Medicine and Science in Sports and Exercise* 23 (1991): 1128–1133.

6. A. M. Lynch, C. Goodman, P. L. Choy, B. Dawson, J. P. Newnham, S. McDonald, and B. A. Blanksby, "Maternal Physiological Responses to Swimming Training During the Second Trimester of Pregnancy," *Research in Sports Medicine* 15(1) (2007): 33–45.

## Chapter 4: Your Third Trimester

1. R. Artal, "Anatomical and Physiological Changes of Pregnancy and Exercise," *UpToDate* (2011), accessed September 17, 2011, at www.uptodate.com/contents/anatomical-and-physiological-changes-of-pregnancy-and-exercise.

2. R. W. Hale and L. Milne, "The Elite Athlete and Exercise During Pregnancy," *Seminars in Perinatology* 20(4) (1996): 277–284.

3. American College of Nurse Midwives, "Omega-3 Fatty Acids During Pregnancy," *Journal of Midwifery and Women's Health* 55(6): (2010): 599–600.

4. R. Looft, "Guest Post by Simply Bike: Cycling in the Third Trimester," *Girls and Bicycles*, April 16, 2012, accessed April 2, 2013, at www.girlsandbicycles.ca/2012/04/guest-post-by-simply-bike-cycling-in.html.

## Chapter 5: Delivering Your Personal Best

1. P. Simkin, "The Fetal Occiput Posterior Position: State of the Science and a New Perspective," *Birth* 37 (2010): 61–71.

2. G. Puig and Y. Sguassero, "Early Skin-to-Skin Contact for Mothers and Their Healthy Newborn Infants: RHL Commentary" (last revised November 9, 2007), *The WHO Reproductive Health Library* (Geneva: World Health Organization, 2010).

3. C. A. Cahill, "Beta-Endorphin Levels During Pregnancy and Labor: A Role in Pain Modulation?," *Nursing Research* 38(4) (1989): 200–203.

## Chapter 6: From Bib Numbers to Bibs

1. S. T. Blackburn and D. L. Loper, *Maternal, Fetal, and Neonatal Physiology: A Clinical Perspective* (Philadelphia, PA: W. B. Saunders Company, 1992).

2. N. F. Butte and A. Steube, "Patient Information: Maternal Health and Nutrition During Breastfeeding (Beyond the Basics)," accessed September 24, 2012, at www.uptodate.com/contents/maternal-health-and-nutrition-during-breastfeeding-beyond-the-basics.

3. R. W. Hale and L. Milne, "The Elite Athlete and Exercise in Pregnancy," *Seminars in Perinatology* 20(4) (1996): 277–284.

4. M. Wolk, "The Vegetarian Breastfeeding Mother," *Leaven* 33(3) (1997): 69.

5. D. Torres, *Age Is Just a Number: Achieve Your Dreams at Any Stage in Your Life* (New York: Random House, 2009).

6. S. T. Blackburn and D. L. Loper, *Maternal, Fetal, and Neonatal Physiology: A Clinical Perspective* (Philadelphia, PA: W. B. Saunders Company, 1992).

7. J. M. Pivarnik, H. O. Chambliss, J. F. Clapp, S. A. Dugan, M. C. Hatch, C. A. Lovelady, M. F. Mottola, and M. A. Williams, "Impact of Physical Activity During Pregnancy and Postpartum on Chronic Disease Risk," *Medicine and Science in Sports and Exercise*, 35(8), (2006): 989–1006.

8. J. P. Newnham, P. M. Dennett, S. A. Ferron, S. Tomlin, C. Legg, G. L. Bourne, and L. H. Rees, "A Study of the Relationship Between Circulating B-Endorphin-Like Immunoreactivity and Post Partum Blues," *Clinical Endocrinology* 20(2) (2008): 169–177.

9. N. Clark, *Nancy Clark's Sports Nutrition Guidebook*, 4th ed. (Champaign, IL: Human Kinetics, 2008).

10. R. Artal, "Recommendations for Exercise During Pregnancy and the Postpartum Period," accessed September 26, 2012, at www.uptodate.com/contents/recommendations-for-exercise-during-pregnancy-and-the-postpartum-period.

## Chapter 7: Mamas on the Move

1. C. Logan, "Pregnancy and Postpartum Exercise," *IDEA Fitness Journal* 3(2) (2006).

2. R. W. Hale and L. Milne, "The Elite Athlete and Exercise in Pregnancy," *Seminars in Perinatology* 20(4) (1996): 277–284.

3. P. Kulpa, "Exercise During Pregnancy and Postpartum," in R. Ag (ed.), *Medical and Orthopedic Issues of Active and Athletic Women* (Philadelphia, PA: Hanley & Belfus, 1994).

4. K. R. Kardel, "Effects of Intense Training During and After Pregnancy in Top-Level Athletes," *Scandinavian Journal of Medicine and Science in Sports* 15(1) (2004): 79–86.

5. J. M. Pivarnik, "Cardiovascular Responses to Aerobic Exercise During Pregnancy and Postpartum," *Seminars in Perinatology* 20(4): 242–249.

6. C. L. Otis and R. Goldingay, *The Athletic Woman's Survival Guide: How to Win the Battle Against Eating Disorders, Amenorrhea, and Osteoporosis* (Champaign, IL: Human Kinetics, 2000).

7. N. Swedan, *Women's Sports Medicine and Rehabilitation* (Gaithersburg, MD: Aspen Publishers, 2001).

8. A. Stracciolini, "Sacral Stress Fracture in a Postpartum Runner," *Medicine and Science in Sports and Exercise* 35(5) (2003): S53.

9. K. D. Little and J. F. Clapp, "Self-Selected Recreational Exercise Has No Impact on Early Postpartum Lactation-Induced Bone Loss," *Medicine and Science in Sports and Exercise* 30(6) (1998): 831–836.

10. C. A. Lovelady, M. J. Bopp, H. L. Colleran, H. K. Mackie, and L. Wideman, "Effect of Exercise Training on Loss of Bone Mineral Density During Lactation," *Medicine and Science in Sports and Exercise* 41(10) (2009): 1902–1907.

11. R. W. Hale and L. Milne, "The Elite Athlete and Exercise in Pregnancy," *Seminars in Perinatology* 20(4) (1996): 277–284.

12. R. Artal, "Anatomical and Physiological Changes of Pregnancy and Exercise," *UpToDate* (2011), accessed September 17, 2011, at www.uptodate.com/contents/anatomical-and-physiological-changes-of-pregnancy-and-exercise.

13. N. Swedan, *Active Woman's Health and Fitness Handbook* (New York: Perigee Trade, 2003).

14. D. Epstein, "Baby Boost," *Sports Illustrated* 109(6) (August 18, 2008); 62.

## Chapter 8: At Home with Your Fit Self

1. Rafferty, "Some Runners Choose Not to Wait for Family," *New York Times*, June 25, 2011. Accessed September 19, 2012, at www.nytimes.com/2011/06/26/sports/some-track-athletes-join-other-parents-on-the-run.html.

2. British Medical Journal, "Active Parents Raise Active Children," *ScienceDaily*, November 27, 2007.

3. K. Holm, H. Wyatt, J. Murphy, J. Hill, and L. Ogden, "Parental Influence on Child Change in Physical Activity During a Family-Based Intervention for Child Weight Gain Prevention," *Journal of Physical Activity and Health* 9 (2012): 661–669.

4. University of Essex, "Poor Role Models: Children Say Two-Thirds of Parents Do 'Almost No Physical Activity,'" *ScienceDaily*, June 20, 2012.

5. A. Terry, "Olympic Moms: 13 Mothers Compete for Team USA," accessed April 5, 2013, at www.csmonitor.com/The-Culture/Family/2012/0808/Olympic-moms-13-mothers-compete-for-Team-USA.

6. Karen M. Appleby and Leslie A. Fisher, "'Running in and out of Motherhood': Elite Distance Runners' Experiences of Returning to Competition After Pregnancy," *Free Library*, March 22, 2009, accessed September 19, 2012, at www.thefreelibrary.com/"Running in and out of motherhood": elite distance runners'...-a0220136004.

# Index

# About the Authors

 **Dr. Kristina Pinto** received her Ed.D. in human development from the Harvard Graduate School of Education in 2005. A specialist in women's health and psychology, she has been a distance runner since 1998, completing 10 marathons and a 90-km run in the Australian outback. Kristina is now a running coach with her business Mile Mannered Running as well as a fitness author who has published in *Runner's World* and *Women's Running*. She wrote the featured blog *Marathon Mama* for *Competitor* magazine and currently writes the blog *Mother Running Rampant* (http://kristinapinto.net). Kristina is mom to son Henry, who bikes next to her while she trains on their country roads north of Boston.

**Dr. Rachel Kramer** completed her OB-GYN training with honors at Yale in 1998 and has been in private practice outside Boston ever since. Her medical interests include perimenopause, menopause, weight loss, nutrition, and fitness. She has appeared on the *Today Show* and been featured in the *Boston Globe* for her inspirational weight loss and evolution as an athlete. She has two sons and competes regularly in triathlon and distance running events.